Motherhood knows no borders.

PRAISE FOR
Knocked Up Abroad Again

"By turns raucous and poignant, a rollicking adventure of motherhood around the world."

-AK Turner, *New York Times* bestselling author of the *Vagabonding with Kids* series

Knocked Up Abroad Again

Baby bumps, twists, and turns
around the globe

Edited by
Lisa Ferland

For my loves—Jonathan, Calvin, and Lucy.

ISBN 978-0-9970624-2-7 (Print)
ISBN 978-0-9970624-3-4 (eBook)

Cover design by Emelie Cheng
Edited by Melinda Lipkin
Photo by Sandra Jolly Photography

CONTENTS

SECTION II LOSS AND HEALING ABROAD

SECTION III PARENTING ABROAD

FOREWORD

Is there anything as vulnerable as a newborn child? Naked, defenseless, limbs flailing, the teensy creature stretches her fine-boned fingers toward a blurry world and what must seem a violent blast of lights, smells, and sounds. Still, she reaches. Headlong she goes, right into the adventure of a lifetime.

The onslaught of stimuli might make her curl into your flesh for refuge, or wail in raw alarm. So you hold her, committed to bearing her as long as needed. She's no more than a couple of handfuls of pulsing magic, this infant you carry. Yet in those handfuls lie both a whole urgent world of need and a throbbing universe of promise.

Nope, there is nothing quite as vulnerable as that babe. But there is nothing quite as magical and magnificent, either.

Unless, of course, it's that babe's mother.

I'm a shameless fan of mothers. A mother of four myself, I know something about how giving birth requires literal but also figurative nakedness. Right off, giving birth strips us bare of any delusions we might have about our own strength. When you hit transition during delivery, didn't your limbs flail involuntarily, your fingers stretch (or claw)? And somewhere near expulsion, didn't you spring sudden lungs like I did and outwail your offspring?

Yes, birthing and, in turn, parenting ratchet up every last scrap of high-pitched anxiety and deep down discomfort we've ever known, then multiply it all by a squillion. And it's exactly because of that massive investment of nerves, grit, and crack-your-ribs love that parenting can foster the kind of heroism, soul expansion, and gratification little else in life can offer.

Which all holds true in ideal, stable circumstances. So what happens when we aren't in those circumstances? When we couple the arrival of our baby with another kind of arrival, that of arriving in a new country? What do we get when fate layers vulnerability upon vulnerability, nakedness upon nakedness, when we are in an unfamiliar setting, speaking an unfamiliar tongue, staring down an unfamiliar medical system, without friends, family, and no semblance of our former competent and composed self?

What happens when we are in Turkey, China, Nigeria, Bolivia? Or maybe in Japan, Hungary, Sweden, South Africa? We've just landed in Brazil, perhaps. Or we're freshly settled in Abu Dhabi? Or surprise, surprise, we find out we're expecting just as we hit the tarmac in Ethiopia?

What you get is knocked broadside with a near-vertical learning curve. What you get is *Knocked Up Abroad Again*. The 25 authors you will meet in these pages have known the scenarios I just mapped out. They know something about motherhood, vulnerability, and heroism in all those countries...plus others. From these women you will get an irresistible compilation of true life accounts rich with firsthand insights and best friend frankness. The result reads something like a whole room of wise, multicultural midwives and cultural integration specialists buzzing with intimate stories of pathos, surprise, hilarity, and tenderness run through with a strong strain of poignancy.

As said, each mother has lived (conceived, delivered, parented, or all of the above) internationally, so each knows what it's like to arrive on foreign soil exposed, practically naked, essentially a newborn yourself. Like you, they've been there battling with a new language, arms flailing indelicately, even spasmodically. They've known about being overwhelmed by the avalanche of urgent needs when setting up life in a new country *and* bringing baby into the mix. And so they sympathize with why a pregnant or freshly delivered newcomer might curl back from it all hunting for refuge, self-medicating, maybe, on chocolate, under a pile of down, in front of Netflix. Programmed on infinite loop. At midday.

Above all, these women are proof that bearing and raising children in your nonnative culture is not only possible but rewarding, and in many instances more desirable than the conventional upbringing many of them themselves knew. They wouldn't call themselves this, but to me they are quiet heroes.

While over 25 years on the global road I haven't birthed or raised my four children in the same countries as have these women (mine were born in Norway and France and raised there as well as in Hong Kong, Germany, Singapore, and Switzerland), I felt while reading their accounts that if we gals were somehow seated next to each other (on an airplane, let's say, since that might be the only place we'd cross paths), no flight would be long enough for sharing all our stories. I understood these women within a page. And I trusted they would understand much about me. I imagined us elbow to elbow with our tray tables down, leaning against our upholstered headrests, comparing notes, laughing, gasping, and at times even weeping without a sound.

Because I have to tell you, birth and life are not all these women have known. Some of them, like myself, have known not only about the cost of bringing a child to earth on foreign soil, but also about burying a child in it. Which means, I'm grateful to add, that this is a volume about *real life*. It offers many parts light and select parts heavy, parts wackiness and some precious parts weightiness. Any volume on parenting abroad (or at home, for that matter) would be shallow and lacking texture without those counterbalancing truths.

So join me in this highly personal, multicultural, and thoroughly human journey. Meet the women who, like their children, have left a certain zone of comfort (for the moms it's a home country; for the children the uterus itself), to enter a new life naked and sometimes squalling, unsure and often vulnerable, but ready to build an existence that shimmers with color, variety, resilience, wisdom, and true beauty.

What a trip! And what a privilege to share it with you.

Melissa Dalton-Bradford
Author: *Global Mom: A Memoir* and *On Loss and Living Onward*
October 2016, Bad Homburg, Germany

SECTION I

KNOCKED UP ABROAD

CHAPTER 1

BIRTH CONTROL, BIRTH, AND THE NEED FOR TRANSLATION

Melissa Uchiyama
Nationality: American
Knocked up in: Japan

"You are 28. You need to have babies, immediately." This from an elderly female gynecologist. She shifts her glasses and looks up, eyes locked on me and then squaring up my body. She really means it. All the obstacles of sifting through language, finding clinics that will accept my insurance, the walk here to this Tokyo clinic today, finally making it through the impenetrable gates of Japanese-only-speaking receptionists, all to hear this. So much for women in business, women working toward something outside of their home.

All I want is birth control, preferably a low-level pill. Instead, she wants me to purchase a basal thermometer and take her Xeroxed form to chart my daily temperature upon waking. Also, the pill I want, nay, desperately believe I *need*, is not available. Not just in her office, but the whole country.

Apparently, I was spoiled from my time in South Florida, USA where my OB/GYN handed me a goody bag full of free samples at every appointment, and I had my range of choices in the birth control department. Forget the popular commercials with women talking about the ring or their miracle pill which also cleared up their skin. Here in Japan, they do not exist. Rather, there is one nearly industrial-strength pill, in the kind of rough, beige hard plastic I would sooner associate with a thick-ankled, compression hose–wearing gym teacher from the 1960s, who delivers the birds and the bees speech with as much delicacy as a bomb.

Also, this particular OB/GYN office does not even offer that particular option. I'll have to visit another office. At this clinic, I may choose for her to write me a prescription for a sponge, which, to anyone remotely near my generation, sounds disgusting. The sponge. What year is this? I am in Tokyo, the city of the future, the city of mega-standards, of convenience, modernity, the city heralded for its expensive, hyper-cleaning, classical music playing toilets with eight kinds of bidets! All this modernity and I can get some crusty sponge with its plastic case that Rizzo probably carried in the back pocket of her Jordache jeans in the musical, *Grease*. Mrs. Carol Brady probably kept hers in the medicine cabinet of her 1970s ranch-style home. Oh, and no sponge until I turn in at least one month's charting of my cycle, temperature, and nightly bedtimes. All homework and no reward. Plus, to make a dismal situation worse, I accidentally step back into the waiting room still wearing the bathroom slippers. Every eye looks. Yes, in Japan, this is a thing—a *faux pas*. All the magazines are in Japanese; the room is tight and claustrophobic with women, and I feel alone.

I've been in Japan almost seven months at this point. Some days it is all mirth at discovering a new, almost romantic culture. I love the exploration with my husband who is Japanese by descent but raised in America his whole life. It's like hunting for poetry and Japan is thick with it. The changes in the air, the fragrance of rainy season, the food—it is new for both of us.

My husband doesn't have to go to an OB/GYN, though. He has the language to use his voice, or at least more quickly find it in this new place. I am loud by nature, excited. I shout when upset. My voice squeaks. I laugh loudly, almost honk, every tooth showing. Here, though? Women cover their mouths. They are demure, and now I see now that I am shrinking back. I don't always know how to manage the tension—there is me, at least when confident, and this new me called "living in Japan on the rough days."

How do I maneuver as a mouse, sidestepping, and wearing the wrong slippers? I learn to bow, sure, but one has to use a voice. That's it—I lost my voice a bit. Maybe it's like my spirit keeps developing an ongoing bout of laryngitis, I think.

I still need the birth control, too, because how can I possibly raise a child when, without a real voice, without language, I, myself, am an infant here? How can I become responsible for another life? I am, as it is, paranoid that someone will collapse nearby, and it'll be up to me to call the police or ambulance. "Please, God, let everyone be okay." At this point, I only know the words "fire" and "earthquake" from the emergency drills I teach the kindergarten kids at The American School in

Japan. I care for them, but all of this takes place within the safe confines of a premier English-speaking, international school in the heart of swanky Roppongi Hills.

My confidence blooms with each new season here, each new restaurant and chic bar in this exclusive, international part of the city, but I still go home to my Japanese in-laws, my husband, and our shared home in a Japanese community with markets and labels and people I cannot understand or speak with. I love it, but I stink at it. I am a child who progresses so slowly in school that she begins to hate it. It's love/hate. It's transition. I'm loud. I'm in shock. I'm shy. I'm emotional. It's a lot to get used to, what with little space, paper-thin *shoji* walls inside the home, and one shower/bath. Gone is any autonomy with my husband, and gone is my birth control.

I find another clinic with the goods—outdated, yet expensive birth control. I spend enough on the pill to go toward a terrific vacation, or at least some fabulous movie and fine dining dates. Japanese health insurance does not cover family planning, so it is big cash I plop down for every cycle of tiny white pills.

Roughly two years later, still as chic in a far different culture with a great language deficit, my husband and I feel like we're ready for the next chapter: pregnancy and kids, or at least letting it be a possibility. Time to get off the pill. It is a faith walk, every night a decision to breathe and trust that I can live here. I am a woman learning to stand with one foot grasping life on this island in the Pacific, and one foot that slides out from under me. That other foot is back in Florida, home with people who understand me, my voice, and all I think I need. It is faith to resist taking more of my birth control, like a winding off of drugs, a chance to believe in something else.

Two months later, I am knocked up. I am pregnant abroad, a woman with child in Japan. We find a large university hospital, the Japanese equivalent of Harvard or Yale. Nurses verify the blip that is our daughter's seven-week-old heartbeat. I wait on benches for hours, waiting to be seen alongside silent Japanese women sitting with their equally silent husbands. Each visit marked by the same lullaby version of The Beatles' "Yellow Submarine." I have no idea what is being spoken by any doctor or nurse. I have no clue what they need me to do or the order in which to do it.

In fact, at this point, my Japanese has little improved from when I had to first call that female gynecologist's office to follow-up on my test for cervical cancer. I bite my nails, deciding I would attempt to make "pap smear" sound Japanese. I state my name and try to convey that I'd had a test. Over and over into the receiver, I state, "Test-o...*papo-soomeeah.*"

The receptionist cannot understand me, so again and again, I state my name followed by, "*testo- and-o papa-soomeeah.*" Finally, I realize the receptionist isn't a receptionist at all but really an old man, and I called the wrong number. This phone call in a nutshell, is the hilarity of being knocked up abroad. Hilarious and sad, for another human being is now counting on you to not only have your life worked out, at least be able to use the telephone, and somehow, somehow advocate and even make baby books for them. I could barely write any more than my name.

These are the moments of becoming, I think, sometimes dodging tears. I sit at these appoint-ments, teetering between glee and terror. I am responsible for operating an old balance scale, responsible to record my height, chart the pH balance of the sticks I must swizzle in a cup of pee, and a host of other tasks all told to me in rapid-fire Japanese. The system is a machine, and I am causing hold-up until maybe the third visit when a doctor tells me I'd probably be more comfortable somewhere else. How racist, right? Clearly, they don't feel up to the challenge of helping me. I have used up their hospitality, and now our relationship is done.

On to the next place, an *au natural* birth house. Here, I learn what is Asian sensibility toward pregnant women. It is the understanding of Chinese medicine that states my ankles must be covered and always, always warm. Even in August when I am accustomed to flip-flops and little shorts. Ankles, they say, are connected to the ovaries. When cold, those poor little ovaries will also be cold and constrict. Cover them up, ladies! I teeter trying to shove socks on my pregnant footsies just before opening the door to the Japanese birth house each week.

I cause great consternation at not keeping my belly wrapped in a cotton cloth, over and over, around, so that my uterus, and my baby are not cold. Everything the midwives are concerned about only makes me feel more alien. Avoid fruit, avoid cold foods. Again, even in the brutal heat of Tokyo's summer. All I want is watermelon, cold and crisp against my lips. Icy smoothies and bowls of frozen yogurt. I rebel. I buck the system. I eat my fruit, cones of ice cream, and take long walks, ankles uncovered.

I want to blend in, but I am different. I am not like the women whom I see in baby shops, not the ones whom I picture as hardly asking questions. I am full of them. I am ripe with inquisitive tones and perhaps I come off brazen. Perhaps I come off as overly confident, but I am an American in Japan, that is, vulnerable, but trying to connect, trying to access humor. I am learning sensitivity and softness of voice, but if pregnancy stirs up a woman's need for a controlled, safe environment, if pregnancy stirs up a woman's need for support and security, then pregnancy abroad is bumpy with emotions spanning the sky. There is a need to connect to our mother. There is our sister, the cousins, a continuation that must find its way to us even through the mystique and frustrations of a different life, one that the women before us have not known. We are the new brave. We dare to have children in a place we've not known long. The culture, the language, and mores will raise up our new babies and they will know two worlds while we still grapple and try to straddle, fling ourselves over two walls.

I grow closer with my mother-in-law. She happens to be wonderful, but either way, it is imperative. I use the resources I have. The long-time family friend of theirs? She is my friend now. I ask these women to help me make appointments. "Where can I buy over-the-counter cream for a yeast infection?" This is hardly a simple interaction, as we must first come to understand the words "yeast infection" via translation. Then there is looking in a store, looking through intimate aisles when I wish I could just be alone. Finally, I learn that it must be prescribed by a doctor. I will need one of these women with me for that, too. I am my most vulnerable in these moments, for I long to be independent. In my own culture, I sure as hell would be. But here? I am a child, a big, fat, pregnant child.

These are the rough goes. The indecisive starts, the doubtful reminders of that voice which taunts, "How can you have a child in a place you can't operate in, not hardly?" And yet, with each week of pregnancy, I grow stronger. I come into my own. This is our branch in the tree my husband and I have joined. It transcends place. Confidence comes as I am becoming a mother.

By the time our daughter is a few weeks old, I am the boss of this motherhood. My own mother flies out for what is her third time visiting us in Japan. Strong and tough, she knows the way independently from the airport to our door. She has come to meet her first grand baby, the granddaughter she has pined for across the sea.

She flings the door open and too excited to mind the narrow Tokyo space, butts into wall and railing on her way up to the tiny baby room we've carved on the second floor. She hasn't bothered to remove shoes or deal with slippers.

"Where is she?" Mom calls, eyes huge and voice high.

And this next part we still laugh about, "I don't care about you anymore! Where is she?"

During her month-long visit, we ladies ignore the tradition that every new Asian mother employs, staying inside for a full month or longer while her mom dotes and prepares every meal, goes out on every errand. I know I need air, fresh oxygen, and skies over ceiling. We three walk to parks and open garden shows, past streams and in and out of grocery stores. Neighbors have never seen such a small baby. I have enough Japanese to understand the old women who balk at our baby carriage, "They will break that baby's neck. It is too early for the baby to be out."

I fling indecision to the curb, nursing throughout Tokyo. We walk rosy neighborhoods in spring, hike Mount Takao in its red maple glory. I maneuver through the Japanese preschool system, making myself known. I write her daily meals, each banana or bowl of oatmeal in her notebook, the inky letters of hiragana making my love known.

I am learning. I am home. I write basic questions and pen simple reports of her health and behavior, "*gokigen*," she is in a fantastic mood, or "*guzuguzu*," crying. I show up on parent days and am lucky enough to bring my visiting mother. My daughter turns one, then, two, and just past that, we are pregnant again with her brother. We grow a community, grow our own sense of place and peace.

Parents like us get to take the best from each culture, I decide. We pick and choose with luxury, knowing that in either place, we may never quite fit. This is the piece that ends tension because our family comes first. I can be myself, a penchant for frizzy hair and laughing with an open mouth. These kids represent the best of us, as parents, as countries and cultures. They are rivers of grass, fields of wheat, and the freedom to hop between paradigms.

There are the *undokais*, the sports days, the challenge and treasure of laughter in two languages. My daughter grows fully bilingual, even translating between me and her teachers, spoon-fed sweets by her Grandparents here, *Ojiichan* and *Obaachan*.

I sit now, rotund and 39 weeks pregnant with our third child. She will be Lana June, a name easily spoken in our two main languages and many in between. She will know love, which I know. And I know, trite as it sounds, I'm in good hands. In whatever land, I have us.

After that, don't get me started on the birth control. Nothing much has changed.

Melissa Uchiyama is a national board educator who has transitioned from year-round summer and key lime pies to sushi during pregnancy and a love of all things nature in Japan. She has three fabulous kids and a husband whom she treasures. She blogs and at www.melibelleintokyo.com. She is a contributor to the anthology Mothering through the Darkness, and she has contributed to many sites such as Literary Mama, Motherlode, and Brain, Child.

CHAPTER 2

HOW TO PREPARE FOR A BABY IN CHINA

Charlotte Edwards Zhang
Nationality: American
Knocked up in: China
Birthed in: China

America puts out some pretty scary statistics saying that parents need to spend thousands of dollars a year to raise a child, what with all the baby gear, outfits for every day of the month and early learning books and toys galore. To some extent, China seems quite the opposite, especially in towns outside of the major metro areas like the one in which my husband was raised, and we presently live. While it seemed anything but fun at the time, my husband and his mother taught me that you only really need a few basics to raise a child, along with plenty of love.

Within our first month of marriage, my husband decided that we needed to replace the spare bed with a slightly larger one, a *mu zi chuang*—literally, a mother and baby bed—so that I could sleep there once the baby was born. Yes, he already assumed that we were having a baby in our first year of marriage. I argued that the baby would sleep in a crib, but either I wasn't forceful enough in my explanation or he wasn't listening. One four-hour shopping trip later, we had a brand new bed on order.

By the end of the next month, we found out we were indeed expecting. Once I got over the initial shock, I quickly began envisioning nursery themes and fun baby gear. Then I realized that the Chinese don't do nurseries. And we already had the requisite *mu zi chuang*. I resigned myself to the fact that, for the most part, we'd be doing this the Chinese way.

I thought I'd be able to change his mind as the months wore on, but my snoring didn't pair well with his inability to sleep soundly, so I ended up sleeping solo in the *mu zi chuang* months before baby arrived.

But I was determined that I would not be co-sleeping with the baby in the *mu zi chuang*.

I didn't plan to go overboard with buying for the baby; it wasn't like we'd be decorating a nursery or that I'd be tempted to blow my whole paycheck on cute maternity clothes to buy, because there were hardly any. I'm not very fashion-savvy, but I know enough that the denim and corduroy bib overalls with embroidered bears and kittens that expectant Chinese mothers wear don't look good on anyone.

I went shopping one day, and in the tiny corner of the store, the maternity department were a few racks of overalls with a few dozen shirts and pants among them. I left with a pair of jeans and plans to have my mom send me a few sewing patterns. A month, a trip to the fabric market, and a day spent communicating charades-style with my mother-in-law (I would have sewn them myself, but she only has an old-school, pedal sewing machine that I couldn't figure out) later, I had a dress and two shirts. Those, with my jeans and a shirt-and-capris set my mom sent would be the extent of my maternity wardrobe. My mother-in-law deemed this plenty as Chinese women typically have only two outfits. I had multiple pieces that could be mixed and matched—a luxury, indeed!

With the clothes issue solved, I decided to focus on necessary baby supplies. I come from a fairly frugal and practical family and knew that I could make do with the essentials. I didn't need a whole closet full of clothes, boxes full of toys or oversized baby gear cluttering up our tiny 635-square-foot home. Keeping things simple was key, plus we were saving every last *jiao* (cent) we had to pay off my student loans as soon as possible.

What I didn't know was how few things are deemed "essential" by Chinese standards. I really wanted to buy a crib despite the *mu zi chuang* staring at me every day. I could appreciate that Chinese moms co-sleep, but I didn't want to. I found an affordable playpen-style crib from the meager selection at the store. I told Santiago about my impending purchase while out walking one night.

"A bed for the baby? Why would he need that? Don't you remember? You'll sleep with him in the *mu zi chuang*."

Suddenly I had a flashback to my childhood neighbors whose parents were hippies and the whole family of four slept together in their over-sized family bed. Surely we weren't going to do such a thing. No, I knew we wouldn't have a family bed. That's not part of Chinese culture. It would simply be the baby and I. Our walk ended in slightly tense silence and, while I still daydreamed about how I'd get the crib, I turned my efforts toward acquiring the other items that I deemed essential.

Being a first-time mom I wasn't quite sure what essential did entail, so I did what any other Internet-savvy mom would do: I turned to Google. I browsed lists on BabyCenter and Target and whittled the hundreds of items down to less than a dozen. I showed my handwritten shopping list to my husband.

He glanced over it and commented, "My mom will take care of this, this and this," as he pointed to the lines listing clothes, diapers, and bedding.

"And why do we need to buy fingernail clippers? We already have fingernail clippers," he questioned. "Besides, babies don't need anything special. If we need something, we can buy it later," he informed me.

To be honest, I wasn't completely sure that we needed them, but I felt they would make it easier to clip a wiggly baby's fast-growing nails as safely as possible. I didn't let my uncertainty show, but just said that we needed them to avoid hurting the baby. I was far more uncertain that we'd find them in this small-by-Chinese-standards town of a million people but with no expat community, which meant that we likely wouldn't find exotic things like breast pumps, baby carriers, and disposable diapers. He accepted my logic and finally, about a month before my due date, we set out to do our first and only preparing-for-baby shopping trip.

With the clothes, diapers, and bedding off the list, the only things left were a breast pump, some bottles, nail clippers and a bouncy chair. I'd spied the chair months before when I'd been shopping for the radiation-blocking maternity smock, and I knew how much my mom had loved the bouncy chair she had for us. It would be perfect to put the baby in while I cooked, exercised, and did things around the house. My husband deemed its 156 yuan ($22, at the time) price tag too extravagant for the little amount of time he felt the baby would be in it. So we left with the only style of breast pump (a manual, of course) they had, four bottles, and a pair of baby-safe fingernail clippers.

A few days after the underwhelming shopping trip, a package, including several onesies, a swaddle, and a dozen cloth diapers arrived from a friend in America. At least the baby will be properly diapered, partially clothed, and warm, I fumed to myself. My mom, who was going to arrive about a month after the baby was born, told me that she'd be bringing a whole suitcase of clothes she'd been buying on clearance sales throughout my whole pregnancy. I just have to make it through the first month, I told myself. My son was due in September, so it would be fine to keep him in a onesie and wrap him with the thin cotton blanket that I'd sewn for him.

Two weeks before I went into labor, I packed my hospital bag with all the things I felt I'd need. Again, I asked Google what I would need and then pared the lists down considerably, mostly because things like physio balls for laboring on, disposable underwear for after delivery, or a car seat for going home aren't used here— never mind that we didn't even have a car. Santiago found this amusing; apparently, our doctor never mentioned doing such a thing during my weekly checkups. Again, he said, his mother would take care of everything. I could appreciate the help, but I didn't understand the secrecy and lack of communication about this. So I kept packing: I put the onesies and diapers in another bag for the baby, along with the blanket I'd sewn for him. I still wasn't convinced that we'd be able to pull this off.

The morning my son was born, I went out shopping in the city center to buy a pair of slippers to wear at the hospital and just to get out of our small community for a change. While walking around the mall, I realized about half an hour into my shopping trip that I was having contractions. Twenty minutes in, and with slippers acquired, I decided to get some ice cream at KFC and time the contractions. They were coming very regularly, at four minutes apart.

Back at home I quickly prepared a simple lunch and then double-checked the bags, still wondering if maybe we should have asked Santiago's mother about the mysterious clothes she was preparing. My husband said not to worry about it; everything would be taken care of. He returned to work after lunch, and I went out for a walk to ease the discomfort of the contractions.

As it neared dinner time, I was certain that the baby was coming that day. Then my thoughts turned to how we would get to the hospital. Our house was a mere three kilometers (less than two miles) away, but we didn't have a car, and buses stopped running at 6 p.m., which meant finding a taxi was slightly easier than finding the proverbial needle in the haystack. I sent my husband to eat dinner with his parents.

All day the contractions had been relatively pain-free, but now they were kicking in full force. As a thunderstorm, with great lightning bolts, settled in, I told him we needed to head to the hospital. A quick call to the doctor who'd been doing my check-ups resulted in him saying that there was no hurry. The doctor proclaimed, from the comfort of her home, that it was just early labor and it would be a day or two until I delivered. My husband believed her and said that if it made me feel better, we'd go to the hospital after the storm was over.

So you know just when this storm will be over? I so badly wanted to retort, but the pain kept me from saying much. Maybe, just maybe, this was the way that I'd get the home birth that I really wanted.

Two hours later my father-in-law came running in, panting from having climbed the 105 stairs to our sixth-floor apartment after having tracked down a van. My husband ushered me downstairs, while my mother-in-law sheltered me from the rain with her umbrella. A few prayers were uttered, asking that the two traffic lights we would soon encounter would be green. They were. Less than 20 minutes later I was in the delivery room holding my son. The nurse yelled for my husband, who wasn't allowed in the delivery room and had to translate from the hallway, to bring a blanket to cover the baby.

We'd left my in-laws back at our house, and my mother-in-law still hadn't produced any baby clothes to set me at ease, so my husband was glad to discover that I was right in preparing a bag of clothes and a blanket for the baby.

I dozed off and on all night in the hospital. My son wasn't catching on to nursing; I was in pain, and the commotion from the mother in the other bed, with her entourage of four parents to care for her new daughter, made for a long night. But in the morning I awoke to see Nathaniel outfitted in a tiny shirt made from a shirt of mine that I'd put in the trash months before, a Chinese-style cloth diaper, and more blankets than a baby could ever need in September.

Sure enough, my mother-in-law had gone back to her house in the midst of the storm to get two huge bags of clothes and blankets and brought them to the hospital in the wee hours of the morning. He mainly wore those clothes in the following weeks, and only wore them when his grandparents dressed him; they deemed onesies too tight, uncomfortable, and unhealthy for his little boy parts.

Two weeks later I woke up around midnight, being rather fiercely nudged by my husband. I'd been sleeping very soundly—hence the unusual forcefulness of his nudging—and discovered that I was lying partially on Nathaniel. That still remains one of the most frightening parenting experiences to date. This shook up my Chinese family and made them realize that co-sleeping isn't always a good or safe choice. Three days later I awoke to find a homemade metal crib in the bedroom. It would never pass American safety standards, with the bars being six inches apart and the depth being less than a foot, but I finally got a crib.

The next month, during my mom's visit, we were out shopping and going through the children's floor when my mom saw the bouncy chair. It was the exact same one I'd attempted to buy months before. That shows just how unpopular those things are among Chinese. She knew the story behind why it was still at the store and not in our living room, so she bought it as a gift from her friend, who'd given her money to buy something that we needed for Nathaniel so that there was no chance of a money fight.

Nearly eight years and another child later, I rather enjoy the simplicity that's found in small-town Chinese life. It's not always easy, not being able to find what I want or being understood by family and friends around me. I've learned a lot about contentment, and that it is truly possible to raise a child with little more than food, clothing, shelter, and love.

Charlotte Edwards Zhang has lived in China for 10 years, with eight of them being married to her Chinese husband. An educator by trade, she's transitioned into freelancing, usually mixing parenting and personal finance topics, such as explaining how parents can save thousands of dollars by raising diaper-free kids and why one might consider doing a Chinese-inspired moon month. Between taking care of her kids (ages four and seven), she writes about parenting in China for Tianjin Today magazine and tries to update her blog, Living in China with Kids to help other expat parents understand the cultural differences between raising kids in China and the West.

CHAPTER 3

MY TURKISH DELIGHT

Rosemary Gillan
Nationality: Australian
Knocked up in: Turkey

It was raining hard as we hurtled down Çevre Yolu No. 1 to Istanbul's International Hospital in Yeşilköy. The operative word was "hurtled" as, thank God, it was 3:30 a.m. on a Saturday morning. At any other time, we would be in stop-start traffic, crawling a meter at a stretch with the patience of Job, to our final destination—weekdays, it took my husband a full 45 minutes from our apartment sitting atop the hill in Ortaköy to drive to his office a mere 2.5 miles away.

Although the odds of this happening were very, very good, I pushed all thoughts of a highway birth to the back of my mind during my entire pregnancy. All I cared about was that I carried the baby to full term—the devastation of miscarrying my previous child at 12 weeks the year prior had shaken me out of my complacent attitude that all pregnancies were a cinch. I carried my third baby with gratitude, wonder, and awe through the entire nine months, praying that this baby would not suffer the same fate as his sibling. So far so good.

We knew we were going to have a boy. Dr. Moshe, my OB/GYN announced it, unasked, with great pride one morning late into my pregnancy, and he couldn't understand why we greeted the news with little elation.

We had an impeccably mannered little girl, so perfect that parents at the preschool she attended frequently requested she spend time with their children so that they could learn and follow the "good example" she set. I shone with pride; she was the epitome of manners— sweet, generous, careful, obedient, polite.

Little boys were from another strain altogether. Clumsy, loud, rough, devil-may-care, sassy. We wanted no part of that. Yes, we'd like another girl, we stubbornly stated to all who presumed we'd like our family completed with one of each sex—as if you simply could not have two of the same kind, unless they were identical twins.

No, we did not want to know what sex our baby was. We wanted to be surprised and delighted at the arrival of another girl—of course, it was going to be a girl— into our lives. Besides, there were too many tales of friends who had been told they were going to have a boy/girl and had bought all the relevant clothes and painted the nursery in "appropriate" colors only to discover at the moment of delivery that the ultrasound had been patently lying. One friend, whose wife had given birth by Caesarean section while he had been relegated to wait it out at Reception, refused to accept the baby boy presented to him some time later, adamantly declaring that he was expecting a girl and the boy was not his. Later, they quietly took down the frilly pink curtains, returned the lacy pink dresses, and painted over the pale ice-cream pink of their nursery walls.

Three times I asked Dr. Moshe, "Are you sure?" and three times he responded affirmatively, for there on the ultrasound screen, without a shadow of a doubt, was the proof that the baby within me was most definitely male.

Over the remaining few months, we came to terms with and welcomed the news. Our baby boy would be different. Sweet, generous, careful, obedient, polite. We'd show 'em. After all, it did all come down to parenting, right? Oh, the smugness of new and clueless parents!

And now my son was about to enter this world, and up until this point, I was contentedly looking forward to his arrival. But whoa, like this? I could feel his head pressing down on the passenger seat of our powerful though aging Mercedes-Benz 500 SEL. Willing the baby not to go any further, I wiggled firmly into my seat, there you go, exit blocked, please wait patiently until further instructed. No way was this baby going to be born on the highway, or worse, in a local public hospital. No, no, he was going to be born in Istanbul's smartest hospital, if you please.

I was a coward where hospitals were concerned, and as with the birth of my daughter almost five years previously in Melbourne, Australia, the hospital was chosen not on the quality of its doctors but on its façade, its feel. Did it look efficient, more like an international hotel with gleaming steel fittings, low lights, hushed voices, immaculately uniformed and friendly and efficient staff, and most importantly, would I feel part of a VIP clientele?

Oozing efficiency in Melbourne was St. Vincent's Private Hospital on Victoria Parade, a big, black, modern building looking so unlike a hospital that it was instantly chosen as the venue for my first child's earthy debut on outward appearances alone. Only then did I look for a suitable OB/GYN practicing there. In retrospect, this order of priority may not have been quite right.

Naturally, I wasn't quite so shallow in Istanbul. I did an inordinate amount of research via the expatriate grapevine as to which doctor I should choose, one who best understood the western female psyche, while also considering the slightly lesser qualities of safety and skill. Based on these criteria, Dr. Moshe was chosen, highly recommended because of his great skill, his understanding of expat women, and let's face it, mostly because of his Jewish humor, and his disarming good looks. His highest recommendation came from Barb, my newly found Canadian friend who had used him for her previous two births—and suggested that just sitting in his office and looking at his handsome face was enough to calm any fears about giving birth in a foreign country.

She was right. But it was his humor rather than his looks that attracted me. You needed to laugh when going through this nine-month see-saw period of emotional and physical hormonal tension, all this being amplified by living in a foreign city and experiencing exotic aromas at every turn and hole-in-the-ground public toilets at perfectly respectable restaurants.

And here you are, newly arrived, in a foreign city, nearly 9,300 miles from your hometown of Sydney, Australia with no family supporting you, a five-year-old to look after, a husband immersed in his work, and a child's birth looming. Thank God for the wonderful

expat community, that unfailingly friendly and understanding support network on tap to hold your hand and
guide you through every new foreign experience.

Enter Barb, the faithful friend/staunch ally and
Diana, the calming prenatal instructor, Canadian angels
both. Completely familiar with and confident in the
Turkish hospital birthing experience, they banished my
initial fears and spurred my appreciation and love for the
wonderful idiosyncrasies of the country into which my
child was to be born.

I was glad to attend Diana's prenatal class, although I
considered myself an "experienced" mother on account
of having gone through the ordeal a whole one time
before. Wanting to share my birthing know-how, I
contributed to class knowledge by quietly suggesting that
the gentle short-short-long, "hoo-hoo-hooo" breathing
Diana was teaching her first-birth-ever students to use
once in the throes of labor was drastically wrong.

"In my experience," I said, "I felt it was more likely a
groan-swear-scream, 'Aarrgghh-*&$#@-AARRGGHH!'
that had a much higher chance of coming out of your
mouth than any shallow breathing."

Startled faces looked back at me, and I hastily added,
"No I'm only joking, it's a breeze," while chortling
knowingly to myself. But I digress.

Along with the need to establish the right venue for
the birth, I also researched which doctor's philosophy
best aligned with mine. There was only one criterion:
They must agree that the whole idea of natural
childbirth was baloney. I wanted them to be happy, nay
willing, to administer all the drugs I needed for a
"natural" birth, or else be happy to perform a Caesarean
section. My aim was to simply feel absolutely no pain
while giving birth.

Surely this was possible, I asked my OB/GYN when heavily pregnant and two weeks overdue with my first baby back in Melbourne five years earlier. She took my temperature and ascertained I was indeed well, then agreed to the drugs as long as I delivered my baby by "natural" childbirth, and not by a Cesarean section. We were on the same page on "no pain" and "yes drugs," though maybe not on the procurement method. Mind you, I was pretty flexible on this last aspect anyway, being largely clueless about childbirth as I had yet to experience it.

At that time, I had an epidural that lasted the duration, keeping me free from pain for the whole eight hours it took for her to enter the world, including huge complications with a torn placenta and a river of blood being lost in the process. The epidural helped marvelously. However, there was a slight problem afterward. When it finally wore off, I felt like I had given birth not to a watermelon but to a field of them, for goodness sake. I walked like a cowboy for six straight weeks afterward, due to the 17 stitches and third-degree tear her 8 lbs. 8 oz. (4,000 g) body, facing sunny-side up, had forced upon me with no conscious effort on my behalf to push and hold when needed, as I was happily in the pain-free bliss of epidural la-la land.

So I had long discussions with Dr. Moshe on this topic.
"Dr. Moshe, under no circumstances are you to allow me to have any pain during the birth of this child," my pregnancy-brain voice spoke out.
"But of course *evet*" (Yes), he confidently lied.
"I want drugs."
"*Tamam*," (Okay) he said.

"And if the baby looks too big, or is facing the wrong way, I want a Caesarean, no natural childbirth rubbish, okay?"

"But of course yes, *evet.*"

"No pain, right?"

He looks at me meaningfully, implying, *"Enough already, I will do all I can, okay?"*

Deal, I sign him up there and then, though somewhere in the dark recesses of my mind it occurs to me that he is a man who has not experienced childbirth, so what the heck would he know about pain. He has only ever probably known the sorrows of man flu. Wait, so there *is* hope.

A whole week after our son's due date comes and goes, we have our next birth discussion.

"*Aman tanrılım* (good grief), you are 10 cm dilated! And I'm worried about your baby's size as he appears to be nearly four kilos (nine pounds)!" Dr. Moshe exclaims.

(Reaching 10 cm dilation before active labor appears to be my body's way of birthing big babies.)

"Noooo! I don't want an encore of my first birth!"

"Precisely. Therefore, we should schedule a Cesarean section first thing tomorrow morning."

"Noooo! We haven't thought of a name yet!"

"You've had nine friggin' months!"

Clearly, he doesn't use the word "friggin," nor any of the other words. He just looks at me in that patient, "I'm dealing with an expat princess, *sigh*, give me a local woman any time" kind of way.

"Can you give me an extra 24 hours please?"

The most obliging smile, and it's fixed—a Cesarean section is scheduled for 11 a.m. on Saturday, November 27, 1993. The next day we agree on a name, send our daughter off to be with friends overnight, pack my bag, and go to bed. *My first Caesarean*, I think, *and no walking like a cowboy afterward either*! *Yay*! Thoughts of my middle being sliced open have mercifully not entered my hormone-addled brain. I sleep.

At 3 a.m. I awake to bad constipation-like pains and notice a little bleeding. I pick up the phone and notify Dr. Moshe, who sleepily asks, "Are you having any contractions?"

"No," I truthfully answer.

"Alright then, go back to sleep and I'll see you in the hospital in eight hours."

He is about to hang up when I decide to panic and lie at the same time.

"Aaaarrrrrgggghhhh. Oh sorry, but that was a contraction right then. Oh dear."

He buys it and says, "Come immediately to hospital," and hangs up.

I too hang up feeling smug, only to be assailed by a long, strong, and extremely painful contraction. Clearly, Dr. Moshe has a truth hotline to God.

Into the car on a pitch black and rainy winter's morning pile my husband, my large suitcase (after all, I intend spending a full seven days of being waited on hand and foot in that hotel, I mean hospital), and I. Contractions are concertinaing one almighty yelp after another, and now feeling the baby's head raring to go, we speed 23 miles toward Istanbul's International Hospital with the intent of arriving there before the baby does the same in our car.

The baby's head pushes down on the seat, and I tense up, it surely cannot be born while I am sitting straight up, I mean it's not that strong, right? Thirty minutes into the drive, my repertoire of swear words knows no bounds when my husband announces he is lost, having missed the highway turn-off in the driving rain.

We take the next turn-off and cautiously venture into the dark street, peering through the fog that has replaced the rain in content but not visibility. Up ahead is a police checkpoint, so we decide to stop and ask for directions. This is 1993 folks, no mobile phones, let alone GPS navigation systems, just a dated Istanbul city map. Dated because twenty-five thousand new highways have been built since it was last published a week ago.

When we pull up to the five policemen, they surround the car, annoyed that their warm smoke-filled bonhomie has been shattered by the arrival of a foreign car with a very large-stomached and scary-looking woman filling out all of the front passenger seat. Said woman points to her stomach and says in broken Turkish *"Bebek var!"* (Baby is coming!) and "Need International *Hastanesi?"* Clearly, my Turkish needs as much help as my desire to find the whereabouts of the hospital as they look blankly at me, light more cigarettes, and get back into their previous huddle to no doubt discuss what this all means. I wind up the window, saying, *"Tamam, teşekkür ederim"* (that's okay, thank you) through clenched teeth and off we go around another corner back onto the freeway and finally on the right route as we see the modern hospital building looming straight ahead of us, the glistening blackness of the Marmara Sea just behind it.

It's now 4:25 a.m., and this baby is not waiting any longer, its head is pushing through, this is *it*. We enter through Emergency, my husband racing in, and me waddling awkwardly behind him. My husband's basic grasp of Turkish has disappeared, and now he's doing the foreign thing and shouting loudly in English, expecting it to be better understood. They ignore him and turn to me, asking politely in stilted English if he can park somewhere other than Emergency, oh and please fill in these forms first.

I am calm, pull out my Berlitz Turkish phrase book, and sweetly say that this baby is going to be born very soon, my doctor is on the way, and would they please take me to Delivery Room straight away. They listen carefully and then gently steer me in the direction of the Delivery Room, accompanied by a couple of orderlies.

Only it's not the Delivery Room, but a third floor room I will inhabit after the baby is born, a lovely corner room with a stunning view of the Marmara Sea, an en-suite bathroom, fresh flowers, light-colored cheerful-looking curtains, and a most un-hospital looking hospital bed. Look this is just for you, you wanted a hotel room and this is the closest we could come to it, don't you just love it, imply their smiling eyes.

Thoughts of hotel rooms are furthest from my mind, replaced by thoughts of murdering several people in quick succession: my husband for getting me into this predicament in the first place; my doctor who has not turned up; and the hospital staff who believed I was more interested in a swish hotel-like room than a highly efficient, caring, and competent hospital environment. What were they thinking?

"*Bebek var, bebek var!*" (The baby is coming, really!) I plead to smiling, caring faces with totally deaf ears. I sit on the bed. I now have three nurses and a doctor surrounding me, looking at me with benign smiles and still talking about my great view that they now have collectively blocked from my sight.

New swear words enter and exit my mind rapidly. I curse all men in the room: those who caused the pregnancy, those who were ignoring it, and those who were late for it. I turn to the three female nurses, repeating, "*Bebek var.*" They huddle together, shooting furtive glances in my direction, and whispering in Turkish.

At this stage, in sheer exasperation I decide to call the shots, removing my winter coat, my shoes, my shirt, and just as I am about to completely disrobe and wheel myself to Delivery if necessary, they hastily provide me with a hospital gown and point to the bathroom as a more appropriate place to get undressed.

I dutifully obey and then waddle back in the room suitably gowned, to see a new and obviously senior doctor who has just arrived. I lie back on the bed, knees up, and he cautiously approaches this totally mad and crazy foreign woman who stupidly thinks her baby is about to arrive when everyone knows it takes several hours at least.

He peers under my gown and nearly falls over in total amazement.

"The baby is crowning!" he exclaims in horror.

"Of course, it is," I say, pleased to at last finally get through, "Get me some strong drugs, this is friggin' killing me!"

He ignores my request and asks if my doctor has been alerted, and I say of course, and relief floods his face at the answer and then back into a huddle he goes with the four other medical staff.

I am rendered absolutely speechless. And at that precise moment, Dr. Moshe arrives, and I am so pleased to see him, my brief vow of silence is not immediately broken with my deployment of every remaining swear word known to mankind. *Where the #&^% have you been?* No, indeed, I smile sweetly and innocently at him.

Wonderful, handsome, calm, brilliant Dr. Moshe now gets things moving along, shouting directions here, there, and everywhere as I get wheeled to Delivery. I join in the chorus demanding general anesthetic or failing that, an epidural.

"No, no, it's too late," says my unkind, horrible, insensitive, unfeeling clod of a doctor.

"How about pethidine, gas, sheesh, even a Tylenol will do!"

"Sorry," he shakes his head. *He's sorry?*

Now starts the real labor, as natural as they come. This is not good, not good at all. I turn to my husband who is stroking my forehead. *What, do you honestly think that is helping?* I turn to Dr. Moshe, who keeps saying all's going well, just hold back on the pushing there.

"Totally agree, Dr. Moshe," I say, "I'll hold back all right, like for the next week, or maybe even month. I've changed my mind, I want to go home."

He laughs.

"No really," I say, "just shove the baby back in. I'll come back later when things calm down a bit, and you've got some drugs for me."

The medical staff is shocked by my humor.

"This is your son! What an honor! And such disrespect toward your husband and your doctor!"

I'll show you disrespect, I think to myself, but the pain is coming heedlessly in huge rounds of killer waves, and I focus all my attention on how I'm going to finish each round.

Within the hour my son is shoved out into the harsh lights of reality and unceremoniously dumped in the incubator while my doctor sews several thousand stitches where my baby clocked in at a whopping 8 lbs. 4oz. (3,800 g).

He is immediately announced, *"Cok güzel"* (of course he is beautiful, he's no longer fighting his way out of my body!) and immediately checked to see that all is well.

My husband dispenses sips of water (water? Where's brandy when you need it?) and countless words of encouragement and praise to which I reply, "This is the last time *ever* in my *whole* life that I will *ever* have a baby. *Ever*."

Everybody thinks it is very funny and laughs. The mad crazy woman has such a sense of humor, aww. They're about to wheel my son out of the delivery room for further tests when my husband catches them mid-stride—wait, please put an ID band on him first. Oh yes, they immediately comply. Phew. My son has my coloring, and I can easily look like a local—no way would be I be able to identify him in a Turkish baby line-up as my very own.

Stitching done, and I get cleaned up, Dr. Moshe congratulates me, saying he'll drop in on me later. I am wheeled back to my room with a view, settled in bed, and now find I am absolutely starving. A nurse pops her head in the door asking what I'd like for breakfast. I start to answer but see that she is directing the question at my husband. He suggests some eggs would be nice, and some coffee, bread, and orange juice if it's not too much bother. "Sure!" she says and heads back out. I am dumbfounded.

She returns shortly with his meal, and I tentatively ask, "Um, may I have some too, please?"

"Oh no," she says, "You've just given birth; you're not allowed to eat for several hours."

I sit and watch my husband heartily gobble down his wonderfully mouth-wateringly aromatic breakfast, oblivious to the murderous stares from his beloved wife, his bride, the blessed mother of his first male child, and the person who has been split in two twice on account of him.

Soon Dr. Moshe pops his head in, holding our baby that he tenderly hands to me. All thoughts of payback have disappeared. This amazing child, with sticking-up thick black hair and eyes the size and color of ripe Turkish olives stares back at me, and I am in love all over again. Feeling that his duty of supportive partner and benevolent father is over, my husband heads for the office, and I'm left alone, exhausted, and hungry.

My ever faithful friend Barb comes over to visit, full of encouragement, praise, and a camera, which incredibly no one had thought of until that moment. I feel uplifted and blessed by her presence, and several hours later my hunger is vanquished when I eventually get served lunch.

Planning to stay in the hospital the whole seven days I've been allocated, I simultaneously realize two things: 1) I miss my daughter very much, and 2) the hospital staff, though highly proficient in French and German, cannot speak or understand English. I cannot explain my problem of blocked ducts, or need to feed outside "schedule." I feel frustrated and helpless and misunderstood, so after two days I check out.

Wrapping my baby in his first ever snowsuit, we venture out into a magical white and snowing Istanbul, heading back out on the very same highway we came on, now starting a life as a whole new family of four. Welcome home, I whisper as I lovingly place my son in the white crib near our bedroom window with its stunning view of the glistening Bosphorus, overlooking the continent of Asia just across the water. I feel fabulous; Dr. Moshe's skills as a surgeon were as expected—legendary even—I've gone back to pre-pregnancy size six jeans, and my son is the most gorgeous boy in the entire universe.

New motherhood bliss is hit with reality when my daughter returns from her prep school that afternoon to announce that there is a concert the next day, and she is to wear a costume with a food/cooking theme. *All* the other mothers have made costumes for their children, she says pointedly. That night, after feeding my three-day-old baby and putting him back in his cot to join the rest of the house in deep slumber, I pull out my seldom-used sewing machine, retrieve some linen table napkins, the only fabric I have available, and fashion a pale green apron for her, complete with frills and tied back bows. I am actually quite pleased with the results. Hmm, my brain had managed to remain intact and not get pulled out with the baby, excellent.

I am beyond tired the next morning, and now another snowstorm is upon us. I put my daughter on the school bus with her costume safely stored in her bag and tell her I'm not sure if we can attend her concert, it may not be wise to take a newborn out in such a storm. Her sad face as I wave her goodbye breaks my heart. I relent, rug up both my son and myself and order a taxi, and soon we are hurtling toward her school in the pelting snow.

It's late when we arrive, and the hall is filled with the dutifully punctual parents who have arrived to watch their child perform. I struggle with the weight of the baby capsule, mindful of the 13 stitches sewn into my nether regions three days ago, scanning the hall to look for a spare seat. There is none, so I stand at the back of the school hall along with a throng of teachers and other late parents like me.

Soon it's my daughter's class' turn to be on stage and there she is, but oh she is so unhappy! While everyone else sings and dances with huge smiles on their faces, she fumbles through her lines, sadness oozing out of her face, and I'm waving madly, I made it, we're here, we're here! Only she doesn't see me, doesn't hear me, and soon the performance is over, and I battle my way to the front, clutching onto my baby in his capsule, racing to tell her,

"I was here, I saw you!" Her smile, when she sees me, is priceless. She lights up like a thousand stars making it totally worth the trip through the snowstorm.

My eyes shine—with pride and with tears—as I look first at my five-year-old daughter and my three-day-old son. Life is pretty much perfect right now, and I would do childbirth all again in a heartbeat.

But on drugs next time.

Rosemary Gillan was born in India into a mixed heritage of Scottish, Indian, Portuguese, Irish and German bloodlines. Emigrating to Australia with her family in the 1970s, she carved out her identity as an Australian citizen, when a decade later her hotelier husband was transferred to England. So began her expatriate lifestyle which was to see her live in 14 countries, having two children, two dogs, several fish, and a divorce along the way (the fish were not the reason for the divorce). Rosemary is currently back home in Melbourne, Australia, undergoing her third attempt at repatriation and continues to struggle with answering the question, "But where are you really from?" Rosemary has been published in Once Upon An Expat and is currently writing her first book, Tales of a Hotel Wife and Other Stories from Hell. You can find Rosemary on Facebook and Instagram.

CHAPTER 4

AN UNEXPECTED DISCOVERY IN THAILAND

Clara Wiggins
Nationality: British
Knocked up in: Jamaica and Thailand

I sat on the edge of the bed in the characterless hotel room and stared at the stick in my hand. There wasn't much mistaking it: two lines. The second had shown up more or less immediately—I had barely had time to get out of the adjoining bathroom where I had first taken a deep breath and then taken the test before it had appeared. As if the tiny baby inside me was impatient for me to know she was there. Come on, Mom, she was saying. Stop eating that unhealthy street food and drinking that beer, and start to think about me.

I was thousands of miles from home in an anonymous Thai hotel surrounded by people I barely knew, in the middle of one of the most harrowing events of the 21st century, and I had just found out I was pregnant for the first time. As if my life wasn't complicated enough, I now had to work out how to disengage myself from the situation I found myself in and somehow get myself and my little grain of rice home. While telling as few people as possible why I wanted to leave. This was going to be interesting!

The events that led to that unremarkable hotel in Phuket started a few weeks earlier on the tropical island of Jamaica. Known as much for its crime and violence as for its reggae and jerk chicken, I was posted to the British High Commission as a second secretary in the political section. Most of the work we did revolved around the ongoing "war on drugs," and so I found myself working alongside my then-partner (now husband) Keith on a regular basis.

To escape the stresses of the job, we regularly fled the confines of the madness that is Kingston and headed for the coast. Jamaica is blessed with beauty in all directions— we could choose to journey any way we chose, and we would eventually hit one of the idyllic beaches that lined its shores.

This particular occasion we had gone west, to Negril— the resort town at the tip of the island where aging American ladies looking for love and partying spring breakers looking for something else meet on the golden sands. We had a few favorite hotels and had chosen one of them to spend that New Year's—swimming, drinking, diving, relaxing. The stuff that all our dreams are made of. Especially those of us who have since had children.

Before we headed off to Negril, we had been following the awful story unfolding in Asia of a tsunami that had swept inland, taking hundreds of thousands of lives with it. This was huge news all around the world—mostly because among those lives had been a not insignificant number of "westerners," including British nationals vacationing in the region. But Southeast Asia is a long way from Jamaica. So while we tracked the tragedy on our television screens along with everyone else, it didn't feel all that real to us as we set off to the beach for our New Year's break.

The hotel was as excellent as ever and we certainly made the most of the facilities. We both went diving, and we both partook of the free alcohol on offer—although I do recall uncharacteristically choosing a softie over an alcoholic beverage at one point. Looking back, I wonder if my body was trying to tell me something.

Once New Year's was out of the way, we headed back to Kingston feeling relaxed and refreshed, ready to get back into the swing of our jobs. I had a stack of work to get on with and official visitors due any day. We had a lot of visitors in Kingston at that time, and I often found myself taking them around to meet various politicians and other contacts, accompanying them to official functions or just being there to help smooth the way for their visits. I knew I had a busy time ahead in my official role.

All that changed with one email.

Sitting down at my desk on the first day back at work— probably January 2 or 3—I opened up my email to find a message from London asking for volunteers to come to Thailand. Over the previous years, the UK Foreign Office's response to crises like the Bali bombing and other similar events had come under increasing scrutiny. They had begun to change the way they dealt with these serious incidents—including employing "rapid reaction" teams to get to the epicenter of the event as fast as possible.

But sometimes, and this was one of these times, the sheer size of the crisis was overwhelming. There were just too many people involved, too many missing British nationals, too many bodies washing up. The embassy in Bangkok sent out a call for help. Its staff had been working non-stop round the clock and were exhausted. Many of them weren't trained to deal with the work that they had to take on—anything from simple data collection to telling relatives that their loved one had died. Other embassies in the region were also having to deal with the aftermath of the tsunami, which affected 14 countries across two continents. About a week after the tragedy hit, an email was sent to every member of the Foreign Office in the world asking for anyone with any relevant experience to come to their aid.

Looking at the contents of the email that morning, my initial thought was that they wouldn't want me as I was such a long way from Thailand. Hold up a globe and you will see that Jamaica is about as far as you can get from Southeast Asia. I almost deleted the email and carried on with my job—but then I thought about my experience and decided I may as well volunteer my assistance.

One of the roles they were looking for were people with press office experience. Before my posting to Jamaica, I had worked in our London office heading up the section of the press office that dealt with consular work. This meant lots and lots of conversations with journalists about why we couldn't give them the names of the people who had fallen off a balcony in Spain. Or gone missing in Brazil. It also meant dealing with some very high-profile cases that needed extremely careful handling—and for which you really did need to know what you were doing.

I had also worked in the press office on 9/11 and dealt with the onslaught of media interest in the British nationals caught up in that awful event. With my small team, we worked long shifts trying to manage what little information we had with the expectations of some of the most persistent journalists in the world.

Part of my role then was to fly out to New York to relieve colleagues out there who had been working non-stop since the planes first hit the towers. It was stressful, but it also meant I now had the experience needed for Thailand. I shot off an email and doubted I would ever hear anything about it again.

Except within hours, they said yes, they would like me to come thank you very much, and here were the people I had to contact about booking my journey. Apparently, the fact that it would take me three flights—including two overnighters—to get there was neither here nor there. They really were desperate for help!

It took about two more days for my flight to be booked, loose ends tied up at work, and suitcase to be packed. At this point, I had no idea how long I would be gone for, so I packed just about everything I might possibly need. I also didn't really know what to expect when I got there—information was pretty sketchy about what I would be doing, as I think this was very much still a moving situation.

Eventually, I said goodbye to Keith and headed for the airport. Because of the late notice, the only flight to the UK available was via Miami, so I started off with the short hop up to America. Here I had a day to kill. *An entire day.* Have you ever spent a day at Miami airport? It isn't the most exciting airport in the world, though you can definitely get enough of plastic pink flamingos and alligator-shaped chocolate.

However, I was flying business class (a perk of the job in those days), and so took myself off to the lounge for a few hours to relax. While I was there, an old man came in with family, causing a stir right through the room. As he left, everyone got up and clapped! Who was this man? I finally got the truth from the receptionists at the lounge gate—the "old man" was none other than former President Jimmy Carter!

Anyway, my next surprise happened when I finally boarded my London-bound flight. As I arrived at the plane door, the cabin crew ushered me not just to the left but right to the front of the plane...into first class! I am guessing the fact that I told them on check-in what I was doing and why helped get me that upgrade, as well as being a single, smartly dressed traveler with an executive club membership. Funnily enough, it never happens these days now that I have kids.

The flight itself was uneventful—I could have had champagne on tap, but given the circumstances of my journey I didn't really feel like it. I had another day to kill when I arrived in London, punctuated by a trip to see the Foreign Office-designated nurse at St Thomas' hospital by the Thames to check what medications/vaccinations I might need for my trip.

"Could you be pregnant?" she asked.

"Well, it's a vague possibility...a very vague one," I replied.

We had started trying but really only just started and very half-heartedly. I was 37, my partner 39. This was bound to take months if not years to happen.

The nurse looked at me askance and made a note. She also adjusted my recommended medication accordingly. I went on my way. Twenty-four hours later and I was finally in Bangkok.

The second leg of my journey had gone smoothly, and we arrived in Thailand as a group of newcomers ready to do our bit. We dumped our stuff in our hotel rooms, and we were taken straight into the office and told what needed doing. There was no standing on attention— this was a serious situation, and we had to be ready to get our hands dirty.

For me, though the work wasn't all that obvious—I had come with a specialty and wanted to use it. It took a few days, but eventually I managed to get moved down to Phuket where the real action was happening. Here I became part of a team of some of the friendliest and most efficient people I would ever meet during my time in the

Office. I am not sure whether this sort of crisis attracts the right sort of people or just brings out the best in them, but I felt immediately welcomed when I started my new temporary role. Which was a good thing as we were all having to deal with some fairly horrific stuff—mounds of clothes, shoes, bags, and other items that needed to be sifted through for identification purposes, families to be taken to visit morgues, very stressed and often understandably angry local British nationals to placate.

I busied myself mostly with dealing with the press—which is what I knew and felt comfortable with, although I helped out in other areas where necessary. At one point I needed to fly up to Bangkok to attend a lunch party for journalists I had arranged for the ambassador. It was around this time I was expecting my period—but with all the traveling, my dates were a little hazy, so I wasn't too fussed that nothing had happened so far. However, at Phuket airport on the way up I remember buying some diarrhea medicine as my tummy felt a little dicky. Again, I just put it down to all the travel and the greasy Thai food we had been enjoying.

A couple of days later and still no sign of my "monthlies." I was just starting to feel a little worried when an opportunity to visit some of the temporary morgues established along the coast came up—something that I didn't particularly want to do, but which would help me talk to the press about why identifying victims of the tragedy was such an enormous task. I knew there were unlikely to be any obvious toilet stops along the way, but the appalling scenes a colleague and I encountered that day took my mind off what might or might not be going on "down below." It was a very sobering day and one that will probably remain with me forever.

By the next day, though, I knew I could put off the task no longer. I needed to know one way or another. Luckily Boots (a well-known UK drugstore chain) happened to have a store right there in Phuket, so I was able to creep in, checking none of my colleagues were in there stocking up on their shower gel or shampoo, and find a pregnancy testing kit on the shelves. After paying, I hid it in my bag and scurried back to my room.

Earlier in the day, I had warned Keith—who was still back in Jamaica—that I would be taking the test. I was still in denial though, and I don't think had conveyed properly in the email I sent him quite how likely it was that the result would be positive. I knew he was waiting for a result—but I wasn't going to call him unless it was a yes. After all, with time differences between the two countries, it was the middle of the night in Jamaica.

Which I pretty well forgot about when I saw that second line and realized where things stood. I returned to my desk feeling shaky and actually told the woman who had been sitting opposite me for the last couple of weeks and become quite a friend what had happened before I phoned Keith. He knew as soon as the phone rang in the depths of the Kingston night that he was going to be a daddy.

It took me another few days to extract myself from Phuket. I decided not to tell anyone the reason why I wanted to leave. It was still very early days, plus I would soon be looking for another posting and knew I was unlikely to be considered if they knew I was pregnant (my instinct was correct—I was unable to secure another overseas role during pregnancy or after my child was born and ended up resigning from the job).

Luckily, the role I was there for was all but wrapped up, and I was able to plead that I was needed back at my own job. As it happened, I was owed some vacation, so I flew back to the UK to meet up with Keith who had hopped on a plane from Kingston to meet me. We ended up getting engaged that week and married a few months later by the sea in Jamaica. By that time, I was nearly five months gone, looking dumpy rather than glowing and wishing I could join in with the tequila and champagne celebrations my now husband indulged in.

Our first daughter Emma was born a few months later in September 2005 in our now hometown of Cheltenham in the west of England. She chose the hard way—after an emergency scan in Kingston, which showed she was still head up, and my decision not to opt for a breech birth for my first I decided to have her by Cesarean section. This was indicative of a little girl who would always know her own mind and do things the way she wanted to. The doctors tried to turn her, but she was adamant she wanted to stay put.

But in the end, she was healthy and happy and in no way affected by her round-the-world journey into a devastating crisis zone while still a tiny speck in my tummy. At least she doesn't seem to be affected by it. Although for a child who has subsequently lived on a Caribbean island she has always hated the sea.

Born in Cuba to British diplomat parents, Clara started traveling as a baby and hasn't stopped. She has lived in 11 countries on five continents and visited nearly 70. Along the way, she picked up a husband, Keith, and produced two daughters. She has worked as a journalist, diplomat, writer, press officer, a prenatal teacher, customer service advisor, PA, coffee shop waitress, school cook (although that was only for one day). She now works from home, managing a journal (the International Journal of Birth and Parent Education), and marketing the Expat Partner's Survival Guide—as well as looking after the kiddies. She is currently living in South Africa. She is a contributor of Knocked Up Abroad.

CHAPTER 5

WINGING IT IN WEST AFRICA

Nicola Beach
Nationality: British
Knocked up in: Nigeria
Birthed in: United Kingdom
Parented in: Nigeria

Our first child was born while we were living in Lagos, Nigeria. For reasons that will become clear, I flew home to the UK for the birth, returning to Lagos a few short weeks later. We were subsequently based in Lagos until our daughter turned two.

It wasn't until we moved back to the UK and had our second child that I realized quite what a baptism of fire we'd been through compared to our home country contemporaries who experienced the whole process of pregnancy, birth, and raising a toddler in the UK.

Lagos, Nigeria is a thrumming megacity. As you are driven (for few expats drive themselves), you are likely to see piles of rubbish heaped along the roadside. You will see street vendors and beggars, the very poorest of all who literally don't even have a shirt on their back and walk naked and dreadlocked, covered in nothing more than a layer of dust, picking through trash for anything of value. It's hot and humid. The traffic is insane. You will sweat a lot. The city and its inhabitants, though, are both vibrant and colorful. Welcome to organized chaos.

Things have been improving over the 20 years since I first visited Lagos. Land has been reclaimed from the lagoons and new roads have been built. The stark rich-poor divide that was evident in the 1990s has been softened by an expanding middle class. This thriving and ambitious socioeconomic group is striving for a bright future.

However, in terms of an expat assignment location, when we were in Lagos it was (and perhaps still is) considered a hardship posting. There is relatively little on offer in the way of cultural entertainment, historic interest, or fine dining. Imported goods can be hard to come by or incredibly expensive. Top quality medical care is another thing that was (I say "was," as we left a number of years ago and a lot can change in such a short time) difficult to come by, and by goodness, it can be a frustrating place to live.

It's the tightest-knit expat community I've ever come across. Everybody knows everybody, and the minute we were married the older expats started checking their watches and watching my drinking habits to try and be the first to know. The question asked wasn't "Do you want kids?" or "Can you have kids?"—it was "Are you pregnant yet?" *No pressure.* I'd actually bought a stash of pregnancy testing kits in the UK, knowing full well that anywhere I went in Lagos I was bound to be spotted, and the jungle drums would immediately start beating, spreading rumors and half-truths, meaning everybody else would probably know I was pregnant before I did. To everybody's great delight, we didn't have to wait long.

Constant cravings and haywire hormones are all part and parcel of pregnancy wherever you are in the world. Pregnant in Lagos, a craving for plantain chips or pounded yam would have been easily satisfied, but this baby was demanding tomato soup. But not just any old tomato soup, oh no, this baby wanted tin after tin of a very specific brand of tomato soup. For days we scoured every supermarket shelf for every last battered and expired tin. I would pace up and down the kitchen each day, opening and closing cupboard doors and then weep in frustration because all I wanted was the elusive soup.

Pregnancy is a fickle bitch though; the minute my husband returned from a business trip, his suitcase stuffed with the yearned-for soup, the craving disappeared.

Then there were the hormones. Although I'm generally very non-confrontational, there was an expat ladies lunch where the service was painfully slow. The food, when it eventually arrived, was revolting. The lettuce was brown, the cheese thin and plastic, the tomatoes were green, and the chicken was virtually raw.

Some of the ladies I was with gently tried to explain to the manager that the food was unacceptable and that word of mouth was a powerful thing. The manager seemed more interested in fiddling with her phone and shrugged in an "eat it, don't eat it, I don't care, you're still paying handsomely for it" kind of way.

The lunch fell during a three-month period of my pregnancy when I would wake up every morning and be thrilled that it was breakfast time. I was constantly hungry. Pregnant, ravenous, and hormonal, I stood in the restaurant and flung my plate across the table. I made it clear that I would not be paying for the overpriced excuse for food, that none of us would, and that the restaurant was a disgrace. (It was a disgrace, but being a group of British ladies, we had all been too polite to put it so bluntly.)

"I'm bloody hungry!" were my parting words and then I flounced out in a huff in full hunter-gatherer mode looking for somewhere, anywhere, to get a meal.

Six months pregnant, I marched (okay, I waddled) purposefully through the sandy car park, then along a potholed pavement until I found an Italian place I recognized. I'd been there once before and immediately sat down and ordered a meal with no care to the carnage I'd left behind (the first restaurant was meanwhile trying to screw the other ladies on the drinks bill).

My sole interest at that moment was food, and I sat like a hungry dog, eyes laser-focused on the kitchen door. I'd hitched a ride to the lunch with a neighbor, as my husband needed the car for work. I had absolutely no idea how I was going to get home, and Lagos is not the kind of city where pregnant foreign ladies hail a cab on the street. But...I didn't care.

Eventually, three of my friends tracked me down and kept me company while I vacuumed up a huge portion of pasta, and then they kindly took me home, marveling at my unexpected outburst.

Over the months, I went for regular check-ups at a clinic recommended by other expat mothers. I can't actually remember what it was called, but there was a lot of waiting around in a dingy avocado-painted waiting room.

I went to my first consultation with low expectations and was not disappointed. I'm not sure I've ever seen such a narrow or unstable doctor's couch. The whole wonky thing shook every time I drew breath. Mid-consultation the door crashed open (*hi there, everybody in the waiting room*), and a perspiring maintenance man in faded blue overalls barged in with his ladder.

"Morning Madame, I just check de A/C unit okay," said perspiring maintenance man. It was a statement, not a question. He continued to crash and clatter about. Meanwhile the doctor continued his checks, seemingly oblivious. I wobbled on the bed and tried to avoid making uncomfortable eye contact with the maintenance guy. The doctor reported that everything was looking fine, but as the printer was broken, he wasn't able to print a much-hoped-for scan image for us.

As my pregnancy progressed, it became increasingly important to begin any outing with an empty bladder. Trust me when I tell you that when you are stuck in a proper Lagos traffic jam (referred to there as a "go-slow"), there is nowhere to go.

In addition to the empty bladder, you would carefully plan your route to include the handful of known public toilets. When I say known toilets and public toilets, they weren't really either, rather a network of secret toilets along off-limit back corridors and behind locked storerooms of supermarkets, discovered by desperate pregnant expats who were close to peeing their pants in public.

This precious knowledge was passed from expectant expat mother to expectant expat mother. Information like that is worth its weight in gold, and it wouldn't surprise me if, since then, some enterprising expat mother or mother-to-be has actually drawn up a detailed map and sold copies for vast sums of money.

The traffic wasn't just a problem for full pregnant bladders. There was an urban legend about the expat woman who had decided that giving birth locally would be fine. She went into labor and set off to the hospital with her driver.

Unfortunately, she got stuck in the mother of all Lagos go-slows and ended up giving birth in her car with assistance from her driver. Please understand, that in a

Lagos go-slow your car will be tightly wedged on all sides, with other vehicles mere inches away. Street vendors and beggars will then weave between the trapped vehicles, selling or begging. All are persistent and think nothing of leaning over your car and staring through the window. The tale turned out to be true. I met the woman, at a party; a whisper went round, "That's her, she's the one."

The expat who stays in Lagos for the birth is (or at least in my time was) the exception rather than the rule. Primarily, this was due to worries about acceptable health care. In the event of serious complications or medical emergencies, the best option was to be medevacked all the way to South Africa, approximately a six-hour flight away. Add running the traffic gauntlet into the mix (nobody wants to be *that* lady in the traffic jam), and virtually all expats return to their home country to have their baby.

I flew back to the UK around the 32–34-week mark, with a doctor's note confirming I was in good health. Being back in the UK for the birth was reassuring, although I would get sideways looks when I went to prenatal classes and insisted that my husband was working in Africa and would be returning for D-Day. There were sideways looks of pity and disbelief; the other mothers and the severe midwife with her demonstration plastic womb all clearly thought I was completely deluded, feeling the need to create such a ridiculous fictional husband and a convoluted backstory of a mythical life in West Africa.

Due to the fact that a C-section was looking increasingly likely, I was transferred from a local midwife-led unit to a larger, better equipped hospital mid-labor. While I was vomiting uncontrollably and waiting for my ambulance transfer, it dawned on me that there was a very real possibility that the paramedic on call would be my brother's best friend, whom I'd known (and teased) since he was 11. Thank goodness karma was kind to me, and he was working a different route. Apart from the hospital transfer and an emergency C-section, the birth was fairly uneventful. In fact, my overriding memory is the frustration that while hot tea and toast were being delivered to my husband at regular intervals, I was limited to sips of water.

Trying to arrange our daughter's initial inoculations before we returned to Lagos was a giant headache. Getting the standard ones done was tricky enough. Then, I booked an appointment with the travel clinic nurse to see which travel jabs our girl could have and when. The nurse was horrified, and that's all-caps H.O.R.R.I.F.I.E.D., that we were taking our tiny infant to such a dangerous place.

Her oh-so-helpful-advice was, "Why don't you wait until she's older, like a teenager?"

She didn't seem to grasp that we already lived in West Africa, that we had lived there for three years and would be there for a further two. Waiting until our child turned 18 wasn't a viable option for family life.

The nurse was also dubious of our living arrangements, and I had to reassure her that we did not live in a thatched mud hut, with a giant mortar and pestle in the corner for me to pound my yams.

She was skeptical when I described our modern and weather-proof apartment with electricity (well, most of the time we had electricity) and running water, in a city, a chaotic city, but a concrete city nonetheless.

I explained that although we prefer the healthcare options offered in the UK, particularly for emergencies and childbirth, that there were actual doctors, who had gone to accredited medical schools in Lagos, whom we would consult in the event of health issues. I suppose she was picturing us venturing to a traditional healer who might use potions, animal parts, and spells to treat maladies.

Eventually, after great persistence our daughter had all the requisite jabs. I would just like to clarify that we took advice from numerous medical practitioners on our best options, our child's welfare being our uppermost priority, but it still took a lot of effort to get the right combination of inoculations in the right order so that we were ready to travel. We stocked up on everything we thought we might need that we wouldn't be able to easily obtain at the other end, took a very deep collective breath, and headed back to Lagos with our tiny, shiny new babe in arms.

Babies arrive with a sack full of love. The other sack they bring is weighted down with worry. Returning to Lagos with a newborn baby brought its own set of additional anxieties and problems.

Malaria was an enormous concern, probably our greatest one. After all, it's the biggest killer in Africa. Children under five are particularly susceptible, and tiny babies are unable to take malaria prophylaxes.

We bought (in the UK) a mosquito net for the car seat and another for the cot. The car seat net had an unforeseen dual purpose. In addition to keeping out mosquitoes, it prevented locals, often wanting to stick their fingers into our daughter's mouth, from poking their hands uninvited into the seat.

But as our daughter grew, she needed a bigger car seat, which was not mosquito net-able. Also, once she was able to stand in her cot, we began to weigh up the protection of the mosquito net versus the possibility of her becoming dangerously tangled in it.

Other preventative measures we counted on included frequent mosquito hunts (I am an expert at obliterating the tricky little buggers with their erratic flight pattern) and stocking up on DEET-free mosquito cream. We would slather our girl in it every time we left the house. Apart from being sticky and stinky as a result of the repellent, she thankfully remained malaria-free.

Once she was old enough (from memory around the six-month mark), we explored different antimalarial options. There was a liquid one that we tried hiding in her milk bottle as per the doctor's advice. She was onto that straightaway and spat the first mouthful out and then refused to touch the bottle, her tiny rosebud mouth firmly closed, doing a resolute head dodge. We sought further medical advice, and I think we ended up crushing a quarter tablet of the malaria medication we were taking, and that worked a treat.

I've already explained that the supermarket shelves in Lagos were not as satisfactorily or plentifully stocked as those in many other countries. Every time we traveled back home to the UK, we would run a full baby goods' stock-take and calculate how long we expected it to be before one of us would travel out again, and therefore how many cartons of formula we would need, how many diapers, and how many clothes for the following three to six months.

As a tiny child, our extrovert daughter was ever-cheerful and completely unfazed by the chaotic city she inhabited. She would wave and smile enthusiastically at the various beggars that knocked on the car window. If they weren't knocking on our window, she would knock at them, bringing them to linger for what felt like an awkward eternity as our girl tried to engage with them.

When we visited the UK, Sweetpea would single out anybody African-looking and shine her beaming smile upon him or her. It confused a lot of people and made us chuckle, particularly when our blue-eyed blonde went through a brief phase of calling all men "Daddy."

The first six months were tough. Like most first time mothers, I didn't have a clue what I was doing. I also didn't have a readymade group of friends from a prenatal class to muddle along with either. Nor did I have old friends or helpful family members rallying round. There was no *Rhyme Time* at the local library. There were no baby swimming, baby signing, or baby massage classes to get us out of the house. There was one international playgroup with a six-month waiting list, but six months was a long time to have to wait to tap into that network.

So, yes, I really did muddle along to begin with. Our house helper, though, was ever ready to impart helpful parenting tips. The two tips I remember best were that we needed to give Sweetpea a daily dose of custard, and that we should regularly oil her hair. It was well-meant, but it wasn't really the kind of advice I needed.

At the same time, I was also grateful, every day, for the things I did have, in sharp contrast to so many around me. The poorest Nigerians would struggle to put food on the table, didn't have access to mosquito nets or childhood vaccinations, and would have to scrape together school fees to ensure the most basic level of education. They probably didn't have medical insurance or even basic first aid items like plasters or antiseptic cream.

I appreciated luxuries such as having a washing machine to deal with onesies/bodysuits covered in up-the-back-poop and a clean kitchen with full cupboards. I was thankful for air conditioning to ease us through sweltering tropical nights, which also helped to keep the mosquitoes at bay.

So despite any challenges we encountered, I made sure to always count my lucky stars, lucky stars that are easy to lose sight of if you're in a first world country and your biggest worries are whether the supermarket has run out of your must-have brand of organic baby goo or whether or not your husband will be home in time to help with bath and bed; or, when the time comes, seriously considering taking a second job to fund private school fees, because your four-year-old didn't get into the most coveted government-funded school.

Despite the dirt and grime of Lagos, the mosquitoes and crushing humidity, all the expat babies and toddlers seemed to grow like robust little weeds. Amazingly, our daughter had barely a cough or sniffle, despite a disgusting phase of shoe-licking and despite finding her, aged two, on her hands and knees happily lapping tap water from a dog bowl at a friend's house.

My friend was quick to reassure me that the bowl was clean, the water was fresh, and her faithful dog had not yet touched it. "It's tap water, isn't it though?" I said tightly. "I'm more worried about her catching cholera or typhoid."

There were some advantages to raising a toddler abroad. From early on, our small child learned to be flexible and adaptable (international travel often doesn't fit with rigid schedules). We were always together and had a lot of quality bonding time with the extreme luxury of not having to go out to work and juggle a job, home and find appropriate and affordable childcare.

By being a little bit off-grid and out of the system, I think we also managed to avoid some of the pressure and judgment of well-meaning "others" either offering advice or obsessively checking and comparing your child's developmental milestones. In that respect those early years were refreshingly stress-free.

We sweated the big stuff (like malaria avoidance), which means we didn't sweat the small stuff (the world didn't end if a biscuit fell on the floor and was subsequently eaten), and I think ultimately that's a good thing.

Lagos is not for everyone—if you are a neurotic, hygiene-obsessed type-A person, a Lagos pregnancy, or even a Lagos posting, might just tip you over the edge, but ultimately I don't regret our experience at all. Yes, I felt like I was winging it the entire time, but then what mother doesn't feel like that? Our girl more than survived those first two years and appears to have developed an incredible immune system. I guess all that shoe-licking paid off.

Nicola Beach is a second-generation expat, who has dodged bullets in Lagos, stray cats in Istanbul, and is currently getting cozy in Jozi. She blogs about her family's far-flung travels and further fetched tales of expat life at www.expatorama.com.

CHAPTER 6

KNOCKED UP IN JOHANNESBURG

Debi Beaumont
Nationality: British
Knocked up in: South Africa

After two years away, we were back in South Africa. And this time, we were thrilled to be there. When we had our first posting in Johannesburg, we were pretty nervous. Everyone knows Johannesburg for its violent crime and poverty. What we found during that first posting was that it is actually a modern, cosmopolitan city, with wonderful people and fantastic weather. Johannesburg is at 6,000 feet (1,700 meters) above sea level, an altitude that makes it one of the highest cities in the world. This means the summers are hot but rarely get much above 86°F (30°C). The winters are mild and short, with beautiful blue skies every day.

The main benefit of this great weather is that if you have young children, they can play outside, get plenty of fresh air, and enjoy the huge range of sports activities open to children living here. The first time we arrived in South Africa, we had a four-month-old baby boy. We moved from London, where we lived in a small house with a postage stamp-sized garden. Suddenly we were living in a secure estate in the northern suburbs of Johannesburg with a large garden, a swimming pool, and miles of walking trails and nature walks. By the time we returned, we had another four-month-old baby boy, and knowing that our sons would be able to enjoy an outdoor lifestyle was one of the biggest draws bringing us back to Johannesburg.

Settling in the second time was smooth. We knew the area. I still knew some of the expats and locals from our first posting. Old friends recommended a lovely school for my oldest son who was now three years old. As an expat in South Africa, it is commonplace to have a domestic worker. Our wonderful domestic worker, Sophie, returned to work for us, keeping the house shipshape and helping with the children whenever I asked. Her endless patience and sunny personality ensured our house was a happy one.

Before you pack your bags and quickly head over to this utopia I am portraying, it is important to remember this is still Africa. My husband likes to refer to South Africa as "Africa for beginners," but it is still a third world country. It was unusual for a week to go by without some bizarre experience or other. When these incidents occurred, they became lovingly referred to as having an "African experience."

For example, when we noticed that our new house had unusual electricity bills, only to find out that our electricity meter was connected to our neighbor's house. This took hours and days and months of time to rectify. Or the time my husband was stopped by the police on his way home from work and accused of being drunk. After being detained for around 10 minutes on the side of the road, the policeman, who was clearly after a bribe, reluctantly let my teetotal husband continue his journey. Or the organized chaos that is "load shedding." This is when the national power supplier schedules rolling power cuts due to electricity demand being higher than supply. Not only does all the power go off in the home during these blackouts, but all the traffic lights stop working, the lights go off in the malls and supermarkets, and the pumps at the gas station cannot pump petrol.

Despite these frequent "African experiences," the first year flew by, and after a long, lazy Christmas break with visiting relatives, my husband posed that question—"Shall we have another baby?" We were so comfortably settled in South Africa that it was tempting to say yes. But after two difficult pregnancies, did I really want to go through the morning sickness, the sleepless nights, the breastfeeding again?

I decided to let fate decide. It had taken me well over a year to conceive my previous two children. I thought the likelihood of conceiving any quicker was unlikely. I told my husband we would give it a year. If I didn't conceive in that time, I would be too old, and we would stay content with two children. I was pregnant the next month. Fate had made up her mind quickly.

Like my other pregnancies, this one proved to be very difficult. The next nine months passed in a fog of nausea with unbearable tiredness, a 30% increase in weight, and almost daily vomiting. I'd been pretty bad with the first two, but this was a full nine months of torture. I don't know if it was my age, or the fact I was tired from the other kids, or perhaps even the altitude, but it was no fun.

I dragged myself to the nearest obstetrician. We were fortunate enough to have health insurance, so I would give birth in a private hospital. I knew the private system in

South Africa was known for its C-sections. Something like 70% of private births are by C-section here. The rate is even higher in wealthier areas. However, my first child had been born in the UK, where elective C-section is rarely an option, unless you are married to a famous soccer player. My second child was born in Australia where the rate is still high at 32%, but a C-section was not something even suggested by my obstetrician in Melbourne. The fact that I had two previous natural births seemed to indicate to the obstetrician at my local private hospital in Johannesburg that she shouldn't suggest a C-section either, and it was never discussed.

The private birth option that I was using meant I saw the doctor often. With my first pregnancy in the UK, I had two scans. One at 12 weeks and another around 22 weeks. In South Africa, I had a scan at least every six weeks, and it got more and more frequent as the pregnancy progressed. During the final few weeks, I had a scan every week. Once again my husband and I had elected not to find out the sex of the baby. We weren't "trying for a girl," so the surprise would be fun either way.

Despite unbearable nausea, the pregnancy passed without incident. The baby in utero was healthy. I had almost everything needed for the baby's arrival—cot, pram, clothes—because this was the third child. And although this was Africa, most things were available at the local Baby City specialist store.

Just as was the case with my second child, I went into labor two days before my due date. Asleep that night, I was awoken by a wet trickle down my leg. My water had broken. I crept to the nursery and called the hospital to inform them of what was happening. It was at this point that my African birthing experience began.

I told the midwife on reception that my water had broken. She asked if I was now wearing a pad, and I replied that I wasn't because there had only been a small trickle at this point. She told me I was mistaken and that I had merely wet myself. Having been through labor twice before, I knew that my water had broken, and I had not merely lost control of my bladder. I told her this but said I would spend some time relaxing at home before making my way to the hospital. After the overexcited labor of my first child, I knew the best thing to do was to relax at home and try to do anything but think of the baby.

Let me take you back to six years earlier and my first labor experience. This time, I was in the UK. I had been so excited when my water broke that I rushed to the hospital only to be sent home. I was told that I wasn't dilating, and that I just needed to relax and allow my labor to progress. Easier said than done. I was so terribly excited and nervous that the adrenalin smothered the oxytocin and contractions would start and then disappear. After two days of this, I was admitted into an overcrowded prenatal ward full of emotional pregnant women who were all having complications with the final stages of their pregnancy.

A few hours after admission I was given a pessary to induce labor. My husband was sent home and told it would probably still be a long time until I got into active labor. However, it turned out this pessary was all I needed to get the show on the road. With no husband and no available room on the delivery ward, I was suddenly in full-blown active labor. There weren't even any nurses to be seen in the prenatal ward, and some poor woman who was suffering from preeclampsia had to half carry me down the corridor shouting for someone to help. I was popped into a side room and left to get on with things.

With no midwife, no husband, and no pain relief, it was a surreal and slightly scary couple of hours, but finally, I managed to crawl up the corridor and call my husband, who shot over to the hospital and got me into the delivery ward.

Another 10 hours of labor, a welcome last minute epidural, and an hour of pushing, and finally out popped Zachary Michael, some three days after my water had first broken. I learned my lesson. In the future, when I went into labor, I would think of anything but the labor and just try to rest and even sleep.

This approach proved very successful with my second son. My husband's work had taken us to Melbourne, Australia. We were provided with private medical care by his company, and the choice of plush private hospitals was amazing compared with my choice-free UK birth. I chose a maternity hospital about a 15-minute drive from our home. As the hospital specialized in mother and baby services, the whole place had a calm and serene feel to it.

The night I went into labor with that familiar trickle of water down my leg in the middle of the night, I chose to ignore that anything was happening. I slept on, waking slightly for a contraction and then falling straight back to sleep.

As the contractions became more painful, my husband lying in the bed next to me became aware that something was happening. I told him the contractions had started to come quite quickly and perhaps we should head to the hospital. I asked him to get things ready while I continued with my approach of pretending nothing was happening and trying to sleep. Some time passed, and the contractions were intensifying. Yet my husband had not returned to the bedroom. I finally decided it was time to wake myself up. I shuffled downstairs to find my husband sat at the kitchen table, enjoying a large bowl of cereal and surfing the Internet on his brand new iPad. Gobsmacked, I asked him why he wasn't getting everything ready to go to the hospital. After the lengthy labor with our first son, it seemed my husband felt there was no need to rush.

I persuaded him we needed to go, and we arrived to find a waiting team of happy, helpful midwives. When they first examined me and found I was already 6 cm dilated, my husband did a dance around the delivery room. Things were going a lot quicker the second time around. I was encouraged to use gas and air when the contractions came, and before I knew it, I was ready to push. The calm but authoritative attitude of the midwife in charge meant it was only a couple of pushes before Jed Samuel arrived in the world, just six hours after my water broke.

Back in South Africa, I naturally decided to adopt this same approach with my third labor of relaxing, half sleeping on the couch in the nursery and trying to pretend it simply wasn't happening. After a couple of hours, I knew the contractions were a few minutes apart. I woke my husband. It was time to get to the hospital. We headed off, stopping every four minutes because I told my husband I couldn't bear the motion of the car when the contractions came.

We hobbled down to the maternity ward. It was the early hours of Sunday morning, and everything was very quiet. When we got to the reception, there was a midwife relaxing in a chair, feet up on the desk, not a care in the world. This was the woman who had told me I had wet myself, and she seemed just as unprepared to believe that I was in labor as I stood before her as she had over the phone.

She slowly rose to her feet and asked us to fill in some paperwork. Then we were shown, in an equally slow manner, to a room on the maternity ward where she said she would check my contractions. I was hooked up to her machines where she continued to ask endless questions about me and my medical history. Twice I was asked if I smoked, and given the waft around the woman, I began to wonder if she was asking for my records or asking because she was hoping I might be able to give her a cigarette.

After a lengthy period of having questions fired at me in between contractions, I asked why she couldn't just use the doctor's records for all this information. I was told the maternity ward did not have access to the doctor's records.

At this point some things about the South African private medical system became clear. As the hospital and the doctor were separate entities, they did not share information, and as such, I was completely unknown to the maternity ward. Second, and perhaps more alarmingly, because this was a Sunday night, in a hospital where the vast majority of births were by planned C-section, there was only a skeleton staff on duty, and this woman didn't seem to be particularly experienced in or have much knowledge of natural births.

I was having a full-blown "African experience."

Thank goodness it was my third birth, and my husband and I were calm. We realized at this point that we just needed to get on with things ourselves. I asked for some gas and air, which had been such a help during my second birth. However, my midwife informed me that this wasn't the delivery ward, it was the maternity ward, and therefore there was no gas and air available. I asked why I wasn't being moved to the delivery ward and was told that my contractions were "very mild" and that I was not properly in labor.

This was something of a surprise as I had done this twice before; I felt fairly convinced things were moving along at a quick pace. I calmly told her that the contractions may seem mild to her, but they certainly did not seem mild to me, and that I would like some gas and air. The woman disappeared. A little later she returned, not with gas and air, but a syringe. She authoritatively said to my husband that she was going to sedate me as I was clearly hysterical.

At that point my husband lost his cool, and ironically, the situation became slightly hysterical. My husband told her to get out of the room as we no longer needed her help and we would call her if and when necessary. Together, and alone, we were calm and focused. The next hour or two were a blur due to the increased intensity of the contractions, but suddenly I knew it was time. There was a huge gush as the rest of my water broke, and I knew the baby was imminent. It was time to push.

My husband ran into the corridor shouting for someone to come and help, as his wife was having a baby. In a stroke of good luck, the clock had just ticked past seven o'clock. It was a shift change, and our useless midwife had just been replaced by the head midwife plus a host of day staff all beginning preparations for the morning's planned C-sections. They rushed into the room, and there was some mild panicking. "Don't push! Don't push!" everyone was shouting. I told them not to be ridiculous; there was a baby coming out of me. It was then that I was reminded that I was still on the maternity ward and not the delivery ward, and that my doctor was not present.

I was painfully moved onto a trolley, and the midwives ran down the corridor with me, still shouting, "Don't push!" There was no time to wait for my doctor. The birth would have to take place without her. The head midwife took control of the situation, and finally in a delivery room, I started pushing. Twenty minutes later the baby was just crowning when into the room wanders my incompetent original midwife. "Goodbye," she cheerfully said to everyone. "My shift is over, so I'm off." She seemed completely oblivious to the fact that there was a baby being born and in fact halfway out. She disappeared, and two pushes later Theo Thomas appears. A third baby boy.

Despite the most bizarre labor with a midwife who refused to believe that I was actually in labor, Theo was born only a few hours after we arrived at the hospital. He weighed 7 lbs. 3 oz. (3,300 g) and was perfectly healthy. I shudder to think what could have been if Theo had decided it was time to appear 30 minutes earlier, but this is not something to dwell on. I can only thank God that I have three healthy, boisterous little boys, and our busy family is complete and happily living in South Africa, a country we still love.

Debi Beaumont was born in Brazil and raised in the UK. Her husband was born in the UK and raised in Nigeria, Brunei, and Holland. Perhaps living abroad was in their blood because together they have lived in the UK, Australia, and South Africa. Debi has had a child in each of these countries and her experiences were hugely different each time. Her family full of boys—she is the only female— still live happily in South Africa. When she isn't busy chasing after, taxiing and cleaning up after all these boys she paints and draws. She is the author and illustrator of a children's book called An Alphabet of Africa.

CHAPTER 7

MACEDONIA TO OREGON—MY TRANSCONTINENTAL PREEMIE

Erin Long
Nationality: American
Birthed in: Hungary, Canada, and USA

I am quite experienced when it comes to giving birth abroad. My first child was born in Hungary, my second in Canada, and so when we found out that I was expecting our third baby the week before we moved to Macedonia, there was never any question that we would have our baby abroad again. I was anxious to experience a new country. And this meant my (somewhat unusual) dream would come true: All of my children would be born abroad and in different countries.

When we discovered I was (surprise!) pregnant with our first child, Audrey, a year after we moved to Hungary, we weighed the options of staying there or returning home to Oregon, USA. In the end, the better Hungarian insurance, comparable level of care, and the call of adventure compelled us to stay. Over the next eight months, I overcame challenges, discovered my own strength, made friends, and oh, did I have a story to tell. Even though Audrey's birth ended with an emergency C-section, I loved the experience. I was hooked. I had no desire to ever birth in the US despite it being my "home."

My second pregnancy in Canada was an entirely difference experience than Hungary, and it did not strictly follow along with what the American pregnancy books said I could expect to happen. Canada was such a familiar environment after all the unknowns I had faced in Hungary. In Canada, I was under the care of a midwife rather than an OB/GYN, and the gentle care and emotional support she provided made a world of difference.

At 32 weeks I started prodromal labor that would see me in and out of triage until our son, Alistair, was born healthy at 35 weeks. Despite the tumultuous weeks preceding the birth, it was the natural and empowering experience I missed with Audrey. While it confirmed that I could have babies vaginally, it did come with a caveat: I was now at risk of delivering early again.

Even knowing this, I could not wait to get on that plane to Macedonia. We had lived in Oregon for a year and a half while my husband, Ryan, completed coursework for his master's degree. He would finish his degree with an internship at a local NGO in the capital, Skopje. We didn't know anyone in Macedonia, didn't have insurance, and didn't know much about the medical system, but we were full of faith and hope as we boarded the plane. We were ready for whatever was next.

We were welcomed to our new country by Ryan's supervisor with a big smile and an open heart. We quickly connected with Robert and Wilma, his wife, and both

Audrey and Alistair took to them like the grandparents they had left behind. We hesitated to share news of my pregnancy with them because we knew it could mean extra time and effort on their part as we learned to navigate the medical system ourselves. But one evening as we shared cups of strong, black Macedonian coffee, Wilma told us she had trained as a general practitioner and knew many doctors, and was more than willing to help us with any medical issues that came up. Ryan and I eyed each other in disbelief. To our relief and their great joy, we shared our news, and Wilma made an appointment with her favorite OB/GYN the next day. Although I was excited about giving birth abroad again, I knew it would come with sacrifice.

My ideal birth is a midwife-attended, natural home birth with a doula as a support. I knew this scenario was not likely to happen outside of progressive Western Europe, but I still hoped elements of it could come to fruition. I planned to start with the OB/GYN and then look into more natural options. Then I found out that home births are not uncommon in Macedonia, they are illegal. Unless I was willing to "accidentally" have my baby at home before I got to the hospital, an OB/GYN-attended hospital birth was my only option.

I had great hesitations with that scenario. What if the doctor or hospital don't support my attempts at a vaginal birth after Cesarean (VBAC) and my only option is another C-section? What if I have complications that lead to my baby being born early, and they don't handle it in a way that makes me comfortable? I was still determined to have my baby in Macedonia, but the reality was starting to set in that I had to give up control.

My first appointment was filled with nerves. I was eager to get back into the routines of prenatal care, even though I had no idea what the routine would be, and anxious about learning the doctor's thoughts on VBACs and my increased risk of delivering early. I was also excited to begin this adventure. Wilma drove us away from our apartment in the city center and the decaying public hospitals to the edge of town to a shiny, new private hospital.

Except for the spoken language and trilingual signs (Macedonian, Albanian, and English) the hospital could have passed for one in the US. There were even receptionists, something we never encountered in Hungary. But the similarities ended when we saw the wall decor: Throughout the whole OB/GYN waiting room there were nude sketches. My Canadian midwife had artwork of women gracefully breastfeeding their newborns, but these were just women lounging about without any clothes on. Nothing erotic or inappropriate, just a gentle reminder of the different ways Europeans and Americans view the female body. Both Ryan and I smiled and then it hit me: Will I have to drop my pants? In Hungary, my doctor did an internal exam at my first appointment when I was six weeks along to confirm the pregnancy, and it seemed like every third appointment included an internal exam. In Canada, I eventually began to wonder if I was ever going to be internally examined at all.

While I was an old pro at being pregnant, I was a first-time mom at being pregnant in this country, in this culture, in this medical system. I liked it because it kept me on my toes. The experience was familiar enough to be comfortable to me but new enough to keep it interesting and force me to grow and learn. Being out of my comfort zone was my comfort zone, and I relished being in it.

The nurse led us into the doctor's office, which had a desk, an examination chair, and ultrasound bed. He greeted us with a delightfully mischievous smile and a handshake, and tried to get our shy kids to laugh. I liked him right off. He asked questions about my previous pregnancies, and when we explained about the C-section,

VBAC, and premature birth, he didn't seem concerned. When we asked about his stance on me having another VBAC, he replied, "Why not?" Thus concluded our interview, which was much more than the single question we asked my Hungarian OB/GYN, "Do you feel comfortable with an English-speaking patient?"

With formalities out of the way, it was time for the internal exam. I laughed to myself as I walked to the exposed corner of the room where I was to undress before walking back across the room half naked. And I thanked God that what sense of modesty I had before my pregnancy in Hungary was long gone.

For the next two months, the pregnancy was hardly on my radar. The honeymoon phase of being in a new country lasted literally 10 minutes, and I dove straight into culture shock. So did my one-year-old and three-year-old. Since I was at home with the kids and the NGO Ryan worked for was very small, we struggled to meet people, which only compounded our feelings of isolation.

Most days I struggled to survive, much less remember or enjoy the new life growing inside of me. I felt good and didn't have many pregnancy symptoms to remind me that part of what was making life so hard right then was my out-of-whack hormones. Culture shock, pregnancy, and raising very young children can each be overwhelming on their own, but together they are a monstrous trifecta.

Over time, culture shock lessened its grip, and I learned to accept aspects of our new country, like cars parked on the sidewalk, so I had to walk down the street with my toddler and stroller. Whatever. We started going to the local international church and immediately found a supportive community there. While it was still rough, things were getting better. Then, at 17 weeks into the pregnancy, I started to feel a lot of pain in my lower abdomen. It wasn't just the normal stretching that happens to accommodate an ever-growing baby—this was something else. And it kind of reminded me of the prodromal labor I had had with Alistair; it was definitely different but similar enough to make me concerned. I tried to rest as much as I could. That helped for a while, and when I brought it up to my doctor, he said not to worry about it.

Then, while visiting friends in Hungary while Ryan was in the US getting our Macedonian visas, the pain greatly increased. Alistair was sick and wanted to be held everywhere we went. He would throw a fit when I put him down because I felt a contraction coming on. I could hardly walk at times because the pressure was so great. I couldn't do anything to relieve the pain once it started. When we got back to Macedonia, I went to my doctor. An ultrasound showed that everything was fine with the baby, and I didn't show any abnormal signs. I just needed to rest and relax. But rest is not an option for a mama of young children.

It was winter, so the kids and I holed up in our apartment; they watched more movies than they had in their entire lives, and I lay on the couch. I felt fine as long as I was lying down, but as soon as I started walking more than a few steps, the tightness came right back. We didn't have a car, so I had to walk everywhere. Even short trips, like one block to the grocery store, took all the energy I had for the day.

Two months after the pain started and 26 weeks along, I began to wonder if it would be better for me to return to the US. Ryan was getting to the end of his internship, so the kids and I could go back and he could finish and follow shortly after. But I didn't want to go. Since we decided to have Audrey in Hungary, I didn't want to have a baby in the US, the land of doctor-convenient C-sections and overmedication. I was certain this baby was coming early too, so my ideal birth was off the table, even in the US. Ryan and I had serious conversations with each other and our parents, and I talked with a midwife in our hometown and an OB nurse friend. Then the prodromal labor hit.

It was like being in labor for several hours until it would subside and start the next day again. I went to my doctor again, and the contraction monitor didn't show any contractions, though I was definitely feeling them. He put me on progesterone and told me to drink water and eat tomatoes. After a week of the progesterone and seeing no benefits, I couldn't do it anymore. I counted regular contractions as I bounced on an exercise ball in our living room in tears, full of fear and overwhelmed by the unknown.

Then Ryan said what we both knew: I needed to go home. I was in too much pain, and we were too far from the due date; we learned that in all of Macedonia there isn't a single NICU for babies born before 35 weeks, and that was seven weeks away. If I went into labor, we would have to drive two hours to Greece and then stay there until our baby was ready to leave the NICU, which could be months. And while we had enough money to pay for a normal pregnancy and delivery in Macedonia, we didn't have enough for a long hospital stay. I still had full insurance coverage in the US and just as important—familial support.

We called our family on Skype, and tears rolled down my face as I felt like we were admitting defeat. Saying out loud that we couldn't stay and have the baby in Macedonia broke my heart. Graciously, Ryan's mom offered to fly to Macedonia to accompany the three of us (me and the kids) back so Ryan could stay and complete the last few weeks of his internship. We didn't know what awaited us in Oregon, other than our parents' basement and three hopefully healthy kids. But I knew it was right. As scary as returning was, staying was more terrifying.

Ryan's parents booked tickets immediately, but the only flight with availability for all four of us was three weeks away. I didn't know how I was going to survive, but thanks to our friends in Macedonia we made it through. They watched our kids and made life as easy as they could. Ryan's mom, Marlene, arrived a week before we were to leave and helped us pack our lives into eight 50-pound suitcases.

For our last night in Macedonia together, our friends rented a luxury hotel room for Ryan and me. We were excited to have one last fun outing together before we left. We went to a traditional Macedonian restaurant and as we slowly worked our way through the courses I had contractions that kept getting worse. By the time the main course arrived, I couldn't sit through them anymore. I had to stand and sway. When I needed to go into my favorite labor position, we knew it was time to leave.

We went to the hotel hoping that some rest would ease the pain. We were leaving in just over 24 hours; I couldn't be in labor now. But shortly after we got there I realized I was bleeding. I wasn't contracting as severely, so we decided to try to sleep and then go to the hospital first thing in the morning if I made it that long.

With only a few contractions and a bit more bleeding through the night, I was incredibly concerned about the 24 hours of transcontinental travel ahead of me. Lying on the couch, I had no idea what that day held for me. I could be on a flight to the US, a car heading to Greece, or already have given birth to a preemie in Macedonia. No option seemed less daunting than the other.

This time, when I was hooked up to the monitor, it did register low-level contractions. Because it was the weekend, I saw the on-call doctor, and he did a thorough ultrasound and exam and couldn't find the reason for the bleeding. Fortunately, the baby was doing great. When we explained our situation and our plan to leave early the next morning, he asked if it was too late to change our tickets. Yes, it was. "Okay." was his response. So with neither his consent nor his objection, we continued with our plans to leave.

At 4 a.m. the next morning, I said goodbye to Ryan, not knowing if I would see him again before our baby was born. Audrey, Alistair, Marlene, and I boarded our plane headed to Vienna, then Newark, and, finally, to Portland, Oregon. We prayed that it would still only be the four of us when we arrived. I felt confident as the contractions had been minimal, and I wasn't bleeding. The flight to Newark went smoothly, and Audrey and Alistair were content to watch movies, sleep, or play with Grandma. So far so good.

Upon our arrival in Newark, New Jersey, my father-in-law had arranged to have a wheelchair meet us at the gate and help us get all of our luggage through customs. I would have gone into labor at the luggage carousel if I'd had to lift our eight suitcases.

While going through security, I could tell I was starting to bleed. I was concerned but not too worried. I'd been sitting down the whole time so how bad could it be? Once in the bathroom, I saw what every pregnant woman fears to see: blood. Lots of blood. My heart shook as I told Marlene. I had no idea what to do. So I did the only thing one can do in these situations: I called my mom.

My dad is a medical professional, and my parents know the director of the obstetrician at their local hospital. Her recommendation: I needed to do whatever I thought was best. That was the last thing I wanted to hear. I just wanted someone to come in and tell me I needed to go to the medical staff at the airport, transfer to a local hospital, and then have this baby in New Jersey or to tell me it was okay to get on the five-hour flight to Portland. Someone tell me what to do!

I knew that if an employee of the airline knew what was going on there was no way they would let me board the plane to Oregon. By this time people all over the world were praying for us as Marlene and I waited until everyone else had boarded the plane to make our decision. Finally, unable to wait any longer, I felt convicted that we should get on the plane. I would have preferred to have felt peace, but I felt comfortable enough to tell Marlene I wanted to do it. I wanted this baby to be born close to home in Portland, not on the other side of the country in New Jersey. We'd made it this far, let's finish it. Marlene looked me in the eye and asked if I understood that if I did go into labor, they would land the plane. Was I okay with that? Yes, yes, I was. So she put her hand on mine, and we pushed the stroller down the jet way together.

In her travel savvy, Marlene had reserved seats A and C in the last two rows of the plane because no one wants to sit in the middle seat, B, in the back rows. In spite of the plane being otherwise full, those two seats were empty, and we had two rows to ourselves. I just might make it. Marlene and the kids took one row, and I laid down and slept for most of the flight in the other. When I woke up, I realized I hadn't felt any movement from the baby for a while. He wasn't usually active, so it wasn't completely surprising but given the circumstances I wanted some confirmation he was moving, much less alive. I put my hand on my belly and prayed, "God, please let him move. Let me feel him move." Before the last word even formed in my mind, I felt a single, strong, solid kick on my hand. My baby was okay. We were okay.

We made it to Portland without an emergency landing. I was met by another wheelchair and all of my family. My mom was the first to hug me, and I cried like a little girl who was finally safe in mommy's arms. After embracing like two warriors who just survived a battle, Marlene handed me off to my mom and headed home for some much-deserved rest. One journey was ending, and another was beginning.

Like many things that didn't go according to my plans, my mom drove me to the nearest hospital from the airport instead of the most prominent children's hospital in Oregon. I'm so glad she did.

Arriving at the nurse's station, all I said was I was 30 weeks and bleeding. Immediately, I was hooked up to every monitor imaginable. I have never been so thankful to be surrounded by modern western technology. I could see that my baby was doing well, and we were safe.

After months of feeling the weight of responsibility of making hard decisions without having full knowledge of what was going on, I could finally relax and let the professionals take over. I did my best to explain that I had just gotten off a plane from Macedonia, recapped all my medical experiences from the last two months, and gave important details from my previous births. I think the nurses had fun looking through my medical records from three different countries in four different languages. I was put on magnesium sulfate to protect baby's neural development if he did come soon and for the added side effect of slowing the contractions.

Several hours later I had an hour-long ultrasound. It revealed a placental abruption at the top of the uterus, which was causing the bleeding and contractions. The Macedonian doctors never looked high enough to see it. So we would wait and see how long baby would stay put, but he was coming sooner rather than later.

Shortly after the ultrasound I talked with Ryan, and he was already in the process of changing his tickets to arrive two days earlier. I urged my unborn son to stay put until his dad could arrive.

The next few days were a blur of visitors, talking with doctors, and learning about the NICU. Since I had never prepared to have a baby in the US, I was suddenly experiencing a steep learning curve. But the more I learned, the more pleased I was. Every OB, even the perinatologist, not only supported me attempting a VBAC, they wanted me to have one.

The morning of the day Ryan was to arrive I was taken off the magnesium. I was stabilized, and I couldn't be on it for much longer without it becoming harmful. I watched the clock, counting down to Ryan's arrival, and heard a cheer from the nurse's station as Ryan walked through my door. Now I could finally relax. I was ready to welcome our baby whenever he came.

By the next morning, the contractions started, and I was put back on the magnesium, but this time the contractions didn't stop. Because everything up to this point was an entirely new experience for me, I felt oddly comfortable in the unknown. I wasn't supposed to know what was going on. But now that I was in labor, something I was intimately familiar with, I felt somewhat lost. I wanted to birth my way. Do I have to wear this annoying hospital gown? Is the nurse supposed to be here now? When can we call the nurse? Who's going to deliver this baby anyway? I didn't know what to expect or what was expected of me. Suddenly, my home culture felt foreign.

After four hours of labor, our son, Edmund Stanley was born, all 3 lbs. 6 oz. (1,530 g) of him. In spite of being born 10 weeks early, he was perfectly healthy. Shortly after his birth he was transferred to the NICU, and I got to hold his tiny body for the very first time two hours later.

We would spend the next five weeks holding him in the NICU while we juggled his two older siblings. In between NICU duty, kid duty, and life, Ryan remarkably finished up the final paper for his degree. We got to tell our fun and exciting travel/birth story to the NICU staff. They all loved hearing about the baby who flew transcontinental to be born at their hospital.

So my dream about all of my children being born abroad in different countries didn't come true. Well, not entirely at least. None of my kids were born in the same country, but one was born in my native land. And I'm okay with that. Each pregnancy and birth stretched me in more ways than just my ever-expanding belly. Each one gave me a unique story to tell, and as each of them grows, I get to cherish how their coming into the world shaped me, my story, and our family's journey.

And I can't wait to find out what adventures await.

Erin Long loves new places, good food, and people. She loves her native Oregon but has spent most of her adulthood outside of the country. With her husband, she has lived in Canada (twice), Hungary, and Macedonia. Along the way they've had three kids and are out to prove that getting married and starting a family does not have to mean settling down. She blogs about faith, family, natural living, and living abroad at www.homeandgrace.net.

CHAPTER 8

NOT ACCORDING TO PLAN

Margaret Özemet
Nationality: American
Birthed in: Turkey

"For God's sake slow down!" Headlines flashed inside my head: "Crash on Turkish Autobahn Kills Hundreds. American and Unborn Half-American Among the Dead." Hopefully, it wouldn't get mistaken for an act of terror. It could be since I would be a lapsed Catholic killed in a Muslim nation, and things were pretty touchy in 2008.

I watched the speedometer continue to climb, "Honey, please! We'll make it there."

"How you know?"

Sweat was pouring down my husband's hairline, and his already shaky grasp of English was beginning to slide away. "Is one hour to hospital. How you know we make it? You never have baby before."

He shifted gears to pass a row of military vehicles while muttering in Turkish about how this frantic rush to the hospital could've been avoided had we just waited until after the baby was born to move. At the very least, why wouldn't I just stay in the city with his parents close to the hospital?

"Screw you!" I roared, guided by my rapidly changing hormones. My husband often forgot I now spoke Turkish too, and his grumblings in his native language were no longer his alone.

"It was your idea to move early. Remember? You were the one who thought I needed to quit teaching and get settled in our new home. 'Turkish women not work when they pregnant like that. You rest now. Not work,' I believe was what you said."

Two weeks before my due date my husband got a new job that came with company housing. While the free apartment meant we were finally released from a yearlong sentence of sharing a two-bedroom apartment with my very traditional in-laws, the location sucked.

Our new home was located on the campus of a waste-water treatment plant, atop a sandy mountain, near a seaside village. The nearest hospital was back in our old city an hour away. When my due date came and went, it was suggested I stay in the city with my in-laws to be closer to the hospital, but considering I'd only recently tasted in-law freedom, I chose to cross my legs and risk it.

"Let's remember, it is not my fault this kid is two weeks overdue."

I'd tried every old wives' tale as well as every relatively sane option found online to get this process moving to no avail. Ultimately, I had no one to blame but his father.

"Americans are punctual; your people are the ones who are always late!"

As he wove between a truck carrying propane tanks and a tour bus, he asked, "Baby is okay? He is moving?"

"The baby is fine."

Though my water had broken more than an hour earlier, I'd yet to have contractions, and while this was my first run at the whole childbirth thing, I knew that contractions were integral to the process.

"Slow this damn car down before you kill us. Wait! You missed the turn. Why didn't you turn?"

"I not take ferry. You are crazy?"

"Why not? It's right there. It cuts like 20 minutes off."

"You want have baby on car ferry? Because I not want have baby on car ferry!"

I was relatively certain that I wasn't going to give birth on the 20-minute ferry ride, and I was also certain that taking the ferry was much safer than risking cross-city traffic, but it didn't matter. The Turk had a plan, and as I'd learned during my first year living and working in Turkey, changing the mind of a Turk is nearly impossible. Unfortunately, I'd also learned that in Turkey, nothing goes according to plan.

We hadn't planned on living in Turkey, and we hadn't planned on starting our family while we were there, but I guess those warning labels on birth control about avoiding extreme temperatures are legitimate. We met and married in the US, but thanks to a colossal goof by our "highly reputable" immigration lawyer, weeks after our wedding we learned my new husband had to leave the US or face deportation and a 10-year ban on reentry.

Six weeks into a new marriage and full of hope, we heard the same thing from every US attorney we contacted, "This is an absolute mess. The best thing to do is go back to Turkey and process his green card through the embassy. It should take about six months." I'd been to Turkey before I met my husband and loved it, so six months seemed manageable.

What I didn't understand was that visiting Turkey is vastly different than living there, and what would take six months on an American timeline would take three years in Turkey.

"Pull over! Pull over!" I yelled.

The Turk spun into a gas station, nearly giving us both whiplash.

"Baby is coming?"

"No."

I flung the door open just in time for my breakfast to leave my body.

"Just needed to barf, KAY? I'm good. Keep going."

By my own admission, I'd handled the whole pregnancy in Turkey much better than I thought I might. Finding a competent, English-speaking doctor proved impossible, and after a frightening test mix-up by an English-speaking doctor suggested by the US Consulate, we opted for a reputable obstetrician who didn't speak English instead. The language barrier was a struggle, and no woman wants to have her husband translate the details of vaginal discharge because the words needed extend beyond her new language vocabulary, but sometimes these things happen. Through most of it, I was able to keep perspective and panic at bay, but as show time was drawing near, the thought of having my son in a language I spoke with first-grade fluency at best was enough to send my breakfast across the parking lot of the AyGaz station. Wiping vomit off my chin, I blurted, "I don't want to do this."

"What?" My bouts of irrational behavior in situations of stress are rare. Irrational behavior is generally The Turk's role, not mine.

"What wrong wit you?"

"I'm scared! I don't understand anything, I've got nobody here but you, and I'm scared. I don't want to do this here." Tears streamed down my cheeks as reality poured in. He took his hand from the gearshift and grabbed mine.

"I tell you when we come here, I take care you. Don't scare. I take care you. This my country. I understand. I will do understand for you."

Though the English teacher in me cringed at his phrasing, I was 100% certain that he would do exactly what he was trying to say. He'd done so up to that point; he wasn't going to stop now.

Fifteen minutes later we arrived at the hospital. The Turk was proud of himself for shredding a full 19 minutes off our previous test runs, even with my barf stop. Our doctor worried that the cultural differences might throw off labor, and recommended a private hospital over the government variety. We'd used the same hospital a few months prior when a fever that wouldn't budge sent me to the ER, where I was soaked in iced towels. Something told me there might be a more modern approach to a pregnant woman with a fever in other countries, but it worked, and the hospital's overall appearance was close enough to an American hospital that I agreed it was the best place for me to deliver. While the hospital itself looked western, the admission process was completely Turkish and something I wish the Turk had prepared me for.

Hospital admission, even for one in labor with amniotic fluid running down her leg, involved standing in line until someone called your number to begin the paperwork—all 25 pages of paperwork. Once the paperwork was completed, we took a new number and waited in another line to pay for services about to be rendered.

"Should we overestimate your needs, a refund will be provided upon your exit." The clerk behind the counter stated. Charming.

The Turk tried repeatedly to get me wheeled off to the maternity ward, "Why you not take her? I paying now. You want my wife have baby here?"

"Sorry, *abi* (brother). All patients must remain in Admitting until bills have been paid in full." the clerk countered.

"This country is mess. I no understand how I leave and when I come back everyone stupid!"

While we waited in these various lines, as is typical in Turkey, all chairs intended for patients were filled with old men chatting, stroking their mustaches, and sipping tea. Old men not in labor. Old men not willing to give up their chairs for a second-class citizen about to provide them with a new countryman. So I stood at the desk, grimacing and leaking until my paperwork was completed.

Twenty minutes and a few gallons of amniotic fluid later, the bill was paid, and I walked, yes, walked, up four flights of stairs to my room, where the doctor and his doula were waiting. After a few cursory questions about my non-existent contractions, I was whisked away for an exam, because policy dictated that no internal exam be performed in the presence of a man. There is not a lot of sex education in Turkey, so why horrify fathers with the realities of childbirth?

From the other side of my enormous belly, I heard the doctor, still clad in a suit and tie, whisper, "*Esim al, problem var.*" Get the husband, there is a problem.

While the doctor and my husband spoke in hushed tones, I was rushed back to my hospital room, and everything immediately went into overdrive. The nurses tried to explain the situation, but everyone was speaking so fast, and the words were so big that I caught only about 25% of the conversation.

"What is happening?" I yelled in English, and when it was ignored, I yelled in Turkish. Something was wrong, but

I couldn't understand what. More rapid-fire Turkish, nods, more Turkish, phone calls, more Turkish.

"SPEAK SLOWER!" I screamed. "I can understand if you would just speak slower!"

As tears filled up in my eyes, my husband explained that the baby's heartbeat was too fast, and there was no fluid left. The situation was dangerous, and I needed a C-section, immediately. Things were certainly not going according to the plan I'd constructed for the birth of my first child.

As soon as I learned I was pregnant I'd ordered various natural pregnancy books from America and crammed like I was back in graduate school. All the books lauded the importance of a birth plan, and since I'm a planner by nature that spoke to my soul.

My plan looked something like this: On my due date, my water would break and I would begin a strong but manageable labor as I was rushed to the one American-style hospital in the city. My husband and I would gaze lovingly at one another throughout the process, as we were about to add to our union. Upon arriving at the hospital, we would be greeted by staff who would whisk me off to a warm and inviting birthing suite decorated in calming hues, with fresh flowers on the nightstand. Through layers of perspiration and he-he-hoo-hoo breathing, a perfect child would spring forth from my loins—sans epidural— and I would be hailed for my amazing feat of womanhood as my perfect baby began to nurse immediately and my husband sobbed tears of joy, just like they do in the movies. Nowhere in my plan was there an emergency C-section. In fact, I was so confident in my plan that I bravely, nay, foolishly, skipped all chapters discussing anything related to C-sections. I'd had wide childbearing hips since I was 12; there was no way I wouldn't be able to birth a tiny baby.

The word "Cesarean" is the same in both Turkish and English, and while I did catch that in the initial flurry, I convinced myself they were talking about someone else. Suddenly I was moments away from being sliced open in a country that was still classified as "developing" in 2008 by the CIA. My husband, being a man, was not allowed in the operating room with me, so I would need to depend on my first-grade level Turkish to get my son and I both out alive.

"Honey, doctor try to get me permission come with you but they no answer." My husband held my hand until the nurses pushed him away to raise the bed rails.

"It's okay. I'll be okay. If I can handle classroom management in Turkish, I can handle this." I tried to assure both of us.

As the nurses began wheeling my bed out of the room, the doctor's doula grabbed my hand and whispered in slow, simple Turkish so I could understand. "I will hold your hand until we sneak him in. He will be there. I promise." This woman and I had shared not much more than understanding smiles and a few sentences during office visits, but in that moment, she was my everything.

Through set after set of swinging doors we traveled, my doula right by my side. "*Yabancı var. İngilizice konuşuyor. Kimin İngilizice konuşuyor mu?*" boomed over the loud speakers in the surgical suite.

"We've got a foreigner. She speaks English. Does anybody speak English?"

A rush went through the room as they searched for anyone who could speak English. A large woman came forward and said, "You are velcome. You are velcome." She smiled, incredibly pleased with herself before turning to those around her and muttering in Turkish, "That's all I know," and disappearing again. The remaining members of the medical staff obviously knew even less as we spent the next uncomfortable minutes sharing awkward smiles before a tiny med student was pushed forward.

"Ehhh, hello Mrs. Özemet." Okay then, maybe there is potential here.

"Mrs. Özemet. You are welcome." Huh?

"Later, I go America." Sweetie, forgive me if I don't share any interest in your future; I am minutes from having my abdomen sliced open, and a small person pulled out.

"I go America. Later." Oh, I see.

"Later. Later I go America. I go. Later."

And it appeared that was the complete spoken English vocabulary of the English ace from the surgical department.

Being a tough American broad, I realized the only person capable of saving me in this situation was me. Perhaps it was the same effect that allows mothers to lift cars off their trapped children, but suddenly I began conversing in beautifully fluent Turkish and everyone was relieved. With the language barrier dismantled, the room again began to whirl at full speed. While I knew this was a routine procedure for everyone else in the room, the gossip about the antics of Turkish celebs against the backdrop of Turkish pop music didn't put me at ease that I was in capable hands.

Moments later room fell silent. *"Hos geldiniz doktor bey."* Welcome, doctor sir.

I'd have gotten up to greet him, but I was strapped to the table. From my position, I heard a giggle I knew all too well. I tried to sit up, but the aforementioned straps made it impossible so instead I screamed. "That is not the doctor! Do not give that man the knife!" My doula was right, they had found a way to sneak my husband in, and because no husbands are allowed, the staff automatically assumed the man in scrubs was there to take care of business.

Fortunately, my husband was followed by the real doctor and following a brief explanation, he was seated at my side, just like in the movies. However, what does not typically happen in the movies is the placing of a reflective incubator directly in my line of sight, providing me with a perfect view of all the south-of-the-drape happenings. I knew I shouldn't look, but that shiny wall was right there showing me everything. It was like a crime scene. I couldn't turn away. My husband caught me and tried to hide my view, but it was too late. I knew too much.

Whoa, that's a lot of blood. Did someone order more? Wait...what is that piled on my stomach? Are those my...intestines? For the love of all that is holy, do you people know how those go back in? Is someone drawing a map? Is this normal? How will I ever poop again? Come on now, is this how they do it in America? Wait...is that man elbow deep in my abdomen?

I was suddenly distracted from the sideshow happening in my midsection by an ear-piercing scream. The Little Turk had arrived, and it appeared he had inherited my vocal cords. The doctor held our son over the drape while saying something in Turkish, which translated to "10 fingers, 10 toes, one wiener, all is well." He then handed our new baby to another masked man who I hoped was a doctor, and who immediately left the room with my child. I didn't get to hold him, or kiss him, or even count his toes for myself. He was gone.

"Honey, go!" I whispered to my husband who was so high on new fatherhood he was nearly comatose.

"Where?"

"Follow them. Where are they taking him? What are they doing?"

"Is fine. They doctors."

"Are you sure? Five minutes ago they thought *you* were a doctor."

The Turk sprang up with that realization and ran into the other room before being pushed back by some burly nurses. However, given the foreign status of his wife, they allowed him to keep watch through the window. He gave me a thumbs up as he chatted with my doctor on his way out. I soon learned that obstetricians in Turkey only handle the opening and removal. Putting the mother back together again falls completely to the interns on duty. Unfortunately, the incubator was gone with my son, so I was unable to supervise the return of my innards to their rightful homes and was left to trust my "I go America, later." friend to finish the job. I crossed my fingers and hoped she'd done all her course work in Turkish.

With the task of delivering a baby into the world completed and danger seemingly averted, it was time for music, of course. The Turks as a people love music, and they love to dance. The lunch ladies at my school often broke into dance mid-lunch service if the right song came on the radio, stomping, waving dishrags, and yelling "Oh-pa!" More than once I'd seen my coworkers belly dance in faculty meetings.

Even my own usually reserved Turk has been known to break into traditional regional dance after a few drinks. By this point I'd lived among the Turks for more than a year so I'd grown to expect a dancing lunch lady or shimmying department head, but when the entire operating room was flooded with music and dancing commenced as my intestines were being returned, I was astounded.

It had to be excessive blood loss right? This couldn't really be happening? But when nurse "You Are Velcome" did a few hip swivels while changing my IV, I realized, yes, this was real. I'd just watched a man pull my first child out of my open abdomen, had not been able to see or hold my son, and now I was strapped to a table in a room quickly resembling a village wedding while a man sang into a mop and another man kept the beat with bloodied surgical instruments. This was certainly not on my birth plan.

An hour and a half later, I was returned to my room to find another group of Turks also in party mode, but this time, the Turks were mine. In Turkish tradition, the entire family had arrived at the hospital to celebrate the new addition. My sister-in-law had assembled a full buffet on the hospital trays in my room, while my husband was emailing photos to my family on the other side of the world.

Turkish music blared over the loudspeakers of the maternity ward, welcoming me as I was wheeled into the party clad in nothing more than a sheet. And there in the corner of the room, nuzzled against my mother-in-law's neck was the beautiful boy I'd yet to even meet. My brand new baby, whom I hadn't even touched, was immersed in a world so incredibly foreign to us both that I nearly busted every stitch in my gut trying to get to him.

Forty-five minutes after returning to my room it was time to walk. My sister-in-law had warned me, "Don't worry if you pass out. Everyone does. They will make you smell the stuff, and you keep going." When she explained this practice in my room I thought I might have mixed something up in translation as no one in my husband's family speaks English, but upon waking with smelling salts in my face, I realized that I'd understood perfectly.

That first night was rough due to some complications from excessive air getting trapped during the process of returning my organs. That's probably why dancing is discouraged during most surgical procedures. There was no nursery, and assistance from nurses was very minimal. In Turkey, once that kid comes out, he's all yours. If you want help, you bring it, just like you bring your own diapers, bedding, clothing, and food.

Twenty-three hours later, with a few Turkish Tylenols and a prescription for an antibiotic, we were discharged. My milk hadn't come in, and our son was a bit yellow but one night is all you get. After all, it's only childbirth.

No one explained what to do if he didn't learn to latch better or if he wouldn't settle or if his yellow hue intensified. No one told me not to lift heavy objects or that I would likely bleed for weeks to come and not stand up straight for a week. I was on my own.

The nurse handed me my baby, and I walked back down the four flights of stairs to the car where my husband was waiting, praying my weak legs would hold up and that my shaky arms wouldn't drop my tiny son. I looked down at my beautiful boy still covered in dried blood—they don't wash them in Turkey—and whispered, "I'm so sorry buddy. This isn't how I had it planned."

I spent my first night at home pacing the floors, hunched over in pain while my son screamed endlessly. My husband was passed out from all the excitement. My mother was on the other side of the world, and my mother-in-law said she didn't want to leave the city and travel to our home. We made it through that night and many, many more like it, just my little guy and I. He never slept, so we watched Turkish soap operas and BBC News all night long for months. He wasn't good at latching and was a failure-to-thrive baby for the first two months, until an old lady from the village shared a few secrets that changed everything. In time we figured things out, but it took five years and a move back to the States before I was ready to do it again.

When our second son was born in the US. I was equally stunned by the ease of it all, though no doctor I spoke with would even entertain the thought of a vaginal birth after C-section after hearing the details of my first delivery. Eventually, I overcame the disappointment and resentment connected to my first son's birth. The payoff of an amazing kid far outweighed how he got here.

Most importantly, I learned that if I can handle childbirth in Turkey, I can pretty much handle anything, and once you tell someone about childbirth in Turkey, they agree.

Margaret Özemet is an American teacher and writer who fell madly in love and suddenly found herself sharing a tiny apartment with her new husband and her surly in-laws in Turkey. After a few years and a couple kids, she's back in the US and trying to adapt. Her work has been seen on numerous online sites, literary journals and anthologies, including New Letters, Hippocampus, Red Fez Magazine, Ducts.org and Scary Mommy to name a few. Her work can also be seen on her weekly blog, Laughter is Better than Prozac. Keep up with her through her website: margaretozemet.com, on Twitter @MOzemet or on Facebook.

CHAPTER 9

WAR AND PEACE

Lucille Abendanon
Nationality: British and South African
Birthed in: Turkey and South Africa

War

"**D**raw your pain, give it shape and form. What color is it? Does it move? Focus on how you feel as you come into the presence of your pain."

In my left hand I clutched a rapidly melting ice cube, a somewhat questionable substitute for how labor pain would feel, and as the cold burned into my clenched fist, water began to dribble pathetically down my arm in tepid submission. I desperately tried to suppress a giggle as I glanced helplessly over at my husband, who was staring at the blank paper in front of him, clearly wrestling with his own icy discomfort, green wax crayon poised, awaiting inspiration. His raised eyebrow was the only indication that he was sympathetic to my resistance.

We had joined a natural birthing workshop in a leafy suburb of Istanbul, and while I had the best of intentions (and the naivety of a first-time mother), I rapidly discovered that clutching an ice cube while trying to illustrate my pain with a clumsy crayon was not the path to my enlightenment.

Pregnancy had come as a surprise, to say the least. We were new to Istanbul, recently relocated from Bangkok with my husband's company. The magnificent ancient city seemed like a return to "normalcy" after our years in Asia, which had included a stint in Vietnam. There was fresh, cool air, clear blue water, and actual seasons beyond "wet" and "dry." However, while my psyche celebrated, my palate lamented the end of the fragrant, spicy food I'd grown accustomed to in the East. Babies were for later. Till then I had too much living to do. But life, as always, had other plans.

I remember calling my mom the day those two blue lines turned my world upside down and wailing, "I'm not ready!" and she just chuckled and chuckled. My father's reaction was so genuine, so deeply overjoyed, that they both almost convinced me that this was a great idea. They were right of course.

Giving birth naturally in Istanbul is like going to war. You need to arm yourself with your strongest warriors and your closest advisors. You need to pick the site of the battle so that you have the best possible advantage and ensure that you control the high ground. You need to be secure in the knowledge that your troops will defend you to their last; that when you are down, they will surround you and fight on, never giving an inch, never allowing the enemy to break through.

The enemy is what I like to call the economy of convenience, embraced so wholeheartedly by the medical establishment in Istanbul. Pregnancy is seen as a gauntlet of life-threatening disasters that can only be negotiated through extreme monitoring by a doctor who appears poised to break the news of your imminent demise at each appointment. I encountered some baffling cultural belief systems: Drinking a cold beverage brings instant doom to your unborn child; walking barefoot, even indoors, evoked such violent rebukes from my doctor you'd think I'd chugged a bottle of vodka. Already paranoid mothers-to-be are guilted and in some instances intimidated into submission by doctors who prescribe Cesareans over vaginal births, intervention over connection, and science over nature.

My first doctor was a rude awakening to the realities of what I was facing. She had frizzy bright orange hair, ice-cold hands, and a look of total detachment in her eyes. I hadn't been to a doctor for decades, was still adjusting to life in a new country, and was completely freaked out by what was unexpectedly happening inside my uterus. I had pitched up without an appointment the day after the positive pregnancy test, stood in front of a panel of manicured receptionists and meekly mumbled "*hamileyim.*" I'm pregnant. During that first appointment, I felt as clueless as a cow being led to slaughter, though vaguely sensing that disaster loomed on the horizon.

"We look for heartbeat," barked the orange-haired doctor. "If no heartbeat, no baby."

And with that, as if she was a knight unsheathing Excalibur, she produced what I can only describe as the most hideously phallic and enormous heart rate apparatus.

The look of horror on my face, while mildly amusing to her, was enough to convince her to use the normal ultrasound machine, and soon I was listening to a rapid but strong heartbeat, that seemed to keep pace with my own thundering heart. Emboldened by my tiny victory I explained that I did not want an ultrasound every month, that I wanted to have as few interventions as possible, that I wanted to give birth vaginally possibly with pain relief, but without if I was able. Her response was a volley of verbal bullets that broke my fleeting confidence and shattered any illusions that she was there to guide and support me.

If I didn't want ultrasounds every month, I could find myself another doctor, and didn't I know that hardly anyone gives birth vaginally anymore? It's too risky. Anything can go wrong.

Seven months later when she all but ripped up my birth plan in front of me, I knew I had to mutiny. I began shopping around for a doctor who shared my birthing philosophy and who had warmer hands. I posted on social media, asked the advice of a few friends who had given birth in Istanbul. I cast my net wide because finding a supportive, pro-natural birth doctor in Istanbul is like asking for a vegetarian kebab—it's just not done. Gradually one name emerged above the rest, a doctor who worked at the American Hospital and whose birthing feats were becoming the stuff of legend in expat circles.

"I've heard she's done a ton of VBACs (vaginal birth after Cesarean)."

"I heard that she runs such a tight ship only approved nurses are allowed in your room."

"I heard that she's leading a one-woman crusade against planned C-sections."

When my husband and I walked into her office for an introductory interview her enthusiasm, gregarious nature and apparent belief in all things natural won us over. I had found my doctor. Little did we know how wrong things would go.

Our preparations for battle included enlisting the services of a doula. She was to be our translator and peacekeeper because while our doctor spoke perfect English, the nurses at the American Hospital did not. Our doula would negotiate on our behalf, keep things running smoothly, and raise the alarm if the enemy attempted a stealth attack. Nothing was going to stand in the way of my natural birth.

The city of Istanbul straddles two continents: Europe and Asia. It is the only city in the world to do so, and the continents are connected via two mammoth bridges that span the Bosphorus like the tenuous threads of a spider's web. We lived on the Asian side. The American Hospital was on the European side, an easy 15-minute drive away if there was no traffic. If the baby decided to come during rush hour when it can take three hours to cross the bridge...I shudder now even thinking about it. But our obliging son chose to begin his journey into the world at one stroke past midnight on his due date, and so it was with much excitement, and relief that we hurtled over a traffic-free bridge to the hospital.

The American Hospital was more like a hotel than a hospital. I had a private suite of two rooms, with a sitting area, flat-screen TV, and a beautiful bathroom. The labor pains had begun at home, and by the time we got to the hospital, things were progressing well. Our doula met us there, and we were all in good spirits. My mom had come for the birth; I felt supported and confident. But as a tornado can change direction in a second, so too can labor. I was handling the pain; I was breathing and walking and resting between contractions. I was ready for the final showdown, my allies were in battle formation, morale was high. The last thing we expected was for someone to break ranks.

Our doctor had been examining me every hour or so to monitor dilation. Things were moving along swiftly, and I had no reason to suspect that she would do what she did. She broke my water without telling me. I'd never done this before, and I didn't know what the sudden torrential liquid avalanche meant. I got the fright of my life because she had given me no warning, no indication that she was going rogue. It was a completely unnecessary intervention. The pain intensified substantially after that, and it caught me unawares. My confidence had been knocked, my trust broken, and I felt all too keenly the breach in our defenses.

Pain and fear locked arms and bombarded me again and again and again until all I could feel was terror and darkness. The enemy was gaining ground, and the assault came in determined waves, never letting up for even a second, and I was engulfed in a vortex of fire and couldn't find my way out. I was wheeled into the delivery room to push, and from within my fortress of agony, I could see that it was a beautiful, sunny winter's day outside. How could the sun be shining? It was baffling to me, as if I was peering down the wrong end of a telescope.

I couldn't stay lying down anymore—nature took over, and I was compelled to kneel on the floor. To her credit, the doctor rolled with it, and I pushed and pushed and pushed.

The baby didn't come out.

After two hours of pushing, I began to black out. Our defensive walls began to crumble, my troops did their best, fought alongside me till the last moment, but even they were battered and bruised and needed relief. I was wheeled back to my room and given an epidural so that I could rest, so that they could rest, so that we could regroup. As the epidural worked its pale magic, I felt relieved and disappointed. Why hadn't the baby come out? What was wrong? The world suddenly seemed hostile and precarious, and I felt the ripples of fear reverberating around me in ever-wider circles. My husband, valiantly faking a cheerful demeanor went off to find some answers. He returned with the doctor, who explained sheepishly that she had miscalculated, that I was only 9 cm dilated, and that the early pushing had caused my cervix to swell. The baby was stuck. Our only recourse was to wait for the swelling to reduce, to monitor the baby's heart rate, and to try again when I was fully dilated. With this news, I dispatched our doula to reinforce my wishes that they avoid a C-section at all costs. The doctor had blithely added that I should try not to eat while we were waiting, and this gave away her intentions: She was laying the groundwork for a C-section.

We waited and waited. I was maneuvered into a giant hammock, my useless legs thick as mud, and with the doula holding one end and my husband the other, I was rhythmically jiggled and bounced in the hope that this would engage the baby's head. The hours passed, and the monitor showed the ceaseless peaks of contractions I could no longer feel, and the quickening and slowing of the baby's heartbeat in unison. We had arrived at the hospital at 5 a.m.; at 8 p.m. the beeping heart rate monitor told us that our baby was in distress.

"This baby is coming out right now," our doctor said as she strode into the room.

Once again I was taken to the delivery room, and I saw that the bright sunshine had been replaced by a blue darkness. Had a whole day passed? The room was obscenely bright, what seemed to me like a crowd of people had gathered, maybe 10 or 15 anonymous bodies in blue scrubs. This isn't what I had wanted. How did this happen?

The doctor attached the suction machine to the crown of my unborn baby's head, and a white-coated man appeared on my left and positioned both hands at the base of my sternum. With the next contraction this man pushed down on my stomach with such force, I thought my ribs would crack. Again and again, he pushed down and as I recoiled against the crushing sensation I grabbed a fist full of his shirt. *If you're going to hurt me, I'm going to hurt you,* I remember thinking as I sunk my nails into his side. As I did so, I looked at him with surprise, for despite his bespectacled face and scrappy facial hair, beneath his battle fatigues was concealed a perfect washboard stomach. I couldn't help but laugh at this bizarre topsy-turvy world I seemed to have slipped into. It was as if I'd fallen down Alice's rabbit hole, and the extraordinary had become ordinary. Not one to be outdone, our doctor who had been diligently pulling on the suction machine with all her might suddenly recoiled violently and almost fell off her stool. "Oh my god!" I exclaimed, "Did you pull his head off?" Utterly farcical. She had pulled so hard the suction apparatus had completely come off the baby's head. A few seconds of fumbling to reattach it, a determined pull from below, a suffocating push from above, and our son was finally born.

He was placed on my chest for a few seconds before being whisked away to be examined by the emergency pediatrician who had been one of the faceless people attending the birth. He was limp, gray, and didn't make a sound. His first Apgar score was two out of 10. His breathing was a concern. But he began to cry, a persistent, angry bleat that reminded me of the seagulls that populated the marina where we lived. After five minutes his score had climbed to seven. He was pink and breathing normally but was taken for observation just in case.

I only got to hold him again two hours later when I practically dragged myself into a wheel chair and demanded that I be taken to my child. Enough was enough. My beautiful son and I met for the second time in a dark room adjoining the observation room, and I held him and nursed him and stroked his perfect pink face, cradled his conical head (it returned to normal after a few weeks), and marveled at how otherworldly becoming a mother is.

This battle was won, but as with any war, there would be others: the agony of breastfeeding, the challenges of being a new mother in a foreign country, the feeling of isolation that comes with being far away from my family. Somehow I managed to get through it all relatively unscathed. Perhaps a survival-type instinct kicked in, and I just got on with things. After all, what alternative did I have? And so our little family lived, laughed, cried, and traveled together as we had before, except with substantially less sleep.

Peace

We were on vacation in southern Turkey when I fell pregnant again. While we were marveling at the ancient ruins of Ephesus, paddling in the travertine pools at Pamukkale, and gorging on grilled fresh fish and fragrant tomatoes, life was blooming within me. Our son was 18 months old, still nursing and co-sleeping, and we simply made space for my burgeoning belly and carried on as usual. Six months in we learned that we would be moving to Durban, a charming, warm, and laid-back town on the east coast of South Africa.

I immediately started researching giving birth in South Africa, and while the hospitals and healthcare are world class, I was dis-appointed to learn that elective C-sections were alarmingly common, with one Guardian article claiming it was as high as 80%. I understand that part of this is the woman's choice, and she should be free to make that choice, but an unavoidable consequence is the normalization of intervention.

Cesareans are more convenient and much quicker than vaginal births, and what doctor wouldn't prefer to clock off at 5 p.m. rather than be on call all through the night, held hostage by the vagaries of nature? I had no choice but to place my faith in Google, and as I sat at my laptop, poised to type in the words "best natural birth gynecologist in Durban," I couldn't help but marvel at how as expats we are forced to fly by the seat of our pants in situations that would otherwise not even be an issue.

Well aware of my fool's errand, I trawled birthing forums, read many articles and pushed on through to the deep recesses of Google's search results. Out of 28,200 hits, a name finally wafted out of the Internet. Post after post mentioned this doctor, her commitment to natural birth, how she had attended a VBAC birth of twins. This was the one, I knew it. And so I emailed her, introducing myself, explaining my situation, requesting an appointment soon after the move.

No response.

I emailed a few more times, reiterating that I was five months pregnant and once we moved to South Africa would be without a doctor.

Still no reply.

Undeterred, I called her office and was confronted by a friendly but stern office manager who was obviously well educated in the art of deferral, as those who work for popular, sought-after doctors nearly always are. "I'm so sorry" she lamented curtly, "We have no appointments left for the next eight months."

I'm not very good at taking no for an answer, and so I politely called back every week asking if there had by some chance been a cancellation in January, which was when we planned to go on our look-see to find a home. This was such a struggle and so stressful that I once again had the feeling that I was preparing for war, except this time we were racing into battle blind with rusty swords and defeat nipping at our heels. And then, a merciful breakthrough! Growing more desperate and therefore exponentially bolder I asked if the doctor could squeeze in 10 minutes before her first appointment just to meet with me. There was a pause on the other end of the phone. "If you can be here by 6:45 a.m., she can see you before her first surgery." I was in!

One week later we flew to Durban to look for a house, and I met with the doctor on a bright and humid summer morning, a lazy sea breeze stirring in the palm trees. She was fantastic. Young, vibrant, yet calm and attentive. We hit it off, and she agreed to deliver the baby. Relief and gratitude washed over me, as if the universe was saying "It's okay, I've got you," and I was reminded again that it always pays to persist, especially in our crazy expat worlds. A month later we said a tearful goodbye to a snowy Istanbul and began our barefoot, carefree life in South Africa.

With each appointment I felt more relaxed. Most doctors insist on an ultrasound every month, but my request to limit them was respected. Instead, the doctor felt the baby with her hands, tracked my weight gain (with no judgment), and joked about how lucky I am to have straightforward, easy pregnancies.

This was a totally different experience from Istanbul, where everything was so tightly controlled, and appointments were rather stressful because I was always on the defensive against being unnecessarily tested, poked, and prodded. So when I went into labor a day after my due date, we headed to the hospital feeling calm and determined.

The hospital was beautiful. Small and personal. I had a private room and was allowed to get on with things in my own time. My husband and I played monopoly, we went for walks, and after four hours the pain blossomed into heaving waves, and I began to feel the abyss of fear looming, as it had in Istanbul. I opted for a walking epidural that would take the edge off the pain but not numbs my legs. It was enough to give me strength and banish the darkness.

The doctor popped in and out checking on our progress, and soon it was time to push. She perched on the corner of the bed in cut-off jeans and a sleeveless summer top and spoke to me in gentle tones, guiding and encouraging me.

She beckoned to my husband, "Come on, you're going to catch your son."

"Wait, don't I need gloves or a gown?" he asked.

"Why? He's your baby!" the doctor smiled. And with that out came our second son with a head full of black hair and a scrunched up little face, right into his father's arms. It was a beautiful, peaceful birth with only four people in the room, dimmed lights and absolutely no freaking out.

As we poured over our new creation, touched his relaxed hands with their perfect miniature nails, and his wrinkly old-man toes, I couldn't help but snort, my heart spilling over, "He's the ugliest newborn baby I've ever seen!" The midwife shot us a look of disbelief. "You two are awful!" she chastised with a huge smile on her face. My mother, who had flown in from the UK to help, took one look at his squashed, wrinkly face, his already luscious lips, and chocolate brown eyes and said, "This child is going to be beauty, you'll see." She was absolutely right.

Giving birth in two very different developing countries gave me two very different birthing experiences. Istanbul was like going to war: stressful, terrifying, otherworldly. Durban was like finding peace: supported, simple, light. Both experiences taught me that it's okay to fight for what I want, that the doctor-patient relationship can be one of negotiation instead of domination, and that stubborn determination can be a really good thing. But it also showed me that birth, like life, is unpredictable; that doctors are not infallible; that pain and fear are brothers-in-arms; and that regardless of grand intentions and the best-laid plans, what's most important is a healthy baby.

Lucille Abendanon is a freelance writer and blogger whose other interests include history and travel. She has three nationalities, and if you ask her where she's from, you'll never get a straightforward answer, because there isn't one. Lucille gets to reinvent her life every three years as she moves around the world with her husband, their two trinational bilingual boys and the family cat. She has lived in England, Vietnam, Thailand, Turkey, and South Africa and currently calls the Netherlands home where she is hoping that her memories of the African sun will see her through the winter months. Lucille writes about travel and the expat experience on her blog Expitterpattica, and her work has appeared in numerous print and online publications.

CHAPTER 10

"YOU SHOULD HAVE A BABY BOY"

Ruth Silbermayr-Song
Nationality: Austrian
Knocked up in: China
Birthed in: Austria
Parented in: China

When I move to China in the summer of 2012, I choose the southernmost metropolis to live and work in. Growing up in Austria, I always hated the cold, and I am sure I'd love living in this place with hot summers lasting at least half a year. Most of the other time, it would still be comfortably warm.

We sometimes make plans for the future, but then fate gets in the way. On my first day at work in a Chinese company, I am seated right next to Yang, a tall, handsome guy in his early thirties, who's originally from Northeast China (often better known in the West as former Manchuria). After finishing work on the second day, our team goes out to karaoke and *shaokao*, or barbecue prepared at street side food stalls. Just when we leave the office, it starts to rain. Only half of us have an umbrella, so two people each share one. I share one with Yang. Since he's so much taller than me, I hand him the umbrella. The other coworkers start joking that we should get a room. They are all around 30, but their sense of humor makes them seem at least 10 years younger. I don't think anything of it, but after a week of talking and joking daily with Yang on a messenger called QQ and getting to know more about him, then another week of doing the same, we start falling for each other. When we start dating two weeks later, his mom inquires via WeChat, a messaging app popular in China:

"Where is she from?"

"From the Northwest. She speaks Mandarin Chinese with an accent."

"In which year was she born?"

"In the year of the rabbit."

"Someone born in the year of the ox would be more suitable for you, but the year of the rabbit is still okay."

Luckily, we still get her blessings after telling her that I'm from a place much further West than Northwest China. It wouldn't have stopped us from dating if she hadn't, but it makes things much easier that way.

We get engaged within a month of knowing each other and marry in Austria half a year later. *Shanhun*, or "lightning wedding" is what the Chinese call a wedding as fast as ours.

Not too long after our wedding and honeymoon, my husband and I are back at work in Shenzhen. When we finish with work on the second day, one of our co-workers asks my husband, "So, when is it due?"

"When is what due?"

"You know, you and your wife..."

"What the hell are you talking about?"

"The baby! When is the expected date of delivery?"

"Huh. That's not why we married."

"Oh. So she's not pregnant?"

Many of my friends in Austria and our coworkers back in China assume we married because I am pregnant (I'm not). I can't blame them. If any of my friends had married so soon after getting together, I probably would have thought the same.

In October 2013, I'm seeing a traditional Chinese medicine doctor, who treats me for menorrhagia. It's the first time in my life that my period is overdue (albeit only one day) when I see the doctor for the second time, which I blame on the herbs I'm taking to treat my heavy and painful menses. Clearly, the early pregnancy test I took a week earlier wouldn't have shown a negative if I was pregnant. The doctor sends me to the next floor for a urine sample. I take a transparent plastic cup, walk across half the hospital to the restrooms, and after peeing into the cup, take it back for everyone to see. The three nurses put a paper strip inside and watch it. The first line is a clear red, the second one a very faint one.

They aren't sure what that means exactly, "You might be a little pregnant, but the result is not very clear yet," is what they tell me before they send me back to the doctor. The doctor congratulates me but says we have to monitor my hormone levels, and that I might have a miscarriage. I'm worried, but my eyes fill with happy tears at the thought of being pregnant. My husband and I had only just started trying for a baby, and I became pregnant on the first try.

At last, the doctor tells me the three no's during pregnancy in China: No lifting of heavy things, no falling down, and no "sharing the same room with my husband."

In the evening, I meet up with my husband in the city. I hand my heavy bag to him and tell him of the three noes. He's concerned about my health. I laugh out loud and tell him that he's going to be a father.

He can't believe it, "Wait, how can you be pregnant when we've only just started trying? You just came back from traveling solo for two weeks—are you sure the baby's mine?"

I forgive him for his thoughtless accusation (and he asks me not to tell anyone he said this) because he just really can't believe he's going to be a father. I walk carefully, being concerned about the tiny new life growing inside of me and thinking that I might fall with every step.

A few days later, nausea kicks in. I crave Nepalese, Italian, Vietnamese, Austrian cuisine and fish in tins, but the one most easily available here—Chinese cuisine—makes me want to throw up just at the thought of it. From then on, after coming home from work at around 8 p.m. every day, my husband first prepares home cooked meals for us, part of which we eat in the evening, and part of which I take with me to work the next day. I'm too nauseous to cook for myself. After enjoying dinner, he works his second job, freelancing from home until the wee hours of the morning, while I go to bed early.

When I'm six weeks in, I have my first ultrasound. It confirms that the egg has found the right spot, and I'm not only a little but 100% pregnant.

When my husband and I wait for the bus after the visit, we jump around (he more than I), and he starts to dance and sings, "I'm going to be a father, I'm going to be a father, I'm going to be a father!"

At two months pregnant, a co-worker asks me how far along I am. I tell her, and she replies, seemingly shocked, "How come your belly is already that big with only two months?"

"That's because it's the afternoon, and I ate a lot today."

We arrange with the in-laws that they will come all the way from their hometown in Northeast China to stay with us in Southeast China and help us with household chores and cooking until I leave for Austria, which is where I plan to give birth. Chinese hospitals scare the shit out of me when I think of giving birth there.

I've heard one too many stories of women being forced to get a C-section once they've been at the hospital for a certain amount of hours. If your doctor tells you that you need a medically necessary C-section, there isn't much to argue about. Who are you to know if what they say is true or just their way of ensuring they get paid more?

Austrian hospitals only do C-sections if they are really medically necessary, and that puts my mind at ease. Staying in Austria for some time after the birth would also mean that I wouldn't be confined to bed for a month after the birth, and that I wouldn't have my mother-in-law around to take care of the baby and do household chores while I stay in bed doing nothing. While I do appreciate a little help, I don't deal well with the lack of space a Chinese mother-in-law lovingly brings with her. And I'd really love to have some time to bond with our baby and get used to the new family dynamic.

During my second trimester, I get a little taste of what life with live-in Chinese in-laws means. On the first day after they arrive, my mother-in-law reorganizes the kitchen to her taste. My father-in-law thinks a bit too highly of the exhaust fan's ability to clean the kitchen air and smokes there first thing after entering our apartment, covering the whole apartment in a cloud of smoke. In the following days, we discover cleaned bowls, the bottom filled with water, and plates with leftover food right next to clean plates in the kitchen cupboards. We also discover that my father-in-law had secretly added MSG to every dish they'd prepared for us, even though we had asked him not to. To him, food doesn't taste like anything without MSG. Putting bowls into the cupboard without drying them first is a common occurrence in Chinese households, but it doesn't agree with the humid and hot climate of Shenzhen, where mold starts to grow on everything as soon as you turn your head. My husband and I discovered this after returning from our six-week-long wedding and honeymoon vacation, where a leather belt, shoes, some clothes, and many more items that seemed to be very much alive greeted us.

My mother-in-law also reminds me not to squat down, and if I do and tell her the baby won't just fall out of my uterus like that, she'll tell me, "Get up, get up, get up, get up, get up, get up, get up," until I find her too annoying and do indeed get up. She never tells me the reason she doesn't want me to squat down. She won't let me lift anything heavy, which I'm glad for. She also tells me not to pop pimples or blow my nose. I'm not sure if these are just some general rules of hers or if they are connected to my state of being pregnant, but I just ignore them. What should I do if not blow my runny nose?

In these early days, my husband fights a lot with his parents about the things we do differently from them, and we try to find some common ground. Some things we can agree on, like having my father-in-law smoke on the balcony instead of the kitchen, others not so much. In China, usually the older you are, the more you have a say in things. It's hard to argue about things with this mindset, but even with all the differences they bring into our home, my in-laws are still very helpful. They do feel very much out of place here in this chaotic city where people speak dialects different from theirs, where vegetables taste different from the Northeast, and they have to live in close quarters with a daughter-in-law they hardly know and who can barely understand them with their Northeastern dialect. But they stay here out of love for their family and their unborn grandchild and put up with their son and daughter-in-law for the time being.

At least once every month, I have to go to the nearby public maternity hospital for a check-up. A sign in front of the waiting area reads, "No men allowed to enter." "Men" only includes husbands, not ultrasound technicians, or security guards who will happily peek into the rooms filled to the brink with pregnant women and their mothers or mothers-in-law, who all talk to the doctor at the same time, thinking that this will shorten the time they have to wait for their appointment. One time, I can smuggle my husband into the room when the doctor asks me an important question I don't understand, and I talk the doctor into letting him hear the heartbeat of the baby.

Because of the one-child policy (which has been changed to a two-child policy in January 2016) and a traditional mindset that only boys can carry on the family name and care for their parents in old age (women marry into the husband's family), gender-selective abortions of girls are very common in China. Therefore, doctors are not legally allowed to tell you the sex of the baby before birth, and men are often not allowed into the room, particularly for ultrasounds. The monitor is turned away from the pregnant woman so she won't accidentally discover the baby's sex. My husband can't see the ultrasound, but hearing our baby's heartbeat together is a very touching moment for us.

In February 2014, I'm five months pregnant. I'm at work, and one of my co-workers who has just had a baby girl stops me in my tracks, "Let me see your belly." After looking at it, she concludes, "It's really big. The clothes you're wearing are quite sexy. You should wear more layers." She says that on a sunny day of 70°F (21°C) that reminds me of spring, on which I am wearing cotton tights, warm winter boots, an undershirt, a dress, and a long-sleeved cotton shirt. And this is only what I'm wearing inside.

After telling her that I'm sweating already, she goes on, "You should have a baby boy. Boys do look more like their mothers than their fathers and since your husband is rather ugly..."

I ignore the last comment and reply, "I've heard that before—that supposedly boys look more like their mother, while girls look more like their father. I have seven brothers and sisters and can't say that I see evidence of that belief in our looks."

She insists, "Well, it holds true with Chinese genetics. Anyways, if you have a boy, he will also be insurance for you."

Being a woman myself, it hurts to hear how men are valued so much more by many here than women. Unfortunately, Confucius is still very much alive in China. From a more pragmatic standpoint, I can understand how the tradition of women marrying out of the family and men and their wives caring for parents in old age is a suitable arrangement in a country where many still don't get a pension. But I can't accept it from a more contemporary and feminist standpoint. There are so many other options of how you could arrange for parents to be cared for in old age than the women-marrying-out-men-carrying-on-family-name tradition.

Fortunately, my husband is on the same page with me, and it doesn't matter for us if the baby is a boy or a girl. On another day during my second trimester, I wash dishes at work during lunch break from the meal my husband prepared for me the evening before.

A female co-worker sees me and says, "Why don't you get your husband to wash the dishes?"

"Because it was only me who ate, and he's napping."

"Go wake him up!"

Comments like these are a fresh respite from the overbearing pregnancy advice I get on most other days. I've been told among others not to squat down, not to have sex, and not to eat sweet rice balls. One time a fruit seller refused to sell me hawthorn fruit after seeing my bump. I know that most people only show they care about you by offering advice, but I can't get over the fact that I'm now seemingly reduced to my bump and not considered a human being with a working brain anymore.

I want to shout at them, "I'm still a human being with interests of my own who's perfectly capable of deciding for herself if she can eat hawthorn or not. Now give me that fruit or else!" But the protective hand of Chinese society does not differentiate between individuals—when you're pregnant, you will be protected, from those around you as well as from your crazy hawthorn-craving self.

Two months later on another day at work in Shenzhen, a female coworker asks me, "How many months along are you?" I tell her I'm seven months in. She then wants to know if I've already had an ultrasound.

"I have."

"So what's it going to be? A boy or a girl?"

"I don't know."

"Has your skin turned darker anywhere after getting pregnant?"

"I don't think so."

"Then you're going to have a girl. At least, that's what people say—that it's a girl if your skin doesn't turn darker during pregnancy and a boy if it does."

At this point in time, I actually do know our baby's sex, but we've decided to keep it a secret from family and friends until birth. People always look so hurt when we tell them we know the sex but won't tell them, so saying we don't know is the easier option.

When I'm eight months pregnant, I take a flight back to Austria. My husband will follow a few weeks later. Having had days in Shenzhen where the only thing I wanted to eat was watermelon to get a little respite from the unbearable heat, I'm glad for the cool weather and the relatively fewer comments on all the things I'm not supposed to do during pregnancy. It will take me until our child is about one year old to be finally able to care less about these comments, put down my own judgment, and be a more relaxed version of myself again.

Just like my Chinese mother-in-law has predicted, Little Song, our son, is born at noon on July 5, 2014, to the sound of church bells ringing. He's born just a day after my birthday and his due date, but we still share the same birthday in the lunar calendar.

Although the 11.5 hours of labor pains were as traumatic as expected and I just wanted to die during the last hour of pushing, never knowing if the midwife was around or not (she had a really busy day at the hospital), and being told that I had to lie on the bed hugging one leg to push, which was the one position I really did not want to give birth in, I am still glad I could give birth in Austria. When our son was finally out, my husband cried. He cried happy tears for both our son and me. He almost thought I wouldn't be able to push him out.

A while after the birth, after having let our son rest a bit on my breast and after having the tear stitched, I feel like going to the restroom. I'm still on the bed I gave birth on, our son and the nurses nowhere to be seen (at least I don't remember seeing him anywhere—he was being taken care of by the nurses). My husband helps me up, and we go to the restroom. When I get up from the toilet, I feel shaky in my legs. I tell my husband, "I think I need to hold..." and faint.

When I wake up again, he's hitting me in the face, shouting at me. He managed to call the nurses who say that I should have called them to go to the restroom. They help me back to my bed. Our son has miraculously reappeared, wearing a pink bodysuit that is way too hot for him in the summer heat and a pink name card. A little while later, they take us to the hospital room we'll be staying in for the next three days. Our son is a miracle. My husband, our son, and I stay in Austria for the next few months.

One hundred days after our son was born, I take a flight from Munich via Dubai to Hong Kong with my husband and Little Song, where we cross the border to Shenzhen late at night, losing our son's car seat on the way. We had stored all of our belongings in self-storage in Shenzhen for the few months we stayed in Austria and made sure that they are being sent to my husband's hometown in Northeast China. We only stay for two days and get on a plane that will take us from Shenzhen to Changchun. Our journey from Austria to Northeast China is the most exhausting journey of our lives so far; we don't know where it will lead us, or of the financial difficulties that will await us in the year of the goat. At that time, we just know we can't stay in Shenzhen, where we wouldn't be able to live on my husband's salary alone and where we'd have no support from my in-laws. I can't stand the thought of leaving our baby in the care of an *ayi*, or "aunt" aka nanny, having to leave for work at seven in the morning and coming back at eight in the evening, past our son's bedtime. So we also send the car we bought a few months prior from hot and humid Southeast China up to cold and dry Northeast China. It will arrive a month after us with cigarette stubs and poker cards scattered across the car's floor.

When we arrive in Changchun, we have an acquaintance pick us up and take us 70 miles (110 km) to Siping, in an old VW Jetta. I sit in the rear, with Little Song in the sling. There's no safety belt, and we're squeezed in between the car door and large boxes belonging to the driver. Little Song sleeps and nurses, and I look out the car at the wide blue skies and the harvested fields that are turned into shades of yellow by the vivid northeastern sun. Northeast China's vast plains are beautiful at this time of year.

It's already quite cold in Siping. During the day, we still get a lot of sunshine. I often bundle up our little one and go for a walk in the early afternoon. When we take a cab, and the cab driver looks at Little Song through the rear mirror, he turns up the heating even more.

He asks, "How old is he?"

I tell him that he's 14 weeks.

"Only three months? It's way too cold for him to be outside.

A few weeks later, my husband, Little Song and I visit his cousin in Changchun. The cousin's wife watches us change diapers.

Before we put on a clean diaper, she says, "Wait a while. Let his pee-pee get some air." She then goes on, "Do you always have him wear diapers?"

After a yes, she says, "Why don't you try split baby pants? We have some at home. I'll get you one. Diapers are bad for his pee-pee. It might start to rot and fall off."

As the weather gets even colder, I visit a bathhouse while my mother-in-law takes care of our son. After finishing a body scrub, the employee looks at my breasts and observes, "Your left breast is smaller than the right one."

"I know. It's even more obvious now that I'm breastfeeding."

"My left breast is also smaller than the right one. You

can let your baby drink more from the left breast. That way it will become bigger."

This is not my first conversation about breasts with a female employee working at a massage parlor or bathhouse, and I'm sure it won't be the last. I don't really mind talking about breasts with other women, though.

In the year of the goat, my in-laws' old house is torn down. They move into the tiny government-assigned apartment they now call their home. We help them furnish it, and our debt grows. My husband is overqualified for the jobs in his hometown and works a few hours a week as a freelance designer for a little more money than local firms would be able to pay him for a full-time job. I find work at the local university, one of the only two jobs I would be able to do here in Siping. Although we're still far from paying off our debt, we have some stability back in our lives. The feeling of stability only lasts until January 2016, when I take a pregnancy test that turns out to be positive. Little Song No. 2 is on the way, making us both happy and anxious for what the future will bring.

Little Song No. 1 is now 22 months old. In wintertime, he'll wear layers upon layers just like any other toddler here—a bright red down jacket and a blue hat with green cartoon worms sewn on the front top off his appearance. Both of these he got as presents from his Chinese grandparents for Christmas—the western spring festival as they have come to call it. A scarf is finally wrapped around his face so that only his eyes have to face the freezing cold winter air. Whenever people tell me that he shouldn't be outside and ask if he isn't cold, assuming that he certainly must be, he'll now be quick to answer for himself, "I'm not cold," making me a proud mom and laughing about this question I've been asked so many times since taking him to China.

Ruth Silbermayr-Song works as a German teacher and illustrator and is a mother of two. She is fluent in Mandarin Chinese, which is the language she communicates in with her husband and in-laws. She currently lives in Northeast China in close proximity to the in-laws, together with her husband and son. Her award-winning blog www.chinaelevatorstories.com features short conversations with locals and posts about cultural differences, parenting far away from home, the challenges of life abroad, and of being in an intercultural marriage. She read some of the unique stories from her blog at the Beijing Bookworm Literary Festival 2016. Her love of solo travel took her to China's Far West seven months pregnant. She makes plans for her next travel destination whenever she isn't busy with day-to-day life.

CHAPTER 11

SEVEN WEEKS AND TWENTY-EIGHT DAYS

Brynn Barineau
Nationality: American
Birthed in: Brazil

The contractions started just before 5 p.m. I didn't know that's what they were. It was my first pregnancy, and I'd never felt a contraction. Everything I read about contractions emphasized back pain. Oh the back pain! I had no back pain. So much for preliminary research. What I had was pain across my lower abdomen that seemed to come in waves.

While watching my students study during the last few minutes of class for the day, I chalked the pain up to intestinal problems. The one classic pregnancy symptom I'd had the joy of experiencing for several months was constipation. I assumed the pain was my intestine finally in revolt, not contractions.

Also, I was only 33 weeks along.

I noted the increasing intensity of the pain as I caught a ride home from a fellow teacher. I thought it odd when I finally scurried into my bathroom at home that I didn't really have to go. Still, I didn't think contractions. It was seven weeks before my due date. I didn't even dismiss the thought of contractions. The thought has to enter your head in order to dismiss it.

By 6:15 p.m., however, I was in sufficient enough pain to ask my husband to call my doctor. He told me to get in a warm shower and sent my husband off to buy some pregnancy-safe painkillers. When the shower failed to lessen the pain, I began to think something was wrong. Then there was blood.

I called my husband. He turned back before ever reaching the drug store. He was on the phone with my doctor when he walked back into the apartment. As I was yanking on clothes in the bedroom, I heard him ask, "How much blood is there? If it's just…" He stopped talking. He'd seen the bathmat. In less than a minute we were in the car on our way to the doctor's office.

Thankfully, my doctor's office was only five minutes from our apartment, and he was working late. It was about 7 p.m. The office was empty except for the doctor and his secretary, as my husband helped me climb the stairs to the exam room. The pain was now so intense I wanted nothing more than to close my eyes and breathe, but we don't always get what we want. Although if ever there were a time when a person should, you'd think it would be while in the middle of birthing a new human being.

In my case, there were questions about pain and Portuguese verbs to conjugate in order to answer. I used to think speaking in Portuguese on the phone was difficult. Speaking in Portuguese during a contraction is much harder.

Placental abruption. That was my Portuguese phrase of the day. My doctor explained the baby's heart rate was elevated and that fact combined with the blood and contractions made him think the placenta had torn from the uterus and blood was now pumping into the uterus. I was headed for an emergency C-section.

After a flurry of discussion between my husband and the doctor, and some quick phone calls made by his assistant, they confirmed no office with an ultrasound was open to confirm the diagnosis, so we would be going straight to the emergency room. At least that's what I was told happened. I was still lying on the exam table breathing through contractions and pain that went from aching to breathtaking, never completely disappearing.

A little before 8 p.m., I was standing on the sidewalk with my doctor trying to have small talk in Portuguese while my husband got the car. I can't think of a less appropriate time for small talk than during preterm labor, but Brazilians are compelled to fill all silences with conversation.

Twenty minutes later my doctor was wheeling me into the emergency room and pushing me over to some nurses who began giving a flurry of instructions in Portuguese. I was being prepped for emergency surgery seven weeks before my due date, but strangely enough I was not panicked. I was too occupied with breathing through contractions and understanding the directions I was given to really dwell on worst-case scenarios. Contractions are a great distraction. Contractions and conjugating Portuguese verbs.

I never thought I would die. I never thought I could die. I never thought my baby would die. In the moment, I never once feared for my life or my baby's. It was only afterward, when researching placental abruptions, that I learned just how serious the situation was. While I lay on my side, curled into a ball, having a needle stuck between vertebrae,

I was worried about the kinds of complications my daughter could have being born early. Would she have eye or ear problems? Would she have some sort of neurological problem? Would her lungs be working yet?

I didn't bring any of this up to my husband as he sat by my head in canary yellow scrubs, pointedly not looking in the direction of my open abdomen. The C-section is certainly one of the most surreal experiences of my life. To be fully conscious while your abdomen is opened and people stick their hands in and root around your internal organs... Well, surreal doesn't quite cover it. I felt tugging, sometimes hard tugging, but absolutely no pain. There was one hard tug and suddenly a baby was crying. I cried for the first time.

My daughter was born at 8:50 p.m. and immediately admitted to the Neonatal Intensive Care Unit or NICU. She was on oxygen for a day and then under a UV lamp for four. At birth she was 4 lbs. 5 oz. (2,070 g) and then dropped to around 4 lbs. (1,800 g). The exact number is gone. I only remember that "18" at the beginning of her weight because I noted it every day. My husband and I had been told that in order for our daughter to be discharged two things had to happen: She must gain weight from breastfeeding alone and weigh more than 2,000 g.

The doctors assured us since she was healthy and without major complications, we should be leaving within a week. Ten days at most. You can guess where this is going.

My daughter spent a month in the NICU.

She's about to turn five, and I'm amazed how much of a blur those weeks have become. Of the many people who cared for my daughter, all but one of the names has been forgotten. Now they're the nurse with red glasses, the perpetually cranky doctor, and the physiotherapist who spoke some English.

What has not faded in any detail, much to my dismay, is my memory of the milking room. This was the place the hospital sent new moms in the NICU to strip them of dignity. It was the room for hand expressing breast milk.

Many preemies are born too small to breastfeed and are fed through a tube and syringe. How do you get these babies breast milk? The obvious answer is pump it, store it, and serve it. Except the NICU did not allow breast pumps of any kind. The hospital said it could not guarantee that an individual mom's pump would be sterile, so they could not give the milk from a potentially unsterile source to the baby. The only way for a baby in the NICU at Vitoria Apart Hospital to get breast milk, other than on tap, was to hand express it.

This is as awful as it sounds.

At least for me. I am not particularly in touch with my body. I'm more cerebral and would be quite content to be a floating brain in space, except for the facts I do like going for walks and eating French fries. I'm aware that my conscious self is housed in an organic Tupperware container that impacts how I feel, think, am, but I don't dwell on it. At least not until I get a stomach virus or have to breastfeed a baby.

And I was going to breastfeed. I'd done my research. Despite my lack of emotional connection to my mammary glands, I was totally committed to breast-feeding. I did not, however, anticipate having to milk myself like a cow. But that's what I had to do. Hand expressing means squeezing out the milk by hand.

Despite this daunting psychological hurdle, I told the nurses I still wanted to breastfeed, so one of them led me out the back door of the NICU, down a hall, through an unmarked door, and into an unused storage closet. Based on the size and lack of any comforts except three chairs, I assume storage closet was the original purpose of the room. White walls, tile floor, no windows, and freezing cold. This was the room I shuffled to with recently sliced apart abdominal muscles, so that I could hand squeeze milk from my boobs.

As I stood there shivering in my hospital gown, the nurse quickly went through the officially sanctioned routine that guaranteed milk I expressed in that closet would be more sanitary than what I could get from a pump: wash hands, don hairnet and face mask, remove the plastic cups from the packaging and take the lids off, wash hands again, wash nipples with gauze, squeeze milk into cup, and seal the cup immediately when full. Fortunately, she demonstrated the whole process because to this day I don't know the Portuguese word for gauze or hairnet.

Then she left.

No medical professional stayed in that closet with the moms. Want to guess how many of the moms milking themselves actually followed that routine when left on their own?

I know because it turned out to be a communal milking closet, and the answer is none that I saw. The next time I went to the closet, two other women were already in the closet happily chatting away, masks down over their chins. I distinctly remember these two women because they were friendly, completely comfortable being half naked in front of strangers, and filling up cup after cup with milk like a competition at a state fair. I was none of those things. I struggled to fill half a cup when alone. Trying to hand express milk in a freezer while confronting small talk in Portuguese and the four largest breasts I've ever seen in person was literally impossible.

I got almost no milk out during that second session or any other. I subjected myself to breastfeeding purgatory every three hours for four days before finally saying,

"Enough." I believe breast milk is ideal. I don't believe it is worth self-torture.

I restarted breastfeeding only after my daughter was big enough to handle it herself. Hand expressing in that closet was one of the worst experiences of my life. And I sat through the Sponge Bob movie.

If I'd had any reserve of energy, I would have been outraged. I was being denied a breast pump on the grounds it wasn't sterile, but there was nothing sterile about that room. They sent a bunch of not-medically-trained women down the hall with instructions to wash their hands and wear a mask. I don't believe a single doctor actually thought the milk coming out of that closet was sterile. They know they're in Brazil, where actual laws are treated as suggestions.

But rules and protocols initially based on sound reasoning yet implemented with such indifference they become nothing but pains in the ass are a tradition in Brazil. The breast pump ban was only one example.

Each morning for 28 days, my husband and I arrived at the hospital by 8:15 a.m. in time for our baby's morning bath. I practiced with the nurses giving our tiny daughter a bath in a metal basin, and then sat with her in my lap until 11:30 a.m. My husband spent those three hours at the snack bar. Only mothers were allowed in the NICU before noon.

Why? "Because that's when the doctors do their rounds, and it gets too crowded."

But why can't the mother and father take turns being in the room? What about a baby whose mother can't come to the NICU? What about a dad who wants to learn how to bathe his preemie baby?

"Only mothers are allowed in the NICU before noon."

This rule based on nothing but archaic gender roles was so rigidly enforced they didn't allow my husband in the

NICU the morning they told me my child had a complication.

Dr. Cranky came up to me before I even made it to my daughter's bed. She began explaining in really inexcusably rapid Portuguese, considering I was the celebrity foreigner in the NICU and everyone knew my Portuguese was terrible. I understood "blood" and "feces" before I stopped her and asked for my husband to be allowed in to help translate. Dr. Cranky refused.

I explained that my Portuguese wasn't good enough to understand the medical terms she was using and that my husband, a Brazilian, could help translate. She reminded me that fathers are not allowed in before noon, and he could speak to a doctor during the daily "face time with a doctor" between 3 and 4 in the afternoon. I then asked that if my husband couldn't come in, could she come outside into the hallway and explain it to us.

I remember pointing at the door. It wasn't 10 feet away. I'd made eye contact with my husband through the observation window, and he knew something was wrong. He'd be right outside the door. I repeated my request with enough volume to turn heads, and the doctor sighed. She sighed. And finally trudged into the hallway.

My daughter had blood in her stools. As there was no infection, they suspected it was due to an allergy, most likely to lactose. Dr. Cranky said the nursing, which I had only just restarted, had to stop for three days, so I could completely cut lactose from my diet and process any traces of it out of my system. My daughter's release from the hospital would be delayed indefinitely until she was able to nurse without any reaction. I cried for the second and last time of my daughter's hospital stay.

The overwhelming majority of my life regrets come from those four weeks my daughter spent in the NICU. I should have gotten a second opinion. I should have gotten our own pediatrician who didn't work for the hospital. I should have asked more questions and argued more. I should have gotten a damn lawyer. I should have gone self-righteous American on them. While unattractive in most situations, the angry, entitled American can get a lot done simply by refusing to let something go. That is to say, I should have fought.

But I didn't have the energy to fight.

We were at the hospital every morning, went home for lunch at 11:30 a.m., were back by 1 p.m., and stayed until they kicked us out at 8 p.m. Once we got back home, we attempted to unpack a box or two, because our furniture and lives had arrived from Rio de Janeiro the day I went into labor. In the end, we brought our daughter home to an apartment that was almost entirely unpacked by our housekeeper and my mother-in-law who flew in from Rio. I still don't where the dessert bowls ended up.

I try not to get too upset about the missing bowls or the lack of fight I put up. I have a beautiful and brilliant future leader in training. She's got the fight I was missing during her first month of life. Ironically, the least family-friendly place I've been in Brazil was the NICU. Children are welcomed and embraced everywhere, and businesses bend over backward to accommodate families. A toddler in the midst of a tantrum elicits sympathy for the parents and support. I'm certain our little banshee queen would have gotten us frequent requests to leave in other countries, so we have ended up in the right place.

True, an electric pump and a private space would have made a huge difference those first four weeks of motherhood, but we all survived, and someday the sound of someone else's breast milk squirting into a plastic cup will fade from memory. Hopefully.

Brynn is originally from Atlanta, Georgia and has a bachelor's and master's degree in international communication from American University in Washington, DC. It was while finishing her master's that she met her Brazilian husband. Brynn eventually joined her then-fiancé in Rio de Janeiro and began teaching. After moving to Vitoria, she taught economics and American literature at Escola Leonardo Da Vinci. Brynn is currently working on building a career as a writer and publishing her first novel. She blogs at BrynninBrazil.com. She has a five-year-old daughter whom she and her husband are raising bilingual in English and Portuguese.

CHAPTER 12

TWENTY-EIGHT HOURS IN ABU DHABI

Kristy Smith
Nationality: American
Birthed in: The United Arab Emirates

"**M**ake *caca*, Kristy!" my Syrian doctor shouted in her beautifully accented English, "Bravo! Bravo! Come on, make *caca*, make *caca*!"

While Dr. Manal took care of the business end, my husband held my hand, or more accurately, he let me squeeze his hand, as the gruff Hungarian head nurse attempted to help me push by plunging my midsection repeatedly, as though my uterus were somehow in need of cardio-pulmonary resuscitation. Being my first time on the delivery table, I had no frame of reference regarding the plunging, but it hurt—much worse than the pushing the baby through the birth canal part, though I'd had drugs for that—so I looked to my husband, Steve, an Englishman, to manage the situation.

Steve shouted to the nurse to stop plunging. His voice, the only male voice in the room, and the only voice I could focus on, drew me in so that I could manage the task at hand and forget, at least briefly, about the plunging and the pushing and the fact that I was in a foreign country with no other Americans in the room—not even my husband—and that I could die here, on this table, surrounded by strange and foreign sounds and experiences, while trying to push this baby out into this world!

Hysterical and overprotective mothers: the bane of firstborn children everywhere.

Back at the other end, Dr. Manal continued preparing for the baby, "I see the head! Get Dr. Hassan! Tell him it's urgent! The baby's coming! One more time, Kristy! Once more...push!"

Three productive pushes later and Steve whisper-shouted in my ear, "It's a boy...We've got a baby boy!"

Dr. Manal immediately placed my son on my chest. He was slippery, and my belly wobbled like a waterbed, so he nearly slipped through my exhausted and shaking hands. But I caught him, and I whispered, "Hello, baby," before he was whisked off to the other side of the room, behind the curtain to get checked over by Dr. Hassan.

Dr. Hassan, a jovial man from Lebanon with a warm smile and kind heart, would be my son's pediatrician the remainder of our time in Abu Dhabi (the capital city of the United Arab Emirates, or UAE), though I never saw him the day my son was born. No men other than the husband of the woman giving birth were allowed in the delivery room, and that included the medical staff. Our situation was unique in that I gave birth in a hospital that was known to cater more to the local Emirati population rather than the western expats and culturally, we had different expectations than many who gave birth there. This uniqueness becomes obvious later in our story. But, let me back up.

My husband and I had moved to Dubai in the United Arab Emirates from New York City in November of 2004. We'd been married a little less than two years at that time, and this would be our second major move—we'd met in Chicago and lived there together for two years before heading to New York. A few short months after arriving and settling in Dubai, I'd had a miscarriage. It was difficult and heartbreaking, but we were young, and my OB/GYN at the time, a matronly but sweet woman from Iraq, assured me that we had plenty of time to have a baby.

A year later, I'd begun to adjust to life in a new country: From shouting, "Sun, glorious sun!" every morning to sighing, "Oh, look, it's sunny again." From aimlessly wandering through and gazing at the architecturally stunning shopping malls, to efficiently and effortlessly honing in on all the best coffee shops in town (Dome in Souk Madinat still ranks in my top five favorites). From timidly setting out to learn Arabic to forging and fostering great friendships with some amazing and talented women in my Arabic classes. From beginning to understand the concept of *wasta* (aka clout) to utilizing it in my daily life; and from cautiously staying in my Jumeirah Jane lane on Sheikh Zayed Road to expertly navigating all five lanes at 100 miles per hour. The confluence of several different driving styles of groups of people from different parts of the world makes for some very specific unwritten rules of the road, whereby the type of car you drive coupled with your outward appearance dictates which lane you should use and how fast you are expected to go. Driving on Sheikh Zayed Road will test one's driving skills to a degree unlike any roads I've ever experienced, and I've driven in several major cities around the world.

I should point out that the UAE, and Dubai in particular, is a dynamic social experiment in international relations and immigration in and of itself. When we were living there (from 2004 to 2008), only approximately 20% of the population was Emirati (that number jumped to closer to 40% in Abu Dhabi, the capital of the country). India provided the highest immigrant population, followed by Pakistan, and other Gulf Arab and Middle Eastern countries. There were also a sizable mix of western expats from the United Kingdom, Europe, Russia, Eastern Asia, South Africa, Australia and New Zealand, and the United States. We had a dinner party at our house once, and though there were only 12 attendees, nine countries were represented: the US, the UK, Germany, Spain, Ireland, Switzerland, Turkey, Finland, and France.

People from varied backgrounds and nationalities lived and worked together, generally quite well, in a country with a smaller geographic area than the state of Maine—and much of that is uninhabitable desert (though to be fair, they have since branched out into man-made islands in the Gulf, so there is a bit more space than there was).

Stereotypes are heightened to the point of exaggeration in this situation. For example, at the beach you could easily spot the German expats with their black socks and sandals, the Indian and Pakistani men playing cricket, the windsurfing Australians, the sunburned Brits, and the loud Americans, to name a few.

All these different people mingling with all their diverse cultural baggage and worldviews create an environment that could easily implode and take scores of well-meaning people with it. But instead, a wonderful thing happens: We laugh at ourselves and our perceived differences. We embrace learning about strange and foreign ideas, and are awed when traditions are so different from our own—or as was often the case, so similar to our own.

Stereotypes aren't a great way of forming judgments of an entire group of people that is different from your own, but when you can see the obvious differences and laugh at yourself, it facilitates conversations and relationships with people you may never have considered before. When everyone is in the same boat—no friends or family nearby—you have a couple of choices: You can dive into life and relationships headfirst, or you can stay at home and wallow in self-pity and fear of the unknown.

I chose to dive in headfirst, and some of my very best friends are the people we met in Dubai and Abu Dhabi. I think this is the best life lesson I've learned from living anywhere. Living overseas forced me to make choices for my own life. No one else was going to come and pull me out of my house; I had to choose to leave it. I'm glad I did.

I went into labor officially at noon on Thursday, November 16. Let's call that hour No. 1. My husband had joined me for a routine checkup at the doctor's office that morning. By then, I was already eight days past my due date and growing larger and groanier by the second, at least according to my hips. (Is groanier a word? It should be.) My hips groaned through the majority of both of my pregnancies. Nobody told me how badly my hips would hurt. I still feel resentful about that.

Pregnancy isn't easy on a body in the best of times, what with all the excess bodily fluids, the expanding and stretching of skin, moving around of organs to make room for another human, and the ever-expanding hips. Add in extra stressors, like living 7,000 miles away from family and close friends (making it so I couldn't even talk about the hip pain and bodily fluids in real time), trying to communicate with everyone in a language that closely resembles English but relies on phrases such as "same same" and "straight and then more straight" to get what you want and where you're going. And throw in temperatures reaching 120°F (48°C) on top of the 60 extra pounds of baby weight, and it takes an even bigger toll on a body (it was baby weight, I've just chosen to hang on to a bit of it still as a reminder of those glorious days of pregnancy and eating whatever I wanted without a care).

Dr. Manal sent me home after the appointment that morning, even though I'd had one lonely contraction during my visit. She said I should come back on Sunday if nothing else had changed. That was three days later—three more days of groaning and expanding. To be fair, Thursday night in the UAE is like Friday or Saturday night in other parts of the world. In Islam, Friday is the holy day, so in Muslim countries, the UAE included, Friday is like Sunday. So, basically, my doctor was telling me that she had plans for the weekend and that I wasn't to go into labor until after that.

Hahaha, sorry doc.

After my appointment, my husband took me to a nearby coffee shop. We ordered coffees and opera cakes. I remember the opera cakes because though I had seen them before, I didn't know they were called opera cakes until we were at this particular café. They're lovely layers of cake, coffee syrup and buttercream topped with chocolate ganache, and they're delish. By this point in my pregnancy, I wasn't concerned about caffeine stunting the growth of my baby. We were well past all that, and mama needed a cappuccino and cake!

After our coffees, Steve drove me home, and then went back to work. His office was only a 10-minute drive, so we both felt no reason for him to stay home. I'd had another contraction at the café, but it wasn't strong, and honestly, at first I just thought I was gassy. Spicy curry, anyone?

I loved the food in the UAE. Our first few weeks were spent living in a five-star hotel, and it showed in the variety and quality of their buffet offerings: strange fruits like dragon fruit and mangosteen, spices with exotic smells and colors creating amazing dishes using otherwise familiar foods, and curries. Indian curries, Thai and other Southeast Asian curries and even Chinese curries populated the menus.

As a Midwestern American girl, my experience with curry was pretty limited up to that point, but once I discovered the flavor explosions from curries, I never went back. One of the pitfalls of being pregnant in a place like the UAE, where you spend 98% of the time indoors wandering around malls and with access to such great food is that you eat far too much. Maybe you wouldn't, but I did.

Being pregnant in the Middle East also skewed my perception of how pregnant woman are, and should be, treated. For example, my OB/GYN in Dubai insisted that I spend the majority of my time sitting and relaxing as though I were a delicate flower. At every monthly check up I would have to answer sheepishly that yes, I was still working at the elementary school, and no, I didn't intend to quit.

On the other hand, I also became accustomed to having others do things for me without my asking, but simply because I was a woman, and I was pregnant (see above re: delicate flower status). So, imagine my chagrin when we traveled to Europe for our babymoon during my second trimester and no one there seemed bothered that I might want to sit down, or that I might expect help with my luggage.

It is amazing how one's perspective changes with one's surroundings.

We moved to Abu Dhabi after our European expedition, when I was about six months pregnant, so I had the experience of fast-moving, shiny new Dubai for the first part of my pregnancy, and spent the final trimester in considerably slower Abu Dhabi. My OB/GYN in Dubai would've been pleased: I'd finally reached delicate flower status.

Around 5 p.m., hour No. 5, on November 16, and after spending the majority of my time at home alone wandering around my house and moaning every 10 minutes or so, I decided it was time to call Steve and get him to come home. These early hours of labor were the easy hours, though I'd had no idea of that at the time.

Overall, being pregnant in the UAE proved to be an easy and fun experience, but being pregnant is a roller coaster of emotions that is shocking and jarring in the most mundane of situations. Add the complications of infertility (we overcame that, but not until after several rounds of prodding, poking, and probing in places and with equipment I never knew existed), and the stress of being 7,000 miles away from friends and family, in addition to the nuances of language and cultural differences, and it makes the process that much more stressful. I would like to point out that I know full well that we chose to be so far away from our loved ones, and Steve and I are and always have been an awesome team (we rock, we really do, just ask either of us), but that doesn't make dealing with emotional stress any less valid or difficult.

What I'm really trying to say is, I missed my mom. We were very close when I was growing up. She was my best friend, and even though I was a social butterfly as a teenager, she was always the person I modeled myself and my behavior after. She lives in the US, and at the time was still working full time, so it just wasn't feasible for her to make the trek to the UAE twice in such a short time span. We'd intended for her to be there after the baby was born, but it wasn't as necessary for her to be there while he was still cooking. So, instead of sharing this experience with her and having her there to hold my hand or rub my forehead or make me a peanut butter and jelly sandwich while I waddled and cried and breathed, I did all of that on my own—except the peanut butter and jelly sandwich part. No way was I going to attempt to hold a knife during my contractions!

Steve made it home around 5:30 that evening. He tried to be helpful, but not much could comfort me. I tried to eat, but couldn't. I tried to take a bath, but couldn't. I tried to rest, but couldn't. By this point, I was crawling around the cool marble floor trying to remember to breathe. The hours passed and the painful contractions intensified, so around 10 p.m. and after 10 hours of labor, I told Steve it was time to go to the hospital. My contractions were hovering around five or six minutes apart, and they were very painful.

I hadn't eaten much since our coffee and cake that morning and hadn't slept all day because it was daytime and I wasn't tired then. And shouldn't the baby be here by now? We made it to the hospital about 15 minutes later, our baby bag having been packed and ready to go for weeks. One vivid memory I have of that moment is getting out of our car at the valet parking at the hospital (yes, they're very fancy in Abu Dhabi), stumbling to the wall, and very dramatically attempting to collapse into it with my arms above my head, but having my belly prevent me from doing more than letting my head fall into the space in the crook of my elbow. And moaning. Lots of moaning. Probably about how badly my hips hurt. Or, maybe how painful the contractions were. Same same.

The moment we arrived and got checked in, they hooked me up to an IV and forbade me from eating, not that I could've focused on chewing at that point in any case. One bit of advice the nurse provided to me was to squat down every time I felt a contraction coming.

Did I mention that by this time, I'd been having contractions every few minutes for about 10 hours? Not gentle tummy tickling, barely noticeable contractions, but heavy, muscle-grinding, breathtaking, non-productive contractions. We spent the majority of the night wandering the halls of Al Noor Hospital, and every few steps I'd squat, and cry, then stand back up, and we'd carry on down the hallway.

We continued with the waddle-waddle-squat-cry-repeat routine most of the night, until I finally relented and begged for the epidural. You see, I had decided very early on in my pregnancy that I wouldn't ask for an epidural: My mom hadn't had one, and by golly, I wouldn't need one, pain be damned! But 20 hours in, I decided I didn't need to be a hero. By this time, it was early Friday morning. Friday being Sunday in the UAE, needless to say the anesthesiologist on-call was not impressed with me. At all. He blew into the room in his track suit (it was his day off, after all), his arms waving wildly, ranting about my insensitivity to his needs, "Why does she call me here on a Friday morning? Why does she do this?!"

Then, he saw the hot mess that 20 hours of labor had created and transformed into Dr. Feelgood: he became my very best friend that morning. You know, after the whole plunging a giant needle into my back and narrowly avoiding paralyzing me as I did my very best to hold completely still during a furious contraction thing. Nearly a full day into this beautiful ordeal, and finally I was able to sleep. Not well, not deeply, but I could rest without feeling like I was being squeezed in the world's largest and most painful vise every 90 seconds. The rest of the morning continued as I would have expected it to in any part of the world: several more hours of drug-induced pain-free calm before the storm.

Hour No. 28 and eight hours after the epidural, it was time for my son to make his grand entrance! I pushed him into this world (and I feel like I've been pushing him every day since) at 4:06 p.m. on November 17, 2006, in Abu Dhabi. He weighed in at 8 lbs. 13 oz. (4,000 g) and measured 21.5 inches (55 cm) in length, and the experience was as miraculous and wonderful as I'd expected it to be. After I'd delivered him and everyone got cleaned up, we were taken back to my humongous private room, presumably giving my husband and I time to adjust to the fact that we'd just brought a new life into the world, and what on Earth made us think we could handle this?

My mom was supposed to have arrived approximately 10 days after the baby was born; instead, she'd arrived five hours later! It wasn't exactly what we'd anticipated. In fact, we'd almost jokingly asked some friends of ours to be on call to pick her up at the airport on the off-chance that I would be in labor when she arrived. We were supposed to have had a chance to get the baby home and get settled into our new, sleepless lives before we had any visitors, but my son, always the one to make his own plans, decided for us, and so my mom was met at the airport, for her first trip outside the US, in a completely foreign land, by our friends whom she'd never met, with a handwritten sign.

My mom visited with us briefly in the hospital that evening, then Steve took her home, and I stayed in the hospital in my private room while the nurses whisked my son off to the nursery with the other babies born that night. This was the norm in the UAE, and I was thankful for the space. I'd just spent the last 28 hours in labor and I needed the sleep. Of course, I'd just had a baby so my mind was on overdrive thinking about all the possible ways that my new baby might get hurt and how I was probably already doing it wrong. And I was alone. I never sleep well when I'm by myself. (My children instinctively know this, so I've not had to sleep a single night on my own since November 18, 2006. Nope. Not one.) Regardless, I told myself I needed the sleep, so I must try.

Just as I was beginning to relax and drift off, the family of the woman in the next room arrived to celebrate their new arrival! And they were so joyous. So vociferously joyous. I wanted to be happy for them, I did. I understood, I'd also just had a baby, and I was also joyous. But, it was after midnight, and I'd just had a baby. Did I mention the 28 hours of labor? Did I mention that 20 of those were without pain relief? This was a moment of cultural learning for me. We'd lived in the UAE for nearly two years by this time, we knew that Abu Dhabi offered more in the way of local culture, and that was what drew us to it, but I'd somehow forgotten that many Emiratis tended to socialize until well into the evening hours. When many of the western expats were headed off to dreamland, the locals were heading out to the malls or to visit with family and friends. And what better occasion than to visit with loved ones to celebrate the birth of a new baby!

But I was so tired!

The vociferously joyful Emirati family went home at some point during the wee hours of the morning, and I attempted, yet again, to get some sleep. Approximately 90 seconds later, the diffident Filipina nurse padded in, gingerly nudged me, and asked if I'd brought any spare clothes for the baby. Even in my sleep-deprived daze, my newly functioning mom-radar kicked in as several worst-case scenarios flooded my mind: Is he bleeding? Did someone take him? Did wild animals somehow break into the hospital and wreak havoc in the nursery?

The nurse quietly informed me that he'd spit up his formula. Formula? My son drank from a bottle? If I'd had the energy, I would've sprinted into the nursery and run all the way home with him tucked securely under my arm. As it was, I was exhausted and all I could do was cry. I'd thought I'd made it very clear that my son was not to be bottle fed. I'd intended to breastfeed and had diligently read the books which insisted that I not allow a bottle to touch his lips for if it did he'd most certainly never accept my breast again. New mothers don't need that kind of fear thrust on them. We have plenty of fears we can make up all on our own, thank you very much.

But, it was a fear I'd developed, and I was heartbroken to have discovered that the nurses, human, well-meaning and fallible, had messed up. I'm afraid I wasn't very kind or forgiving at the time, though I was effusively thankful and overly polite the next morning. Another cultural difference had reared its head: Breastfeeding was not common among Emirati women at that time. Giving birth in a mostly Emirati hospital, we were subject to the routines normally utilized by the staff for Emirati families. So, my son spat up on his clothes, and I had a meltdown.

Having a baby is every bit what the clichés say it is: wonderful, amazing, tiring, heartbreaking, heart-swelling, exhausting, confusing, beautiful, messy, smelly, tearful, lovely—have I forgotten anything? I can't remember. I blame baby brain (my children are 10 and seven, but the condition is known to last years, I'm afraid).

Having a baby in a foreign country is all of those things, and it is also stressful on a level that is difficult to articulate. And, I mean that literally. It's sometimes difficult to articulate exactly what you mean when each person is speaking in a language that is either foreign to themselves or speaking their own language in a way that sounds foreign so as to make sense to the person to whom they are speaking. Make sense?

For example, our neighbors in Abu Dhabi were Emirati, and therefore somewhat a rarity (see my previous comments about population demographics), so I would attempt to speak Arabic to them whenever I saw them. We usually made it through "*salaam alaykum*" and "*wa alaykum issalaam*" (that translates to "hello," and "hello to you") before my neighbor gave up on trying to understand me and switched to English.

I recall one evening when I was quite far along in my pregnancy, and I saw my neighbor and his 12-year-old daughter outside. We all stopped to chat briefly, and after the initial greetings, there was some discussion about how his daughter one day would be fat like me. I think we all left the conversation feeling a little confused and thinking that our neighbors were a bit strange. I'm still not sure exactly what either of us was talking about—did he think she'd get pregnant soon? Did he think I thought that? Did he think I thought he thought that?

I was mortified, but sometimes smiling, nodding, and walking away is the best choice. We were both well-meaning in our conversation, but neither of us was making ourselves clear. His daughter just giggled. But, it's not always words that cause misunderstandings. Sometimes having expectations that everyone celebrates your traditions in a similar way can muddle things up and lead to hurt feelings, at least until everyone has the chance to explain their perspective.

One tradition from our culture that I completely missed out on was the baby shower. I get it, it seems a bit frivolous and maybe I'm being petty to even discuss it. But, once I got pregnant and became comfortable with the idea that I'd have a baby, I had certain expectations based on what I'd experienced with my own friends and family. But, I soon discovered not every country or culture values early preparation. At least not in the form of celebrating something that hasn't actually happened yet.

Many of my European friends were superstitious about welcoming the baby before he makes his debut. So, no silly quizzes or baby bingo for me, but shower or no shower, the baby still came along and still needed to be celebrated—eventually!

My friends took pity on me after my son was born and made the trek from Dubai to Abu Dhabi to celebrate his arrival and catch up with food and drink—that I'd prepared, in my house, so I was responsible for the clean-up afterward. Not sure I got the best deal there, come to think of it.

The trek is about an hour and a half drive along Sheikh Zayed Road in good traffic and takes you on a tour through several decades. You travel in your sparkling clean SUV from shiny, architecturally intimidating buildings with perfectly manicured surroundings and immaculately kept landscaping to an older, more Bedouin-type setting: The buildings are noticeably shorter, squatter, dustier, and appear well loved, in an outwardly neglected kind of way. The landscaping is minimal and not nearly as green, but feels more appropriate for your drive through the desert.

As you approach the capital city, the bougainvillea creep into view, bursts of pink and green crawling up trellises and along fences. The date palms stand tall down the medians, and provide an ever-changing canopy as they produce and shed their fruit. The desert city is beautiful, and feels Arabian.

We spent an afternoon celebrating the birth of my son and catching up with each other. Still no silly quizzes or baby bingo, but that's okay, I had my friends and family with me. No matter where we live or what traditions and cultures are prevalent locally, we always have each other, our family, and our friends, and that makes any strange or foreign experiences less strange and more exciting because of the wonderful stories we can tell.

Kristy Smith is a stay-at-home mom and trailing spouse who has traveled to and lived in several parts of the world, including the UAE and the UK. She is a bit of a dabbler and likes to try her hand at most anything: writing, gardening, DIY, running, teaching, and child rearing, to name a few. She's mother to two spunky and inquisitive children, both of whom were born overseas. Currently, she can be found gator-hunting while she walks her dog in the suburbs of Houston, Texas.

CHAPTER 13

THE BEST THING ABOUT A DUTCH BIRTH

Amanda van Mulligen
Nationality: British
Birthed in: The Netherlands

Giving birth in the Netherlands can give rise to a few cultural shocks but if you can navigate your way through the midwife-led, pain relief-free natural home birth system then the best part of having a baby Dutch-style awaits you: *kraamzorg*. A maternity nurse comes to your home to help you with your newborn for eight days following the birth.

Nine years ago, however, when I was pregnant for the first time in the Netherlands, I didn't know just how wonderful *kraamzorg* would be. I had no idea then that the *kraamzorg* visit would be something I would come to not only want, but an experience I would cherish for the rest of my life.

The pink cross was freshly formed on the pregnancy stick when I was introduced to parenting "Dutch-style." We were vacationing in France in May 2006 when my husband and I discovered we were to be parents. We called our *huisarts* back home; our doctor's assistant was happy to give us some advice.

"In principle, your doctor won't be involved at all in your pregnancy; you need to find a midwife as soon as you are back. Don't go to a French doctor—they'll tell you that you can eat anything you like, but that's not so. Avoid pâté, unpasteurized cheese, and raw meats and fish," she explained.

"What about cycling?" my partner asked.

"Oh cycling is fine; just don't fall off."

My British friend had been told by her doctor in England to leave her bike in the shed until the 12-week point of her pregnancy, but it takes more than the small matter of a growing baby to part the Dutch from their beloved bicycles.

So no doctor involvement, just a midwife. And lay off French delicacies. We'd been on vacation for a week already, and the local red wines had been a daily guest at our dinner table. I'd inadvertently eaten chicken gizzards and knowingly eaten pâté. And now I realized I was pregnant while doing so—mother guilt started early.

Getting pregnant had been the plan all along, but for five months the plan seemed to be faltering, and so I'd relaxed while we were on vacation. I'd let the rules slide a little. Okay, I'd let the rules slide a lot. Two evenings previously I'd felt a little strange but put it down to the French red and the rich meats. The next day when I was still not feeling quite right; I began to suspect there may be more to it.

I rifled through the Dutch-French dictionary we had brought with us for *zwangerschapstest* and found *test de grossesse*. Reasonably confident I could competently acquire a pregnancy test, we headed off to the local pharmacy. In actual fact, it was the only pharmacy around for some distance, vacationing as we were in a small rural French village where our presence dramatically lowered the average population age.

"*Bonjour! Je voudrais un test de grossesse s'il vous plaît,*" I said in the best French accent I could muster.

After a few minutes of watching a pharmacist clad in white rifle through drawers and carry out an animated discussion behind the counter, we emerged from the pharmacy with a pregnancy test.

It was positive. I didn't believe this first test, though— after all, I had no idea how long it had been lying in that drawer in the "French pharmacy that time forgot." It was anyone's guess the last time a pregnancy test had been needed in this village. So we went back to buy a second test the next day. This time, the madame behind the counter knew exactly where they were, or it was; I imagine we wiped out the local pregnancy test supply.

That too was positive.

And so now I was in a foreign country discovering there was life inside of me. And it was a different foreign country than the one I lived in.

Two weeks later we were back in the Netherlands, back to real life. I set about finding a midwife, and two months into my pregnancy I had my first appointment. I answered more questions in quick succession than a Mastermind contestant.

"Do you want to give birth at home or in the hospital?" she asked me (in Dutch).

"Home," I answered without hesitation.

Why the hell not? If so many Dutch women can do it, then I can too. The midwife sitting opposite me raised her eyebrows.

"Really? Most English women here opt for a hospital birth," she stated.

We discussed prenatal testing. We discussed breastfeeding. We never discussed the topic of pain relief—there's no question of pain relief if a home birth is in the planning, I realized later.

"And who is your *kraamzorg*?" she asked.

"Erm, I don't know. I haven't registered with one yet," I explained.

"Well, best do it this week—they fill up quickly! There are a couple we work closely with, so maybe check those out first?"

So I did. I scoured information online about local *kraamzorg* providers, and I read everything I could about what exactly *kraamzorg* entailed.

"But I don't want a stranger in my house after I've given birth," I whined to my Dutch husband-to-be. He looked at me and shrugged. He'd had no previous experience with all this either and had little to say on the topic.

"Whatever you want is fine with me," he said to close the conversation out for the umpteenth time.

I picked a *kraamzorg*, filled in the forms, and then set about planning for the mother of all home births. Music, candles, aromas, lighting, breathing techniques—I had it covered.

One afternoon the doorbell rang, and a delivery man stood on my doorstep with a box for me. It was the *kraampakket* from the health insurance company, a box of items we would need for the home birth and the first few weeks after the birth: a clamp for the umbilical cord, alcohol (the cleaning anything and everything kind and not the drinking kind), mattress protectors, disposable gloves, cotton wool, antibacterial hand gel, and various sizes of compresses. It was quite an eye opener, and I began to see a different side to my envisioned home birth. It was going to get messy. In our bedroom.

The bed was put on *klossen* (bed raisers) as is customary in the Netherlands to make a more comfortable working height for the midwife and *kraamzorg*. It meant I had to use an Ikea step stool to get in and out of bed for nearly four weeks.

Thirty-seven weeks pregnant and we were ready, come what may: There was a mattress protector under the bed sheet (making getting into bed a rustling affair), two shiny new plastic buckets on standby, and a bed pan under our bed. I was never really sure if that was for toilet use or for putting the placenta in or whatever else came out during a birth.

And I never got to find out.

Contractions woke me at 4 a.m. Definite contractions. I danced like a baby elephant around the living room, trying to get comfortable with the help of my big red yoga ball, puffing away contractions. Three hours later I moved to the bath. Two hours further, and the contractions were close enough together to call the midwife. The *kraamzorg* was on standby, and my midwife, Lorraine, who had recently given birth herself, would pop round during the morning.

By the time my midwife did the internal examination to see how far dilated I was, I had been sucking up contractions for seven hours. Seven long lonely hours, just me, my helpless partner, and my red yoga ball.

"If she tells me I'm 3 cm dilated when she gets here I'm throwing her out of the window," I half joked.

It was worse than that.

"You're 2 cm dilated," she said with a grimace, "But you're doing a great job; keep doing the breathing techniques you've learned. You can bet on an hour per centimeter, so it'll be a while yet. I'll be back in a few hours." She returned at 4 p.m. By then contractions had been ongoing for 12 hours. I was exhausted and in pain. And I was still only 2 cm dilated. Lorraine grabbed her phone to talk to the gynecologist at the local hospital—the one I had not planned to give birth in.

Lorraine broke my water (with what looked like a divining rod, but let's not go there), and they were green.

"There's meconium in the water. You need to get to the hospital," my midwife calmly said. "Now." And just like that, my home birth shattered into pieces.

My son was eventually born at 9:52 that evening. I was exhausted, hooked up to monitors, and full of drugs to induce the birth and dim the pain. It had been an unpleasant, stressful experience. There was no gynecologist available when my body gave the signal that my baby was ready to be born—I had to breathe away the urge to push for half an hour so that the gynecologist could finish off another birth before making her way to me. By the time the maternity staff turned its attention to me, the contractions had skulked away. My son came into the world with a nurse sitting astride me, pushing down hard on my stomach, while a gynecologist performed an episiotomy without an anesthetic.

His nighttime appearance meant that we both had to stay the night in the maternity ward. It was at this stage that I realized I hadn't packed any clothes for myself in the suitcase. My newborn son had an array of beautiful, newly bought or gifted outfits to choose from, for any occasion he should find himself needing clothes for directly after his birth. I, however, would be going home in a blood- and sweat-stained nightdress, unless my husband came with wardrobe supplies early the next morning. After a restless night, we were allowed home.

"I've rung the *kraamzorg*," my partner said as he drove us home, a new family of three.

"I don't want a stranger in my house," I said huffily as we pulled up in our street, and I clambered carefully out of the car, trying to avoid inflicting further pain to the inconveniently stitched up area.

"I know. She'll be here soon," he retorted.

I'd just sat myself gingerly down on the sofa, my partner nestling our newborn into my arms after cautiously releasing him from his Maxi-Cosi car seat, when the doorbell interrupted my gazing at him sleeping peacefully, wrapped up cozily in his furry blue winter jacket.

Kraamzorg calling...Our maternity nurse had arrived. I was too tired to even bother scowling.

"I'm Gerrie. *Gefeliciteerd mama en papa!*" she congratulated as she breezed into our living room, into our home, into our lives. She asked about our birth experience; she asked how I was feeling. She tutted and gasped as Lars, my husband, and I recounted the past 24 hours.

"Right. Rest!" she commanded.

She ushered me upstairs, supporting me as I made my way slowly upward, one stair at a time. She helped me clamber up onto the raised bed. She settled my baby peacefully into the Moses basket next to me. I sank away into sleep while she got on with her job. That first day back home is a blur, but I do know it went like clockwork because of the help we had in our home.

Each morning she let herself in around 8 a.m. with the house key we had entrusted to her. I'd hear her come in, hang up her coat and then pad up the stairs to us.

"How did the night go?" she'd ask. We'd tell her how our son had cried all night long. She'd give us tips and advice; she felt like a safety net after the uncertainty of a restless night. She'd reassure us that we could do this.

Then she'd make breakfast. She cleaned the bedroom, changed the bed linen, and ran a hoover around the room while I took a shower. She'd put a load of washing on. Then she'd do the medical checks: check my blood pressure and temperature, my stitches, the position of my womb, and write it all down for the midwife to check when she came to do her rounds.

She helped tirelessly with breastfeeding, helped me bulldoze my way through the problems we had latching on. She showed us how to bathe our newborn (who it turned out was no water baby), and she completed all the newborn checks: his temperature, his weight, his diaper-filling habits, powdering his naval stump. She helped us distinguish between a cry of hunger and a cry of discomfort.

She laid my son on our bed facing the window with the blinds pulled back to help him soak up all the natural daylight that a gloomy January morning had to offer. He was a little jaundiced. She told us not to worry.

Then she'd make lunch, clean the bathroom and vacuum downstairs. She welcomed visitors, prepared drinks and the traditional Dutch *beschuit met muisjes* (a buttered baked biscuit with aniseed sprinkles on top—blue for a boy and pink for a girl) for them and cleared up after she had encouraged their exit. The rest and recuperation of both me and my baby were her priorities.

Gerrie spent eight days with us, from 8 in the morning until just after lunch. My "I don't want a stranger in the house" meant she didn't work the maximum hours we were entitled to. I had compromised. It was a mistake I'd never make again.

For over a week she eased our fears and insecurities as new parents, she built up our confidence, and she did less and less as each day went by. Without noticing, we picked up what she was no longer doing.

When her last day with us arrived we tried everything to get her to move in with us; we tried bribing her to stay longer but all to no avail. She tottered off at lunchtime on the eighth day, and we never saw her again. For her, we were one of hundreds and hundreds of families she has helped to get on their feet after a new addition to the family; for us she was one in a million. And she had set the bar high for future *kraamzorg* experiences.

When I was pregnant the second time around (three years later and not without some difficulty), we signed up with the same *kraamzorg* agency and specifically asked for Gerrie. She was still working there, but they couldn't guarantee she would be our *kraamverzorgster* come the day I went into labor. One thing about unborn babies is that they are quite unpredictable.

My second labor and birth experience was almost a carbon copy of my first, except this time around we knew it would be a hospital birth right from the start, and we had a doula, Malua, at our side cheering us on (something I would recommend all expat women to consider). We met her when we attended the *Samen Bevallen* birthing classes during my first pregnancy. She gave the course, but she was also training to be a doula back then and had offered her services for free to attendees, as she needed the experience.

We figured that yet another body in the delivery room would make it crowded, and yes, I may have uttered "I don't want a stranger..." After we recounted the awful experience we'd had in the delivery room at our birth class reunion, Malua confided in us that her instinct had been to approach us about being our doula, but as we hadn't come forward she had left us alone. If I could turn back time. It brings tears to my eyes to think about how different that first birth experience would have been with Malua at my side.

So the second time around Malua was on our call list, even before telling our parents. I wanted her by my side, advocating for me. The whole experience was more pleasant than the first time around, less traumatic, and it took less time. My second son was born late afternoon, and after some dinner we were released from the hospital and home by 7 p.m.

A maternity nurse was again at our home within minutes. She checked that we had what we needed for the night ahead and helped us get settled. She said a new *kraamverzorgster* would be with us bright and early the next morning. And she was.

Simone crept meekly into our home, almost as if on tiptoe. She was quiet, unassuming, and young, very different from Gerrie. But she laid the groundwork for an amazing *kraamweek* as a family of four. She entertained my eldest son, she reminded us to capture the memories of this amazing time that would speed by before we knew it.

We have a canvas hanging in our stairwell with three sets of male footprints on it, made when my newborn was just a few days old. It's a precious keepsake, and all the credit goes entirely to Simone. Of course, this time around I knew that I absolutely wanted a stranger in my house after the birth, and we plucked every hour we could benefit from our entitlement. When the eighth day rolled around, and it was time for her to say goodbye, we again unsuccessfully tried bribing her to come and live with us. I watched her leave with tears in my eyes.

The third time I brought a baby home from the hospital, the postnatal experience was a completely different one. Two *kraamverzorgsters*, José and Jessica, came to our home this time around, Jessica being a trainee. I guess the idea was as a mother of two, an old hand at this *kraamweek*, was a great home for a trainee. For us, it meant twice the attention, twice the effort, and twice the kindness. And as it turns out, I was able to repay the trainee with quite the experience.

It was Jessica who found me in an unresponsive state lying in my bed on the third day after the birth. I was transported back to the hospital in an ambulance. It seems that my body had gone into shock. The labor and birth itself had been easier than the first two times, and my third son had been quicker to make an appearance than his brothers, but I hadn't slept for a number of nights by the time he was a few days old. Contractions that had started and then stopped, a birth, and then a newborn with reflux (though we didn't know that at the time) who couldn't lie on his back made sure that sleep eluded me as I became a mother of three.

My husband had followed the ambulance with our newest addition in tow, and the *kraamverzorgsters* stayed with our older sons until friends arrived to take over. It turns out that *kraamzorg* may not stay with a family while the mother and baby are not present. Our impromptu disappearance to the hospital meant that they both made a hasty exit, with the message that they were to be called the moment there was news about me coming home.

My baby and I were kept overnight in the hospital and released the next morning. My two trusty *kraamverzorgsters* were there to greet me. And so we made another attempt at the *kraamweek*. Rather than the focus on learning everything there was to know about caring for a newborn, as was the case during the first *kraamweek*, or about creating memories as our family expanded like the second time around, the third time around was about physically recovering, about trying to make our newborn son comfortable, and about reassuring his two brothers.

Because our *kraamweek* had been disrupted with an emergency trip back to the maternity ward, we were granted two extra days of *kraamzorg*. We hadn't needed to bribe or beg for our *kraamverzorgsters* to stay longer with us this time around, but it was a dramatic way to get additional hours of help. Ironically, by the time we said goodbye to them both, we knew that it was a good sign. Our family was getting back on track, despite the hiccup. My youngest son would continue to be a terrible sleeper, he still is in actual fact, but around seven months the reflux dissipated.

Three different births. Three different *kraamzorg* experiences. I can put my hand on my heart and say that the best bit about a Dutch birth (aside from the baby you get to keep) is the *kraamzorg*. Inadvertently, the Dutch have created a postnatal system that supports an expat woman, a new mother who is living in a foreign without the love, help, and presence of her own family around her as she welcomes her own child into the world.

Amanda van Mulligen is British-born but was whisked off to the Netherlands on a promise of a windmill wedding in 2000 and now raises three sons there with her Dutch husband. In addition to mother, wife, and expat, she is also a writer, published author, and blogger. She writes about expat life on her blog Expat Life with a Double Buggy, and on the topic of highly sensitive children over at Happy Sensitive Kids. You can find more of her writing on Mamalode, Bonbon Break, and Brain, Child Magazine, among others. She contributed to Dutched Up! and Once Upon An Expat and has translated the Dutch children's book "Langmuts is een held" into English (available as "Long Hat is a Hero"), a book written specifically with highly sensitive children in mind.

CHAPTER 14

EXPLORING PETRA INDIANA JONES-STYLE

Jennifer Malia
Nationality: American
Knocked up in: Jordan and
the United Arab Emirates

My six-month-old daughter Noelle, strapped to me and facing outward in a Baby Björn carrier, led the way up the Nabataean processional path with my husband Dave following close behind us. To take a break from navigating the narrow switchbacks and crumbling stairs, we paused on the mountain to admire two rock obelisks that represented the main male and female Nabataean deities: Dushara, the god of strength, and al-Uzza, the goddess of water and fertility.

Our fearless leader was nodding off from all the bouncing as we moved up the mountain, looking more and more like a bobble head with each step we took on our way to the High Place of Sacrifice. The Nabataeans were an ancient nomadic Arabian tribe that performed rituals, including sacrificing animals, and likely humans, here. Children were known to be offered up to the gods as sacrifices in other nearby Nabataean cities. Just to be clear, Dave and I were not involved in a reenactment of any ancient rituals. Bringing an innocent baby to a place of sacrifice was not what I had in mind when I chose Petra for a vacation. As a mother, I was horrified to learn that the Nabataeans purposely killed children, but as a literature professor, I was fascinated to know the story behind the High Place with all its gory details.

When I reached the High Place of Sacrifice, I was exhausted, out of breath, and nauseous. My exhaustion and breathlessness could be explained by the extreme heat and the steep terrain. The strenuous exercise, though, should not have been enough to make me sick to my stomach. In college, I used to lead backpacking trips in the backwoods of Maine; in my twenties, I ran half marathons up mountains in southern California; and in my thirties, I was fighting in tae kwon do tournaments. Sure, I was still working on losing the last 10 pounds I had put on from the 50-pound pregnancy gain with Noelle, but a few months ago I was trail running in the Blue Ridge Mountains of northern Georgia with no problems at all.

Maybe I was queasy from imagining all of the bloodshed that must have taken place on this mountain. I could picture an ancient procession of Nabataeans draining the blood of a baby in the main altar and channeling the blood down the mountainside.

My husband Dave was standing next to me on the flat summit of the mountain, trying to catch his breath. He tossed down our backpack full of water, granola bars, trail mix, diapers, wipes, baby bottles, formula, and extra clothes for Noelle that he had lugged up the mountain. Being careful not to get too close to the nearly 600-foot cliffs, we gazed down at the royal tombs carved out of the sandstone below us. Looking down at the rose-red city of Petra carved into the mountainside, I realized I was in one of the most amazing places I had ever been. I took deep breaths and drank (maybe chugged is more accurate) water, desperately trying to knock out this bout of nausea so I could enjoy the stunning view all around me.

Dave turned to look at me. I started to hunch over in response to the pain, but I was careful to keep Noelle, whose legs were dangling out of the Baby Björn, from touching the ground.

He wiped a drop of sweat from his forehead and asked, "Are you okay?"

The only other time I remembered being this queasy was when I had morning sickness with Noelle. At that time, it was too early to use a home pregnancy test, but I just knew. I wrapped my arms around Noelle, which made it easier to stand back up.

I looked at Dave and said, "I think I'm pregnant."

Two days prior, we took the three-hour flight from Sharjah to Amman on Air Arabia, a budget airline similar to EasyJet in the UK. At that time, I was a professor at the American University of Sharjah, located midway between the cities of Sharjah and Dubai in the United Arab Emirates. Air Arabia was probably the only airline I would fly out of Sharjah International Airport, which was only about a mile or so from my on-campus faculty housing.

One of my colleagues flew on an old rickety Soviet-era plane that had remnants of tobacco smoke in the cabin from the days when passengers were allowed to smoke cigarettes on board. The only smells on our more modern Air Arabia flight were the concentrated flower oils of Arabian perfumes from the passengers, which were preferable to smoke even though the perfumes made my nose tingle.

When we arrived at Queen Alia International Airport in Amman, we requested a smoke-free car rental. After sending a few cars back that reeked of Arabian perfumes to cover up the tobacco smoke, Dave negotiated with the Arab car rental salesman, who also reeked of smoke, so he could go with him to the parking lot to smell the rental cars. I wasn't about to let Noelle breathe third-hand smoke for the three-hour drive to Petra.

We stayed at a local family-run hotel about a mile from Petra called the Alanbat Hotel in Wadi Musa (Valley of Moses) because we thought it would be a more authentic experience than international chain hotels. Alanbat is the Arabic name of the Nabataeans. On the balcony of our hotel room, we were greeted with large Arabic script painted on the sandstone rocks of Wadi Musa below, which translated to "Welcome Petra visitors." We were happy with the spectacular view and the simple and clean hotel room, but we knew we were in for some sleepless nights when we saw the crib we had requested for Noelle on Expedia's website with our room booking. The crib was in reality a travel bassinet made out of a thin fabric that stretched around metal bars, forming a small rectangular box less than a foot high. This would have worked for a newborn baby, but Noelle was well beyond the stage of rolling over, let alone crawling. We took turns trying to rock her to sleep in hopes that we could still use the bassinet, but we eventually gave in to co-sleeping with her.

Early the next morning we entered Petra Archeological Park, a UNESCO World Heritage site where roughly 15% of the ancient city has been uncovered, and 85% remains underground. At Bab as-Sīq, the gateway to the ancient city, a Bedouin, one of many nomadic Arabs in Petra who makes a living on tips from tourists, offered us horse rides. I watched the tourists gallop by kicking up the packed sand from what appeared to be a makeshift race track.

"No thank you. I have a baby," I said, figuring that that was enough of an explanation.

"The horse safe for you and baby," he said, patting the red and black hand-woven saddle bag on his horse.

While I would have enjoyed racing through Petra on a horse Indiana Jones-style, I wasn't about to take an infant with me. Within a quarter mile, Dave and I declined horse rides from two other Bedouin men only to come to another Bedouin man who offered us a ride on a horse-drawn carriage through the Siq. We politely refused all animal-powered transport in favor of traveling on foot to enjoy the sites at a slower pace.

About a mile long, the Siq or *thaniya* is a crack in the mountain or gorge that serves as the main entrance to Petra. With an ancient cobblestone road that is really narrow at some points, the Siq is still wide enough for horse-drawn carriages to pass through. Walking past men wearing the armor of Roman soldiers and carrying shields to guard the Siq of the ancient city, we were in a swarm of tourists speaking Arabic, French, German, Spanish, English, and a number of other languages that I couldn't recognize. I couldn't see far enough ahead to know where the path led.

We passed an Arab woman fully covered in a black *abaya* (robe-like dress) and hijab (headscarf), and followed behind another Arab woman wearing jeans, a long-sleeved T-shirt, and a cowboy hat on top of her hijab. Noelle was by far the youngest child in the crowd, but a lot of Arab kids were running through the Siq dressed like American children in jeans, T-shirts, and baseball caps. Bedouin men dressed in traditional attire, a white *thawb* (ankle-length tunic) and a red and white *keffiyeh* (headdress) could be seen off in the distance casually sitting on dangerously high sandstone cliffs where most tourists wouldn't go.

About halfway through the Siq, we realized Noelle's canvas bucket hat with a hand knitted bear on the front was missing. Since she was born, she had worn this hat on all of her hikes in the Baby Björn, including the previous summer she spent in the Blue Ridge Mountains. The sentimental value was enough for us to retrace our steps through the Siq to look for it.

We were ready to press up to the sandstone walls at any moment when the occasional horse-drawn carriage passed by on the cobblestone road. I would put a hand in front of Noelle's face to block the sand kicking up from the carriage. We backtracked to the armed Roman soldiers, the last place we remembered seeing the hat on her head, but didn't have any luck finding it. We figured that either someone had already picked it up, or the hat blew over the jagged cliff of sandstone near the armed soldiers. In either case, we weren't expecting to get it back. We turned around to continue our pilgrimage through the Siq. Having watched *Indiana Jones and the Last Crusade* enough times, I was anticipating the path to end at the massive Al Khazneh (the Treasury) carved out of rose-red sandstone.

It was on a bench next to the Treasury that I first breastfed publicly in the Middle East. Attempting to be as discrete and stylish as possible, I used a fuchsia nursing cover that was like an oversized apron but with wire around the wide neck.

In Dubai, one of my favorite places to go was Fashion Avenue in the Dubai Mall, not to buy purses at the Coach boutique, but to take advantage of a mother and baby room located next to it with leather changing tables and comfortable cushioned armchairs. If I couldn't find a comfortable place to nurse in Dubai, I would escape to my Dodge Nitro with tinted windows to breastfeed.

While it is not against the law to nurse publicly in Jordan or the United Arab Emirates, women are encouraged to wear modest clothing or to be fully covered with an *abaya*, making public nursing uncommon.

From the bench next to the Treasury, I could see three camels with colorful striped cushioned seats on their backs awkwardly bending their legs to sit on the compacted sand in front of the monument. I too was sitting awkwardly on the bench trying not to smother Noelle while pulling the wire of the nursing cover as close to my body as possible. No one was paying much attention to me, though, with the chaos of Bedouins trying to get passersby, including Dave who was taking photos of the Treasury, to hire a camel or purchase souvenirs.

Feeling exhausted from an hour of walking, I was happy to sit down, drink a bottle of water, and rest, even though nursing inevitably made me more tired. Dave took my place at the bench, giving Noelle her formula supplement as the sun peeked over the cliffs and lit up the red-rose monument.

Happy to have my turn to take pictures of the Treasury without Noelle weighing me down, I tried to zoom in on the carved lions, representing the fertility god al-Uzza, and the giant urn at the top of the monument, which was riddled with hundreds of machine gun holes from the early 20th century. As legend has it, Bedouins shot the urn because they believed an ancient pharaoh stored treasures in there. In reality, the urn is solid sandstone.

Entering the Treasury with Noelle leading the way in her Baby Björn, we weren't expecting to find the Holy Grail, but we were hoping to see something more impressive than the bare squared walls of sandstone that felt like a dark cave, making the Treasury little more than a façade. The original use for this monument is still a mystery. Perhaps more will be known about the history of this place when the centuries-old flood debris built up in front of it is excavated. One theory is that it was a treasury or tax house for passing camel caravans, which is how the Treasury got its name. Many archeologists now believe that it was a royal tomb. As a literature professor, I prefer a little-known theory that the most impressive structure in Petra was actually a library for scrolls and parchment. I made a mental note that someday I would have to return to Petra with Dave and Noelle when more of the ancient city is unearthed, and she would be old enough to remember her time here.

Leaving the Treasury behind, we took what started as a leisurely stroll along a colonnaded street and ended as a race to find a less populated place to change Noelle's diaper. Passing by the ruins of the Temple of the Winged Lions, I imagined Nabataean women going to the temple to worship the fertility goddess al-Uzza to whom the temple was dedicated. Beyond the end of the street and away from the crowds, we settled on hiding behind Qasr Al-Bint Far'oun or the Palace of the Pharaoh's Daughter to take care of Noelle.

Dave put our American football Steelers changing pad on a massive yellow sandstone block lying flat on the ground behind the ruins of the temple. This monument got its name from a local folktale about a pharaoh's daughter who tested potential suitors by challenging them to bring water to her palace. The structure was, in reality, another Nabataean temple, not a palace, and it had nothing to do with a pharaoh.

"Are you sure you want to use that block?" I said, looking up at the ruins of the yellow sandstone temple.

"Do you have a better idea?" Dave said.

"I guess not," I said, looking around at the piles of yellow blocks surrounding us.

Besides, we were probably changing Noelle's diaper on sacred ground no matter where we set her down.

We packed up our backpack, including Noelle's poopy diaper, which helped us remember that we needed to find the nearest trashcan to dispose of it. By now, Dave and I knew what role each of us played in our routine: change diaper, breastfeed, bottle feed, eat, drink, hike, and repeat.

At the head of the trail to the Ad Deir (the Monastery), which was more likely to have been a temple than a monastery, three different Bedouin men approached us offering donkey rides. Watching kids who were about four years old ride donkeys up the steep trail, we politely refused while being repeatedly told that "the donkey safe for our baby." Dodging donkeys on the way up the 850 steps to the Monastery, I was feeling nauseous and dehydrated. Though the timing would be horrible, I wondered if I was finally getting my period, which was already five days late. We were prepared to go off the trail at any moment when we heard the clattering hooves of donkeys on the carved sandstone steps of the narrow pathway, which accommodated donkey and foot traffic in both directions.

Resting on a pile of sandstone rocks on the side of the trail, I took Noelle out of her Baby Björn so we could both cool off in the shade, while Dave wandered off to take pictures. A Bedouin woman selling scarves and jewelry approached me with her arms wide open. She started cooing over Noelle and smiled at me. I smiled back but moved a step away from her. Moving closer to us, she continued to reach her hands toward Noelle. Then she proceeded to put her hands on Noelle, trying to take her from me. I pulled back and said, "I'm sorry, but you can't hold her."

She didn't respond. I backed away further from her, holding Noelle tight.

She yelled, "*Haram!*"

The scream caught Dave's attention, and he came running toward us. She shouted *haram* over and over again, which in Arabic means something is forbidden by Islam. We were slowly gaining an audience of passersby who must have wondered what atrocious act we committed to deserve this. Even though I would never ask a woman I didn't know in the US if I could hold her baby and wouldn't expect anyone to ask the same of me, I adapted to what was a fairly common practice in the Middle East by allowing some strangers to hold my baby.

One time in Dubai, I let Filipino waitresses hold Noelle while Dave and I ate lunch at California Pizza Kitchen. Another time, I let an Indian woman hold her for a few minutes during a long-haul flight out of Dubai, keeping my hands within reach to take her back at the slightest sign of turbulence. But I had to draw the line with the Bedouin woman in Petra. The rough terrain with sandstone boulders and steep cliffs was simply not a place I was willing to hand over my baby. With the Bedouin woman continuing to shout *haram*, Dave and I quickly gathered up the items in our backpack, put Noelle back in the Baby Björn, and continued our journey up the crumbling sandstone stairs.

We viewed the Monastery, which resembled the Treasury with its elaborate design carved into the sandstone, while enjoying cold drinks and sitting on the floor of a tea shop in a cave across from it. Tourists are forbidden to climb the path that leads to the top of the Monastery, which is nearly 150 feet tall, but local kids will take daredevil tourists with them to not only climb the trail but even jump on the uppermost parts of the monument.

We watched a local Bedouin kid, who couldn't have been more than 12 years old, lead another Arab kid, who was about the same age, up the Monastery path. When they emerged on the top of the monastery, the Arab boy's family, who were standing near us, cheered as they watched their son climb around on the urn at the top of the Monastery. I didn't think the situation could get any crazier until the Bedouin boy got a running start and launched himself from the urn across a 15-foot gap to a sloped ledge of the Monastery. Presumably, he got the attention he wanted from tourists like us who were so in shock with what we were witnessing that we just stood there dumbfounded snapping photos of this performance. As a mother, I thought about how irresponsible this boy's parents were for allowing this to happen. As a lover of history, I didn't like to see this sort of wear and tear on the ancient monument.

The next morning, we followed the crumbling stairs next to the theater that didn't look like they led anywhere and could easily be passed by if it weren't for the tourists or the occasional donkey riding up. These were the stairs that led us to the High Place of Sacrifice, where I finally acknowledged the possibility that I was pregnant. When my nausea was tolerable enough to make a descent down the Attuf ridge, we returned a different way than we had come up, passing by ruined Crusader walls.

"Are you sure we're going the right way?" I asked Dave.

"Don't ask me," he said.

Eventually, we found ourselves tailing a tour group. This wasn't the first time we were tour crashers. When we were on Big Island in Hawaii, we didn't have flashlights to light the path through a 500-year-old lava cave, so we followed the tour group in front of us to hike in and out of it. About halfway down the Attuf ridge, I realized that I shouldn't be carrying an infant (or two) on this hike, but by the time the terrain became difficult enough for me to admit this to myself, it was too hard to turn around and go back up, especially since carrying the weight of Noelle in front of me threw off my balance. The hike down from the High Place of Sacrifice was by far the most dangerous path we were on in Petra. I felt like Indiana Jones when his quest led him to what seemed to be an impassable cliff. In our case, I wasn't willing to take a leap of faith, doubting that throwing sand would reveal a bridge across the valley. We surpassed the tour group, which was moving slowly to get a history lesson on the way down, and continued our descent very cautiously, with Dave leading the way. He admirably took on his newfound role as a rock climber, checking footholds every step of the way, shouting out, "Don't step on this rock!" or "Watch out for this branch!" We didn't see any Bedouins offering donkey rides here for good reason. Noelle was perfectly happy facing outward at the mounds of yellow sandstone all around her, and even smiled when I was forced to go down on all fours to do a crab crawl with her weight on top of me.

The best part about having completed this difficult descent was that I somehow managed to get Noelle down the mountain without a scratch on her. The Lion Fountain at the base of the mountain was another reminder of how grateful I was that not a drop of Noelle's blood was shed on this journey.

As legend has it, blood from the High Place of Sacrifice would travel down the ridge and feed into this Nabataean-engineered water fountain shaped like a lion that was carved into the sandstone rock face. To the Nabataeans, the lion represents the fertility goddess al-Uzza. Though the head is missing now, I imagined the blood of Nabataean babies spouting out from the lion's mouth of the fountain

During the heart-pounding descent, I was too worried about getting myself and my family safely down the mountain to realize how nauseous I was. I was as queasy as ever standing in front of the Lion Fountain, but at least I didn't have a swarm of tourists around me. Since it is less accessible than the other sites in Petra, few tourists even bother to go to Wadi Farasa.

We explored the Roman Solider Tomb, which had a carved body wearing the recognizable armor of a Roman solider but missing a head, both legs, and an arm. Exploring this tomb without a soul around us made it easier to imagine what it might have been like for the ancient Nabataeans to live here when Petra became part of the Roman Empire. My time in Petra made me secretly want to be an archeologist who discovered monuments like these for a living.

Exiting the gate to the Petra Archeological Park, we were immersed in a row of souvenir shops lined up along the sand compacted road. We passed the "Indiana Jones Snacks Shop" that was advertising anything from ice cream to Arabic coffee. The permanent sign on the front of the shop had the movie poster image of Harrison Ford from *Indiana Jones and the Last Crusade* with the tagline, "The man with the hat is back, and this time he's bringing his dad." We bought glass bottles full of the colorful sands of Petra from one of the vendors. Since we had trouble finding a Christmas ornament to purchase, a tradition we have in every country we visit, we ended up converting one of these small bottles of sand into an ornament.

When we realized we didn't have enough formula to make it through the rest of our trip, we drove our rental car away from the ancient city bustling with tourists back to the traffic circle filled with shops in Wadi Musa, where mostly locals seemed to go. We figured even Jordanian babies had to eat and hopefully formula wasn't too uncommon to find. We came across a pharmacy, which was the only store we could find that had a chance of carrying formula. I sat in the car nursing Noelle while watching Arab men drink tea and smoke flavored tobacco called shisha from hookah. I was relieved when Dave walked out of the pharmacy with a can of Nestlé formula. Luckily, Noelle was happy to drink her formula.

At the Amman airport, I bought a pregnancy test at a pharmacy right before my flight back to Sharjah. I would have had just enough time to take the pregnancy test in the bathroom next to my departure gate, but I decided not to take it. Having spent the past few days exhausted and nauseous, I know I should have jumped at the opportunity to know if I was expecting. But if I were pregnant, I didn't want to celebrate this news in the chaos of the airport among a crowd of passengers emptying carry-ons for airport security checks and getting patted down to check for forbidden items.

I finally took the pregnancy test when I arrived back in my apartment in Dubai. I was not at all surprised to find that I was indeed knocked up abroad again.

Jennifer Malia is a professor and writer with a doctorate in English from the University of Southern California. During her four years as an American expat in the United Arab Emirates, she worked as a writing professor at the American University of Sharjah and gave birth to her first daughter in Dubai. She currently teaches world literature and creative nonfiction as an English professor at Norfolk State University. All three of her kids are enrolled in a Spanish immersion preschool in Virginia Beach. A professional globetrotter, she has traveled to more than 20 countries to study world languages, teach English as a second language, present research on world literature, and write about her treks around the globe. She and her husband are a writer and photographer couple that travel the world with three munchkins in tow. They are the Founders of Munchkin Treks, a new family adventure travel website where they will share their adventure travels with three munchkins in tow. In her free time, she practices yoga and tae kwon do and explores the beaches and hiking trails around Virginia Beach with her family.

SECTION II

LOSS AND HEALING ABROAD

CHAPTER 15

THE GIFT

Amy Johansson
Nationality: American
Knocked up in: Bolivia and Sweden

There was a lot of magic in the air that summer, dark or light magic, I don't know. Because there was a lot of both. Down below the equator in Bolivia, high up on the Altiplano, mingled with the scent of winter harvest fires, coca leaf, and cold sweat, I got the message that my beloved grandmother had died. She'd had a stroke 18 months earlier, and was in palliative care at home in New Jersey when we had left to Bolivia, where I was finishing off the last few months of a Fulbright grant project.

The project had started the previous summer, and I had traveled to Bolivia fresh off a late-term miscarriage, a two-year-old and my husband, a busy Swedish architect who had a corporate design job in Manhattan. He was going to take his Swedish *pappaledighet* (parental leave) by hook or by crook, and this was the perfect window for him to take time off to be with our son. Our initial stay was interrupted in October with the news that my grandmother had taken a turn for the worst, and was leaving the ICU so that she could receive hospice care at home. So I talked to my grant admins at the embassy, and to the director of the museum where I was working in Bolivia, and flew home.

"She's waiting for you to leave so that she can go," was the advice given to me, seated on the front porch of my parents' home, in the company of the hospice nurse, hospice chaplain, and an elder care social worker. I had come home to New Jersey to be by my grandmother's bedside during her last months on earth. I wanted my two-year-old son to have some memories of her, and I wanted her to feel shielded and comforted by our love and energy.

Her name was Rose; she was a twin born in 1922 on the 10th of the month. Rose was my idol, my best friend, and a person who radiated love. Her death was something I'd been dreading since I first learned what death was. Here she was, fully conscious and sharp, but in terrible physical pain. I was angry; I was devastated. Mostly I was miserable.

When I found out that I was pregnant with child No. 2, in summer 2010, it was just as she was admitted to the ICU again. I (maybe foolishly) believed that she would wait for my baby to arrive, that this new life would bring her joy and heal her. No, the baby died, and Rose continued to die slowly. I went to Bolivia in August and returned in November when she was transferred to home hospice. During this time, I was also suffering the physical and psychological aftermath of a late-term miscarriage. And my marriage was teetering. My husband made it clear to me that he did not want any more children until I was on more stable mental and physical ground. And of course, his insistence on this made all of my pain far worse. I felt abandoned, alone, and unwanted. The only person I felt any genuine undulating affection from was my two-year-old son. It was like healing nectar. It was the only thing that kept me from tumbling off the earth to join my grandma.

On May 2, Bolivia was calling, and I said goodbye for the last time to Rose. I knew I wouldn't see her again, and I had a caul over my heart. In one of our final conversations, she told me how she was looking forward to seeing her twin sister again. And that I need not worry, as she'd be able to hear me whenever I spoke with her, no matter where we were.

After Rose died on May 11, 2011, the normally sunny skies on the Bolivian Altiplano opened up, and there was a terrible rainstorm. It was autumn in the summer hemisphere, and winter was approaching. Harvest fires were ignited, and indigenous Aymara autumn prayers were invoked to shield us from the darkness and the cold. On the 21st of June, it is *Midsommar* in Sweden, the first day of summer in America, and the winter solstice in Bolivia.

We greeted the sun in Tiwanaku at 7 a.m., after arriving at 5 a.m., driving through the chilly darkness of the pre-dawn Altiplano, higher and higher into the frigid heights. Aymara firewater, dancing in rings, spinning faster and faster as the dawn neared. Bolivian President Evo Morales arrived and joined the gathering crowds for the sun-greeting ritual, and then was promptly spirited away in a helicopter worthy of Mr. T in the 1980s. (Evo is a character. I have grown fond of Evo.) As a group of obvious gringos, we were, of course, offered loads of cocaine. Which we politely turned down. We ate egg sandwiches and drank *mate de coca* and watched the sun creep up over Tiwanaku, an ancient spiritual site. I felt a pang of happiness as I felt that I was ovulating.

I was home by midday in La Paz, where I joined Simon and Liam at the table. Their day had just begun, and they were eating lunch. I was off from work, and Liam's daycare was closed.

"Let's go to the Amazon," I said.

We booked via cash and a dot matrix printer at a travel agency, the only one that was open on the holiday in downtown La Paz.

We flew to Rurranabaque on a 20-seater plane. Rurre is at the mouth of the Bolivian Amazon. It's a sleepy little village populated by Ticana indigenous group. "The hand of the government does not extend here," said our guide as we rode motorcycle taxi to the luxurious hut that was our home for the vacation. Liam went to sleep, and Simon and I went upstairs to the roof hammock where we listened to the chattering monkeys and drank beers.

"I want to have another baby. I'm ready to try again." In true silent Swedish fashion, Simon said nothing, did nothing, but looked at me thoughtfully. And then went to bed. I felt my eggs slipping away and my heart turning to ice. The heartbroken feeling of abandonment returned. I went into Liam's bed and went to sleep stroking my son's hair and wondering why I wasn't good enough to have more children with.

As the sun rose the next morning, Simon gave me his answer, silently of course. He quietly led me half asleep to the other room, and we did what people who want to conceive a child do.

Later that day, we traveled up the Amazon River; observed monkeys and exotic birds; spied a lazing crocodile; picked coffee beans, bananas, and chocolate. Liam decided of course that in the middle of the jungle, he needed to poo in one of the terrifying ancient concrete toilet structures erected by Paraguayan prisoners in the 1940s. I held him carefully over the teeming, steaming hole while he did his business. Simon continued to stay silent.

A few days later, he broke his silence, "I've gotten a job offer in Sweden. Would you want to try living there?"

Then I understood his silence. Now that my grandmother had passed away, I did not have the same need to live in the States permanently. And I then understood his silent physical consent to our attempted pre-dawn conception in the Amazon.

"Sure we can try living in Sweden," I answered.

Simon printed out his work contract, and despite finding no working scanners in La Paz, he managed to fax his agreement back to Sweden. A few days later, trying to position himself in just the right spot to get cell phone reception, he negotiated an apartment rental in Sweden.

All the while, I tried to forget that I was trying to conceive. After my miscarriage, I wanted to be joyfully blindsided by pregnancy, as I had been with my first son, whose presence I detected two months along. I wanted to be a happy pregnant idiot. And with an international move, a two-year-old child to care for, and the pain of my grandmother's loss to contend with, it was easy enough to trick my mind into not thinking about the contents of my uterus.

On July 4 we flew back to New Jersey. July 17 we flew from New Jersey to Ireland, where Simon had a gallery exhibition. July 21 we arrived in Växjö, Sweden, stepping off the train in Alvesta to a darkening July sky, still uncertain of whether I had a tenant in my uterus. July 30, my curiosity got the best of me, and my sister-in-law helped me select a pregnancy test at the pharmacy.

We rummaged through the moving boxes at our nearly empty new apartment and found a *glögg* (mulled wine) cup for me to pee into. The language barrier gave me comfortable privacy and no chitchat as I awaited the results. A very prominent positive signal appeared almost immediately. I was pregnant, and at that point about six weeks along. We returned to the playground where our kids were playing, and I told my husband in hushed Swedish tones. Which he returned with a silent hug.

November 8, I had my 20-week scan at the midwife's office. In Sweden, ultrasounds are doled out carefully for normal pregnancies, which thankfully this one was. I felt good physically though not great mentally, the pain of losing my grandmother, my homeland, and my language in one swoop was still gnawing away at me. And in Sweden we don't wear our wounds, I learned. Coming straight from my Swedish language course, I tried out my newly won knowledge, "Can see the gender?" I asked carefully in Swedish. "Which one?" She asked. "Didn't you know you are having twins?" The bomb dropped, my husband went pale, and I felt like I would faint.

It turns out that my grandmother's parting gift for me was twins. In the spring, two weeks overdue, I gave birth to girl-boy twins, born on the 10th of the month. Just like their great-grandmother. My daughter bears an uncanny resemblance both in appearance and personality to my grandmother. They share a name and those same clear green-yellow eyes. Now she is with me forever.

Amy Johansson has gone from being a gatekeeper/taste-maker/that bitch with a clipboard in the upper echelons of New York City's media world to an expat mother of three and librarian/teacher on the sleepy coastal countryside of Southern Sweden.

CHAPTER 16

MY FOREIGN MISCARRIAGE

Vanessa Jencks
Nationality: American
Knocked up in: China

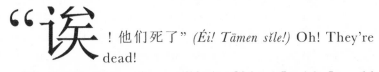! 他们死了" *(Éi! Tāmen sǐle!)* Oh! They're dead!

For the first time in my life in China, I wish I could truthfully respond, "我听不." *(Wǒ tīng bù dǒng.)* I don't understand.

In disbelief and a faint hope that I misunderstood, I ask the translating nurse,

"Did she say they were both dead?"

"Yes, they don't have heartbeats."

As soon as she notices tears under the arm covering my face, she brings me tissues, "Don't be so sad."

A procession of people suddenly appears in the ultrasound room.

I hear my prenatal doctor commenting, "是的. 他们." *(Shì de. Tāmen dōu sǐle.)* Yes. They're both dead.

The nurse probes her, "她年轻, 是？" *(Tā niánqīng, shì ma?)* She's young, right?

"是的。很年轻， 她已经有两个孩子" *(Shì de. Hěn niánqīng, tā yǐjīng yǒu liǎng gè háizi.)* Yes. She's young, and she already has two kids.

Angry from the chatter, I interject, "他们是男性还是女？" *(Tāmen shì nánxìng háishì nǚxìng?)* Are they boys or girls?

The technician answers, "我看不见." *(Wǒ kàn bùjiàn.)* I can't see.

The nurse states, "They're in a bad position."

The doctor questions, "她觉得他们什么时动了?" *(Tā juédé tāmen shénme shí dòngle?)* When did she last feel them move?

I respond in English, "I felt them yesterday."

The nurse translates.

"不可能," The doctor adds, "他们已经死了两个星." *(Bù kěnéng. Tāmen yǐjīng sǐle liǎng gè xīngqí.)* Impossible. They've been dead at least two weeks.

That sinks my heart desperately low. Two weeks ago? Could I really have missed that they stopped moving?

Later in the dark and silence of my hospital room, I jolt suddenly from a slow drift of weary sleep, frantically touching my stomach to see if I feel them. I put steady pressure on my womb with my hands. I shake my bulge gently. Nothing. I realize what I've been feeling has been their bodies shifting and trading places.

I reach back to the only distinct memory of their kicks before that night. Several weeks ago, my daughter wanted me to hold her at church while I stood: Her legs and my hands straddled the top of my bump. Even though I kept most of the pressure off of my belly, they kicked her, and the force almost knocked me back into my seat.

The doctor inquires, "她朋友来了吗？" *(Tā péngyǒu láile ma?)* Did her friend come?

She was referring to my also pregnant expat friend, Daviana. We scheduled most checkups together when we could so we could chat together as we waited to be seen.

The nurse whispers, "她自己来的." *(Tā zìjǐ lái de.)* She came on her own.

Sharon, the nicer translating nurse is by my side now, holding my hand. She searches my face. In return, I search her face gelled with worry. My tears pool and burn behind the dam of my eyes, preparing to leak, but I fight them. My face sours in battle. "Don't worry," she says. I only stare in response. Both nurses help me up. I wipe my belly and follow Sharon outside, averting my eyes from the pregnant women waiting for their turn in the ultrasound room; women who have nothing better to do than wait and study the bellies of other patients. I feel shame since my tears publicly disclose my secret.

Sharon walks and talks in imperfect English about what to do next. Thrice, she encourages me to contact family members before I decide to have the "surgery" at their hospital.

Sharon tells me to sit down in the waiting area and to call my family. She sits next to me with her face still gelled with worry.

"Don't be so sad. You're still young, you can have another," she tells me.

I gently respond as I hold her hand, "I understand you are trying to make me feel better, but you shouldn't say things like that to mothers. That doesn't make me feel better, that makes me hurt more."

Her face reflects horror and shock, but also reveals her genuine intentions.

I sit down facing the window in one of the big, pleather seats lined in an L formation in front of her desk. I pick that seat because I can turn to the window if someone notices my tears from within; I can avoid eye contact if someone avoids my tears while outside. As is normal with Chinese culture, the whole family is involved with everything, and Sharon encourages me to call my own family to make a decision about staying in this hospital or going someplace else. Calling my husband, Bobby, satisfies this request in my opinion.

Nervous, I bite my lip as I wait for him to answer.

"Hey, hey! Is it a boy or a girl?" He asks excitedly. I had frustrated him by waiting a bit longer to go in for my mid-pregnancy check even though I could have come in before 24 weeks. At 20 weeks, the ultrasound technician in China might have said they were too small to be sure, so I waited to avoid that frustration.

"They're dead."

"What?"

"They're dead. The technician was going to check the gender, but they're dead. There's no heartbeat."

"What's going to happen now?"

"We need to make a decision if we're going to stay here or go to a different hospital. The nurse wants us to decide before she'll admit me. The procedure they need to perform doesn't involve a knife. I made sure it wasn't a C-section they were suggesting."

"Okay, yeah, of course. Where else could we even go?"

I hear his students laughing and shouting in the background. I imagined them playfully hanging from his arms and wrapping their arms around his neck as usual while he sat at his desk in grave silence.

"I have to teach class. I'll call you back soon and be on my way there."

I send WeChat messages to several friends, arranging childcare and asking for help, including a message to Daviana. She calls me.

"Oh Vanessa, I'm so sorry. I should have come with you today! Please let me know if there's anything I can do to help."

"Yes, could you pick up Rizpah from school?" Other friends have already agreed to pick up my three-year-old, Ki, just a year and four days younger than his sister. He was just a tad too young to start school at the school where my husband works.

I then call my supervisor, then my friend, then Bobby again, then my husband's boss. With each call, I cry, dry up, and calm down; cry, dry up and calm down. Sharon interrupts me to tell me I need to call my insurance for preauthorization. I call and then hand her the phone once I realize explaining so soon to a stranger is too difficult in either language. I've already cried and dried up so many times now.

I stare out of the window again, this time with an ache that feels like someone shoved the raw handle of a street sweeper broom into my throat.

Approval is granted, so Sharon asks me to sign, agreeing to my own torment. She takes me to my room. Our first 24 hours of the 96 we spend trapped inside the hospital are filled to the brim with sober meetings with Chinese doctors; pestering, mixed-English questions from busy nurses; and phone calls and messages from eager friends and acquaintances, wanting to express their condolences, offer their notes of prayer, reference appropriate Bible verses, or to visit.

Our first group of visitors is a throng of student nurses, who have come to "study me." My normally patient and ever-bearing husband forcefully says, "This is not the time for that. Please leave." Friends who arrive need my comfort more than I need theirs, and one steely coworker surprises me with her quivering cry and quick breath. Even a superior forgets his propriety to argue the benefits of Chinese medicine versus western ways. Without fear, I reprimand him, "Let's talk about that another time." In the face of death, the famous Chinese composure melts away.

The next day in the early morning, both nurses and our friends translating frequently confuse "procedure" and "surgery." Bobby and I give an emergency English lesson to explain that a "procedure" is a general medical term to describe a medical event while a "surgery" involves a knife and strikes fear into our hearts. The dowdy doctor with pants too short assures me that the procedure requires a small needle and hurts just a little. Jolie, the teacher assistant in my office and thankfully good friend, is assigned the responsibility to translate. I'm relieved she wants to be here for us.

A few hours later, the nurse comes to tell me that I need to go to the ultrasound room. There is no explanation of why; Bobby, Jolie, and I must follow. First they take me in a wheelchair down to the general ultrasound room. The crowd is dark, with migrant workers in black jackets, sweaters, shoes, and pants. When I first arrived in Beijing with my husband and two kids in August of 2015, I used to wonder why everyone wore such dark clothes. But I now know that black hides the particles from the sky. Black hides the earthen ground in a shared shack. Black hides thinning, faded fabric. Black at least can slide into disturbed gray.

Not only is my coat a blood red, but also my face was a pale shade from lack of sun this winter and a day of crying. I search for pockets of people who are too caught up in their own pain to notice this pregnant 老外 (lǎowài) foreigner. Sometimes I misjudge and my eyes connect with others.

I feel ashamed to cut the obviously long line as the nurse wheels me into the back. We wait for a few minutes as the nurse checks behind every curtain to find an empty machine. After 10 minutes, nothing is open, so I'm wheeled out again to find another ultrasound room.

As they come to an outside door, they shove a blanket on top of me to keep me warm for the brief seconds I'll be outside in the cold. Usually I protest out of principle against traditional Chinese medicine, but I'm tired of fighting little disagreements in medicine and sickness for the day. Plus, they just want to care for me out of their conviction of what is best for me.

We enter a different building and go up an elevator into a darkened corridor. We stop at a door decorated with hearts and little bears. I can hear babies crying. I have to get out of the wheelchair and walk because the waiting room is actually just an extra small corridor lined with grandmothers, mothers, pregnant women, and babies. Some are crying. Some are sick. Some are nursing. We step over feet and wiggle past kneecaps separated only by a handful of inches. I hate them for taking me here. There are only two inadequate yellow lights in the whole miserable corridor.

This time I can't cut line so easily. The nurse enters one of only two ultrasound rooms and shuts the dingy door behind her. There is no safe place for my eyes. Do I look at the sleeping baby? Do I look at the tired mom? Do I look at the auntie who is staring me down, probably because I'm not wearing enough clothes so far into my pregnancy? I look down at my shoes. I look down at Jolie's hands and feet. She rests her head on my shoulder. I don't want to look at Bobby. Seeing his face will make me cry. I just want to sit and stay numb.

A pregnant woman opens the door, and her mother follows her out of the ultrasound room. The nurse comes after her and motions for me to follow her inside. She tells Jolie to stay outside in this tiny area, but Bobby comes with me. The room I enter is even darker, but the glow is different, pale but natural. I'm surprised by two machines in the room with two clumps of people waiting for each bed. One woman finishes wiping the gel of her belly then gets up. I'm told to lie down and expose myself, and this makes me glad I rebelled against the hospital gown to this point.

I meet my soon-to-be surgeon. Bobby wanted to make sure the babies were definitely dead, and the ultrasound technician reconfirms that the heartbeats are gone. They search all over my stomach, chattering in Chinese I can't understand. Then I hear someone say 笔 *(bǐ)* pen, and the nurse and technician look for one. The surgeon cleans the gel from two spots on my stomach that the technician has indicated. She makes small ink circles on my stomach. I am told not to wash them off.

I get up, wipe off the gel from the rest of my belly, then follow the nurse back into the small corridor. Jolie searches my face for news, but I avert my eyes. We walk back to my wheelchair and go back to wait in my room until the procedure.

In the 25th hour of our stay, I'm scared and grief-stricken as they wheel me on a bed toward the operating room, where I'll be without a translator and without my husband's hand to hold. I fight back tears as I glance at the nurses' faces from under my blanket. One is an older woman, who looks at me with knowing, empathetic eyes. The other is a young man with Korean-style glasses and a shaggy haircut.

At the door of the surgical wing, my husband obediently stops, and another busy nurse continues on with me.

She asks, "小床在哪里?" *(Xiǎo chuáng zài nǎlǐ?)* Where is the baby bed?

The others ignore her.

She calls out, "嘿！别忘了小床!" *(Hēi! Bié wàngle xiǎo chuáng!)* Hey! Don't forget the baby bed!

The old nurse hushes, "他们死了" *(Tāmen sǐle)* They're dead.

The loud nurse's eyes meet my eyes and linger. I wonder if she wonders if I can understand.

Inside the operating room, the older nurse leaves me with two young, fresh nurses and a stocky male nurse. They're laughing and joking around. I wish that the older nurse had stayed and held my hand, or that I would have had the courage to reach for hers.

As everyone waits for the surgeon to arrive, two of the nurses busy themselves with something to do, while one fresh nurse comes to inspect me.

"你会说普通话吗?" *(Nǐ huì shuō pǔtōnghuà ma?)* Can you speak standard Chinese?

"一点点." *(Yī diǎndiǎn.)* A little.

"你很漂亮." *(Nǐ hěn piàoliang.)* You're very pretty.

"谢谢." I respond as usual. *(Xièxiè.)* Thanks.

"你不要了, 是吧?" *(Nǐ bùyàole, shì ba?)* You don't want them right?

"他们都死了." *(Tāmen dōu sǐle.)* They're both dead. Tears begin to fall down the sides of my face into my ears.

As she tries to wipe my face, she hurries to say, "啊！别哭了！你很漂亮！" *(A! Bié kūle! Nǐ hěn piàoliang!)* Oh! Don't cry. You're so pretty.

I turn away from her, disgusted, and she walks away.

I continue to cry, slowly, quietly letting out tears and whispering to my heart that this is goodbye to my twins. I'm telling them goodbye with this procedure; I feel like I'm ejecting them from my body. The older nurse returns to the room and comes back to my side for a second. She sees that I'm crying, but she responds with merciful silence. She is whisked away again to another duty. The fresh nurse walks back toward me and sees I'm crying.

"别哭了！" *(Bié kūle!)* Don't cry!

"你是母亲吗?" *(Nǐ shì mǔqīn ma?)* Are you a mother? I ask her, hiding my irritation.

"不是." *(Bùshì.)* No.

"我需要告诉他们再见但是我不要告诉他们再见，所以我不能别哭了." *(Wǒ xūyào gàosù tāmen zàijiàn dànshì wǒ bùyào gàosù tāmen zàijiàn, suǒyǐ wǒ bùnéng bié kūle.)* I have to say goodbye to them, but I don't want to say goodbye, so I can't not cry."

She doesn't wipe my face, and she walks back to the desk station in the room. She doesn't return to talk to me.

I cry angrily in my heart, "Oh my dear twins, I want you. I want to hold you. Your daddy wants you. We want to name you. Your brother and sister want you, too. We don't want to say goodbye. We value you and treasure you. You are both unique and special. I cannot have others like you."

The surgeon arrives to end my bright white hospital purgatory. Her ruby earrings and her ornate glasses match. I try to steady my breath and heartbeat when I see the needle. The needle is not small. I want to be able to watch so I can deal with my pain, but my lifted gown obstructs my view even with my neck weakly bobbing my head in the air above my bed.

The ruby studded surgeon looks at me and says, "一点点." *(Yī diǎndiǎn tòng.)* A little pain.

I'm breathless from the sting when she inserts the needle. I try to control my body to keep it from moving, as everyone yells, "别动！别动！" *(Bié dòng! Bié dòng!)* Don't move! Don't move!

But every muscle tenses from the aching flood spreading across my stomach. I feel heat emitting from my body and sweat tickles my head at my roots in protest. As she moves the needle inside, I cry out in pain.

Again they rebuke, "别动！" *(Bié dòng!)* Don't move!

I wonder if Chinese women bear pain better than I do, or if the doctors lie to everyone. The rubies flash as the surgeon fills my womb with liquid. My stomach feels full now, but my heart is emptied.

After the insertion and filling from the second needle is finished, I'm not bothered for a few brief moments as the staff prepares for my move back to my room. I whisper, "Goodbye. I love you, both."

The familiar pressure in my eyes starts again and my nose burns at its tip. Soon new trickling streams are sliding down the sides of my face as I am ejected from the surgical wing's womb. My husband is patiently standing at the double doors opening. They all push me back silently to my room Bobby and I have been sharing. He took up residence on the floor using the cushions from the couch that's just a bit too short to be a bed. Our battle turns into waiting for something to just happen. I have to wait for the normally fetal-death-causing liquid to induce contractions.

Jolie goes home, since all we can do is wait. Her workday is over. Her children need her. More importantly, she needs to go home to hug them. Bobby and I fall asleep without saying much to each other.

The next morning passes by slowly. I dutifully update friends and family. I continue to coordinate with others. I put my teacher certification program on halt after I attempt to finish another assignment. I sleep. I drift in and out of conversations Bobby and Jolie have. They leave to get food and coffee. I study the room.

Most Chinese medical locations are tacky. Whoever decorates new Chinese buildings and venues is in love with Victorian style with a slap of the American 1980s. The combination is so odd. This hospital managed to escape the design trend, probably because the buildings have been around for a while, or the CFO wants to cut costs. I like the warm wood colors reminiscent of the 1930s in Beijing.

Sharon checks on us so many times and keeps reminding me that if I am in pain I should tell her as soon as possible.

Later that night, I do start to get contractions, but I don't tell anyone, even though nurses come and ask several times if I'm in pain, like they did the night before. I just want to sleep; I know it's going to be a hard and long labor. The more I let the contractions do their work, the faster the whole process should take. Through the whole night I contract and tense and release. I try to rest and get comfortable.

Early in the morning, before even Bobby has woken up, I wake up in a sweat and extra active bowels. After I relieve myself and start to walk back to my bed, brown, medicinally putrid liquid splatters onto the ground from between my legs. I call out for Bobby to call the nurse. In retrospect, I wish I had waited. My cervix was just beginning to open. I thought my water had broken, but in fact, no one explained to me that when my cervix begins to open, the deathly concoction would begin its waterfall.

A large bed is rolled in again, where I'm set under a plethora of blankets to stay warm. Sharon and another nurse roll me out of the room, on to the elevator, down two ramps to a door leading to the outside that needs a specific badge, which no one has been able to find in all of these rollaway trips. Luckily no badge is needed to get into the next building, which is a mere 50 feet away. I'm rolled into another elevator and into the labor and delivery wing, through double doors and a dark corridor. Bobby is stopped and told to put on nurse clothes, and that he must wait. I'm rolled into a shared room where my cervix is checked again (I have been to this room earlier during a false alarm, since Sharon told me to tell her if I had any pain at all, resulting in a completely ridiculous trip to be told I had no dilation at all). This time there's blood, but I'm only open to a finger and a half.

A room is prepared for me, and I'm wheeled in, then transferred onto the delivery bed. My husband and Sharon are allowed to come in to be with me as I wait for the group of other doctors and nurses to come in and essentially watch my labor, since there's no need for so many pairs of hands.

At this specific hospital in Beijing, and maybe in others in China, epidurals are frowned upon. This is my first natural labor, as my first two labors were given with plenty of medication. Earlier this year a friend explained to me that she loved natural birth, but she tried to delay the arrival to the hospital as much as possible, because once she was in the hospital, she wouldn't be able to walk around and deal with the pain. The release of pain was very similar to relieving herself after constipation. Now that I've been through the process, I agree.

I need my husband's help to keep my mind distracted from the pain. We have been in the process of memorizing the book of Romans, and I begin to recite the scripture, and he finishes the verse when I need to push.

We talk about vacations and joyful moments we've had as a family. We pray. Sharon is already a pale Chinese woman, but her skin tone is bleached under the bright surgical light. Her eyes are shaped more like lemons than almonds. She has an uncommonly deep and raspy voice, which doesn't change when she switches languages. As I pray, recite, and push, I hear her voice get lower and lower, then crack high as she stammers over questions and mentions she learned about religion in the Philippines. She asks questions about what we believe, but she's just being polite, since she quickly changes the subject after we answer.

As I cry out in pain from an extended push, Bobby's face begins to turn red and tears line the top of his bottom lids, like water reaching the top of the sides of a bathroom sink.

His lids fill up as though they're about to fall, and I gasp to see them tip over, but they don't spill out. When Sharon turns away to help change the bloody square sheet cover underneath me, he cracks, "This has been the hardest thing in my entire life. You're in so much pain, but I can't do anything."

My cervix finally reaches four fingers in dilation. The first baby is in a breech position. They try to reposition the body, but they have no luck. A leg makes it out first, and the doctor holds on. She seems to reach for scissors and in brief moment of horror I think she's going to cut off the leg because the baby is already dead, but in fact some of the placenta was bulging up under the leg and had liquid pooled in a bubble. She cuts into it and more liquid falls out. She has to pull as I push so there's more progress made than just with my pushing alone.

I try to count the number of pushes, as my first delivery was three pushes, and my second was one. I lose count, and it's pointless anyway. When am I going to brag about how easy this birth was? Never. So I focus on the silence of the verses no longer being spoken and the sweat sliding down the sides of my temples. I focus on my trembling. The hips make it through, then the shoulders and surprisingly the head is not too hard to push out after the shoulders. It's a boy.

I'm surprised to see that he looks more like an alien, and when the nurse offers him to me, I'm still in incredible pain before I push out the second so I can't bear to hold him. I just look and shake my head meaning, "Yes, I see him," but my arms don't go up to meet him.

The next baby is positioned correctly, head starts to push through and they yell in Chinese first then English to push. I push so hard, harder than I had to push in my first two deliveries. I can't anymore so I take a shallow breath, noticing that my hiked up legs are quivering. I'm drilled to push more, so I pull back on my knees and I feel relief as his head makes it through, and my cervix swallows around the rest of the body. Push again, and the body makes it out. Another boy.

Next to each other on the table, they don't reach for each other like twins should. They don't cuddle. They don't cry out. Their faces are torn, I assume from either the hungry, eating liquid or from decay. Bobby does not take a picture. He doesn't want to have a picture. They are slimy, wiggly, and dark from death. I have no chance to say goodbye in my own way, and the doctors and nurses didn't really understand what I meant when I told them earlier I wanted time with them. Maybe they don't understand my need to say goodbye because the boys never really entered the world alive in the first place. Maybe they don't understand because this is something too painful to talk about.

After a quick procedure to clear every remaining tissue from inside me, I'm cleaned up and pushed back.

Our room feels empty with just Bobby and me. We agree to name them Perez and Zerah, the twins of Judah and Tamar in Genesis. Perez means "to burst forth" and Zerah means "sunrise." The nurses checking up on us no longer feel urgent. We're left alone for hours on end, and we're told I can go home in about 24 hours. But home means going back without babies to reminders of what we've lost. The pregnancy pillow waits for me on the bed. A beautiful white crib forever to collect dust sits in the planned nursery. Baby clothes never worn hide in the closet collection.

After I am home again, I ask Jolie, also a mother of two, what she thinks about what was said during my hospital stay. I'm so confused by what has happened. How can such a normally warm and hospitable culture be so harsh in such a somber moment?

I tell her how others have said, "At least you have your body."

"Do you know, your husband is great? He is a great man."

"At least you have two children. Be thankful for them."

I tell her how others scolded me about taking care of my body in the process of my grief.

She tells me she wouldn't like their words either. She tells me that these doctors and nurses, and others, they don't know what to say to comfort me. Especially for the elder Chinese, they have experienced famine, drought, and revolutions. They just want me to focus on what I have, focus on the good still in my life.

Yet, birth and death are the most powerful, uncontrollable events we all experience in life. Birth and death humble us all and shatter honor. Birth and death connect us all. What can a baby say to birth or anyone say to death?

And for the second time in China, I wish I could truthfully say, "我不明白." *(Wǒ bù míngbái.)* I don't understand.

Vanessa Jencks primarily works as managing editor of beijingkids magazine, an essential resource for international families in Beijing. She writes on her personal blog, vanessajencks.com about topics related to education, expatriation, society, social justice, and womanhood.

CHAPTER 17

FOOTPRINTS LEFT BEHIND

Marcey Heschel
Nationality: Canadian
Birthed in: Malaysia

My husband and I are Canadian expatriates enjoying our second relocation. We spent three years in Midland, Texas before our overseas move to Kuala Lumpur in December 2014. We were accompanied by our American-born one-year-old frequent flier Sophia Victoria, whom by that time had accumulated over 50 flights traveling around the US, Mexico, Canada, and South East Asia. With barely two months of settling into this foreign tropical metropolis, we discovered we were pregnant with baby No. 2, but unforgettably, pregnancy number three.

West Texas

I'd suffered my first miscarriage in Texas on April 14, 2012, due to undiagnosed hypothyroidism. The events of that day were grim, to say the least, as I miscarried while waiting to be seen in a Dallas hospital. We were on a weekend getaway when it happened. We had visited the grassy knoll and place of President JFK's assassination, eaten a Thai lunch and were making our way through an aquarium when I started to bleed. Just like that. We rushed to the hospital, but it was too late. The staff obviously didn't understand the emergency, and I was not given a bed nor a painkiller while I squealed in agony from the cramping.

Unforgettable, it was.

Aside from that hospital in Dallas, the treatment and care I received in Texas were excellent, comprehensive, and proactive. I can remember vividly how my OB/GYN, Dr. Saintly, offered his hopefulness to us by explaining how likely it was that I could and would carry a healthy baby. He made us feel comfortable, cared for, and confident in the process by answering our questions in detail and taking the time to do so regardless of how many people were in the waiting room. Without family near to listen, it was relieving to find a doctor who would. The only questionable incident that occurred in his office was when I asked his nurse when I could expect my period again, and she hadn't heard me correctly. She turned to me and with that Texas drawl she blasted out, "Do, what?" Um... It was a shocking way to speak in a fragile moment.

Sometimes Texan vernacular is a little less than gentle around the perimeters. Apparently, "Do what?" may take the place of "Pardon me" or "Sorry, I missed that. Could you repeat?" With my hormone levels vacillating like a yo-

yo, I took a moment to release some estrogen on Nurse Glenda. I'm certain that, bless her heart, she will know when not to respond with, "Do what?" again. In retrospect, it wasn't her fault—it was my hormones and sensitivity as much as it was just typical Texas. We apologized to each other later on. Texans' hearts are as big as their hair.

Months went passed until finally, I became pregnant again in early January. Dr. Saintly ensured my human chorionic gonadotropin (hCG) levels were tested repeatedly and doubling nicely. My thyroid and progesterone needs were attended to diligently without me having to do anything but give blood. My pregnancy progressed through 17 weeks of nausea, vomiting, constipation, and a plethora of other healthy but heinous pregnancy symptoms.

I was induced a week early and led through the delivery with no surprises. The staff allowed me to fill the room with essential oils and spa music, and thus Sophia was born into a setting of lavender, eucalyptus, and softly flowing water sounds. Even my contractions were tranquil, which likely had less to do with the essential oils and more to do with the epidural, a marvel of modern medicine that I plan never to deliver without. For many women, the word "tranquil" alongside "contraction" could define the law of contradiction.

I'll never forget the moment my doctor handed me the most precious gift I had ever received. As daddy took her to bathe, I experienced a moment of sincere gratitude for the entire process, including the miscarriage, because in my arms I held the inexplicable joy of an answered prayer, along with eternal love for one that was not.

During the post-delivery appointment, Dr. Saintly gave baby Sophia a pink onesie with a picture of a stork on it and the words "Made by God, Delivered by Doctor

Saintly." I truly don't know if without his impeccable care we would have Sophia today. She's the most incredible soul I've ever met and the strongest reason that I believe everything happens for a reason. Everything happened to deliver Sophia into our lives. She's our lucky Texas star.

Malaysia

We were transferred to Malaysia in December 2014. In February, I visited Prince Court Medical Centre in Kuala Lumpur to confirm the third pregnancy. I found the OB/GYN, Dr. Dismal, chilly and uncongenial. She did not congratulate me, nor warmly celebrate the moment. In fact, her words were something like, "The pregnancy has been confirmed. Please schedule a follow-up to test for viability." It could have just been that traces of ammonia were found in her morning cornflakes, or that this woman was just a complete bitch.

Regardless, I believed at the time that it was preferable to have a doctor with excellent medical knowledge and skill over jovial bedside manner. I now believe this woman perhaps has neither. I've met a multitude of Chinese women throughout my time in Malaysia who are both warm and loving as well as professional and hardworking, so I don't believe her coldness was cultural.

During my follow up appointment, I let Dr. Dismal know about my first miscarriage, my healthy pregnancy, thyroid condition, and prior progesterone treatment. I requested the progesterone, but she scoffed at my request, deeming it an overprotection. She did prescribe it nonetheless, but I was complacent with it as I now doubted its necessity. I'll never truly know if it was needed or not but in future I will take it religiously as a precaution.

Thankfully, a healthy heartbeat was detected, but it was nerve-racking just to have the scan done. You see, once a woman has had a miscarriage, she can never look at an ultrasound screen the same again. I was thankful to have had my husband with me at that moment to comfort me and witness the doctor say, "Heartbeat confirmed, please schedule your next appointment." We truly should have gone on the hunt for a new OB/GYN right then and there. It dawned on me how a woman's pregnancy needs are not only medical, but spiritual, emotional, and most certainly psychological. Finding comfort from this woman was as likely as finding a tropical beach in Antarctica.

It became clear that at Prince Court, each issue was referred to the appropriate specialist. There was no comprehensive treatment as I had experienced in Texas. For my blood work and thyroid tests, I was sent to an endocrinologist. To discuss depression and anxiety, I was sent to a psychiatrist. It would have been preferable to have had the doctor in charge of my pregnancy manage all of these pieces, understanding the innate inter-connection between them. Instead, I was off seeing specialists and dealing with proud medical personalities that didn't like to be questioned.

Each time I had my thyroid bloodwork done, the endocrinologist came back to me with the same answer. "You're in the normal range." I now know that the "normal" range is large and subjective. I found myself studying up on endocrinology and thyroid medicine because I couldn't comprehend why Dr. Saintly had altered my dose repeatedly, yet in Malaysia, I was told simply that I was "in the normal range." I was frustrated, confused with the doctors and almost felt that a "Doo whhaatt?" would be appropriate. I felt so very far from Texas, and even further from our Canadian home.

The symptoms of pregnancy were strong and felt endlessly exasperating. I could barely stomach anything, and the sight of Malaysian food with fish heads, heavy spices, and dried minnows for garnish was the antithesis of appetizing. I swear I could smell Durian everywhere, and this is the fruit that is banned from covered buildings due to its rotten aroma. It permeates the air, and it's not uncommon to see signs in apartment buildings that actually ban the fruit from entering.

Cab rides through constipated traffic jams from the hospital to home took over an hour and a half, and the repeated momentum of the stop, go, stop, go filled many a plastic bag with bile. Cabbies use the parking brake in back-to-back traffic, moving an inch and pulling the brake. It feels like six thousand rounds of whiplash by the time you make it home. The drivers also often reek of body odor, as little deodorant is used, and they burn incense or hang little jars of jasmine instead to even further permeate the recycled air. I eventually learned to pay the extra 10 Ringgit ($2.50) for the luxurious Blue Taxi Van. Those usually are big enough that you can't smell the driver, and they rarely use the parking brake.

Now I drive myself after finally biting the bullet and learning how to drive on the opposite side of the road, therefore saving myself from the retching rollercoaster ride of taxis. It was terrifying to learn, and I almost killed many motorcyclists as they swerved right in front of me out of nowhere. However, I control my own airspace, and there is no jasmine incense allowed in my Kia Rio. The body odor is my own.

My husband worked long hours and so I thanked God daily to be in a part of the world with affordable domestic help. Our young Filipino helper was able to care for Sophia and boil up ramen noodles to serve me in bed. I so longed for the comfort food of home and Lipton chicken noodle soup made by Mom. Perhaps it was the soup, or maybe I just longed for the familiarity, comfort, and support of my loved ones. I remember sitting in the bottom of the shower barely able to move but drawing the numbers for the weeks to go on the glass in steam. I had the goal of 17 weeks in my head as that is how long it took to feel well during my successful pregnancy.

I was also not-so-patiently waiting for that 12–15-week mark where we might find out if we were having a boy or a girl. It didn't matter, but the daydreaming had begun, and I found this to be somewhat of an escape from the nausea.

On weekends, I conjured up enough energy to escort my little family to the various malls to establish a new household with all of the necessities like appliances, cutlery, and dinnerware. It was a headache buying all of the electrical adapters for our American-styled cords.

It was also a headache listening to Malaysian salespeople answer our inquiries with, "No, no have," when two minutes later we would find it on a nearby shelf. Through our time here we have learned that "no, no have" really means, "No, I don't understand you," or "No, I'm not going to help you."

Shopping with morning sickness in Malaysia was a maddening cultural experience. As sick as I was up until nearly 13 weeks, I started to feel better and was surprised that relief had come that early. I wondered whether I was having a boy, as I'd been told that pregnancy symptoms vary by sex. It was now only days until that three-month checkup and the chance to see that little soul on the screen once again. The last time it had been merely a flickering heartbeat but preeminently a visible sign of life.

On the night of April 14 (the exact date of my first miscarriage) I had a dream in which I was with my mother at the top of the staircase at our northern Canadian cabin and gave birth to a stillborn. I woke up frightened, and I called my mother on FaceTime before I left for my appointment. She calmed me, and I felt relieved and excited again as I ordered the blue taxi. The appointment with the sonogram specialist started well, and I was given the option to pay a great deal for an early test that could determine gender. It was expensive, and I wanted to call my husband to assess together if it was worthwhile. I was already envisioning nursery themes, colors, and gender reveal announcements. He wasn't answering at the time, and the doctor said, "You can think about it, and we will go ahead with the sonogram." I don't think I felt much other than excitement and anticipation when I took a breath and eased my way onto the table.

The eerie silence that followed felt like a nine-month term itself.

"What?" I said, "What's wrong?"

I could see the technician was mouthing the anatomical observations but seemed uneasy. I felt it in my gut. I felt it in my heart. I felt it in my soul. Somehow at that moment my own heart swallowed itself as I was told that our baby didn't have a heartbeat at almost 13 weeks. I could see it. It looked like a baby. There was a little head, a body—the whole thing. But it wasn't. It wasn't alive. I think I screamed.

In utter confusion, disbelief, and fear I shouted emphatically, "What do you mean? What are you talking about!?!"

But that was it. The sonogram technician just said, "I'm sorry," and ultimately stopped probing my belly with that icy instrument of life or death.

I couldn't quite reconcile the desire I had had moments earlier to reach my husband regarding the gender test with the inexplicable truth that the gender was now ultimately, heartbreakingly inconsequential. I was shaking. They asked if I needed a moment. I started to sob.

The technician started to recite some statistical information with me regarding miscarriage which sounded more like, "Well, 25% blaaa blaaa blaaaas." As I sobbed, I noticed the nurses wanting to calm me down somehow as to not disturb the other patients. They placed me in a room to settle. This worked for less than a minute because as soon as I entered the room, I turned to discover a massive 3-D shadow box display of fetuses at various stages of development. They looked like our baby, and I couldn't believe the insensitivity I was experiencing.

I was called into my doctor's office, and she sat me down and again reiterated the commonality of the loss. Again, there was no empathy, certainly no sympathy, and she suggested that I call my husband, take some time, and we could decide what to do. I wasn't offered a place to cry comfortably; I wasn't offered a hug nor a hand to hold. I wandered the hospital for around half an hour alone. I called my husband.

How do you tell your spouse that kind of news? He was a rock in my time of need and undoubtedly as devastated as I was. He was on his way. I called my mom, but I could barely speak. Somehow I had known it from my dream. My mom felt my pain, I know she did, as only a mother can.

I couldn't help but wonder at that moment if something I had done had caused this loss. Had I not taken my progesterone as I should have? What did I do wrong? I was blaming myself, searching for answers where there were none, and ultimately just processing the shock. I wasn't sure if I could believe that it was true. I needed to see our baby again.

My husband arrived, and he just held me there as I sobbed. We made our way back to Dr. Dismal, who told us that we were overreacting and that we should "get it together." After another ultrasound, there was no denying the facts. We were both emotionally destroyed. We were given the options of letting the baby pass through in a week's time or so naturally, or having a dilation and curettage (D&C) the next day to remove the fetus. I couldn't comprehend the idea of waiting with our baby who didn't survive still inside me almost as much as I couldn't comprehend having a surgery to remove it.

Ultimately, we chose to have the surgery in the morning. It was a long night. We went home and took our daughter to the pool. We held each other, we prayed a bit, and we shed many tears. I kept my hand on my belly all night.

Saying goodbye to something (someone) you never really had is a bizarre form of grief. The *"what ifs"* and the *"if onlys"* run rampant through the mind, and the longing to hold it and love it encapsulates the heart. It's painful, and it takes a long time to come to grips with. I can't even imagine how it must feel for the women who carry their babies to full term only to be shattered into a million pieces. I felt so broken.

That morning we arrived at the hospital to sign paperwork to have them "remove the waste of conception." To the surgical room employees, a D&C is simply a standard practice. A surgical procedure. For us, it was devoid of emotion or caring, which are two of the things I value the most. If it weren't for my husband, I wouldn't have made it through the procedure. He made me laugh and read me magazines after I was wheeled back into the room following the surgery.

Perhaps it just wasn't our time. Perhaps all things happen for a reason. At least I could get pregnant. At least we already have a child. For months after the miscarriage, those sentences came at me from all angles. Many people who don't understand the devastation of miscarriage believe that they are helpful statements when in fact they're aggravating.

What I needed was someone to say to me, "I am so sorry, this is horrible, and I am here for you," or, "Nothing can make it better right now, and it's okay to feel this pain. It's a loss."

Through discomfort in discussing personal matters, people often revert to statements that are supposed to help you look on the bright side. Sometimes, you need to enter the dark side with someone and be there with them while they cry.

Recently, I was at an expatriate dinner party during which some women were discussing morning sickness and how horrible it is, but how thankfully it always leads to the most amazing gift. I wanted to lovingly remind these ladies that in fact, sometimes it doesn't. However, I kept quiet because sometimes a truthful disclosure can breed contempt instead of empathy, something I learned while at a yoga retreat when I spoke of the miscarriages with some women I didn't know personally. I was asked whether I had children and if I wanted more. I gave an honest answer. The response I received was awkward, and a friend of mine told me later that I had made some of the women uncomfortable.

Loss makes people uncomfortable, and I guess that "getting to know you" dance doesn't include discussing things such as this. Apparently, western women are far more open than women of many other cultures. I can respect that without agreeing with it, but realistically, why is it such a taboo?

We suffer in silence as the first trimester completes because we are told not to disclose the pregnancy in case it doesn't work out. The conundrum is that women need the most support during that first trimester. We can be sick; we can be worried; we can be afraid.

So why shouldn't we talk about it? Perhaps silence gives some women strength. Silence, however, will not liberate women and benefit women's issues.

I hope nothing more than that my story may provide some loving support and encouragement to the mommies who have had a miscarriage or lost a baby while traveling and living abroad. It's heartbreaking at any time, but even more so when your loved ones are nowhere near to hold you up through it.

A couple of weeks ago, my husband and I were notified that we are being transferred back home to Alberta, Canada. Just today, and much to my absolute bewilderment and surprise, we received a positive pregnancy test result. I am beyond hopeful that things will work out well this time, but regardless I can now be certain that we will not have to experience another birth or loss somewhere foreign. The synchronicity of becoming pregnant again and being moved home feels divine.

Hopefully in nine months' time we will hold another rainbow baby in our arms. Rainbow babies are the children born following a stillbirth or a loss of pregnancy. They are loved in a special way, as they somehow make sense of an otherwise inexplicable trauma.

I read this chapter to my husband to let him know that we're pregnant. He's still in tears. I guess I am knocked up abroad again while we anxiously await our rainbow.

Marcey Louise Heschel is a 35-year-old Canadian mother, wife, and therapist living abroad in Kuala Lumpur Malaysia. Marcey spends her time as an expatriate raising her daughter as well as seeing clients at a marriage and family therapy practice. With an undergraduate degree in anthropology and a graduate degree in counseling, she has found a niche working with people of varying ethnic backgrounds.

She recently started an expat support group for struggling spouses dealing with relocation stress and anxiety. She is an avid traveler, half-marathon runner, and advanced scuba diver. She enjoys writing about her adventures, travels and cultural experiences on her blog www.marcey.me. Follow her on Instagram and Twitter @missmabes. Her most recent publication was in the anthology, Once Upon An Expat.

SECTION III

PARENTING ABROAD

CHAPTER 18

WOVEN BETWEEN CULTURES

Michelle Acker Perez
Nationality: American
Parented in: Guatemala

When I was eight months pregnant, and my belly swelled over my black leggings, my Guatemalan mother-in-law surprised me with a handmade, woven textile. I assumed it was a blanket. She explained it was to carry my baby. "It's a *cargador*," she informed me.

I fumbled over the pronunciation, as she showed me how to fold it in half and tie a knot at my shoulder to secure it. It seemed heavy and awkward. "*Aqui*," here, she patted, "is where the baby's head goes." I thanked her, nodding politely. I was sure I wouldn't use it.

My daughter was born a month later on the full moon of summer solstice, and that woven piece of fabric became the only way I could get her to sleep. I learned to tie a knot behind my head without looking and slip my little girl inside during the dark, early morning hours. I tucked the fabric up tightly around her legs and swayed back and forth until her eyes closed.

About a year later I sat across the table from my Guatemalan sister-in-law, who has three kids, all much older than my own. The plastic covering on her dining room table stuck to my sweaty arm as I adjusted my now 20-pound daughter, who still preferred to sleep in the *cargador*. I was tired and hoping for a three-step plan.
"So how did you get your kids to sleep independently?" I asked with slight desperation, explaining how my daughter only fell asleep while being held.

She listened, and nodded empathetically, but seemed puzzled by my question. "All kids eventually learn," was the most she offered.

I knew that one day my daughter would in fact learn to sleep by herself, but I think buried beneath the syntax of my words was a deeper question on my heart: When would I feel comfortable being a mother in a country different from the one I grew up in?

The first time my daughter was really sick, like any new mom I was worried, so I turned to Google. But not to look up symptoms, but rather to translate "rapid heartbeat" and convert 103.5°F to Celsius before I called our pediatrician. As I held my sweaty baby in one arm and my phone in the other, our pediatrician gave me the name of a medicine. I scribbled it down in Spanish. My husband was out of town on a work trip so I called our local pharmacy.

One of the perks of life in Guatemala is free pharmacy delivery. Forty minutes after I hung up the phone and spelled out the name of the medicine letter-by-letter, a man on a motorcycle showed up at my door. I handed him 55 Quetzaels, the equivalent of about $8, and whispered, "Gracias," as I helped my sleeping daughter in the *cargador*.

I opened the box and tried to make sense of the Spanish directions listed on the side of the box. Did that say one *cucharita* or *chuchara* (teaspoon or tablespoon)? What was the difference again? It was one of many times I wished for instructions and information in my first language.

There is much in my mothering that I have had to convert. When my husband and I decided to send our daughter to preschool, I eagerly attended the parent meeting at the beginning of the school year. I smiled nervously and found a seat near the back so I could see the director's lips moving while also simultaneously watching what the other parents did. Careful observation is my favorite cross-cultural coping skill. The director explained about the classrooms, the uniforms and then reminded us to have our payments in before the 5th of each month. She rattled off a number in Spanish while I typed the number into my phone. 7-8-3-2-5...I knew I had missed something. Was that an account number for the payments or a phone number? I wasn't sure.

I wanted to ask a question, but the desire to appear competent felt more important than seeking clarity. I am an educator by training. I have studied best teaching practices and classroom management, but I had never felt more lost at a school event. I missed the confidence that comes when you intuitively understand a system.

I felt a bit like a preschooler myself. It was the first time it hit me. I will be learning right alongside my daughter. After all, this was her first experience in the Guatemalan school system, and it was mine, too.

This wasn't an entirely new feeling. Maybe all mothers feel like they are learning alongside their children. However, my sense is mothering in a cross-cultural setting offers more layers for learning. I remember the first time I realized my daughter knew a Spanish word that I didn't. She was barely two years old. We had celebrated her second birthday the week before, and my mom had flown down to visit. One of the many gifts she had brought down for her only grandchild was a wooden puzzle of sea creatures with a magnetic fishing pole attached. My daughter adored it, and daily asked to "go fishing."

One afternoon while we sat on the floor playing with her puzzle, my daughter pointed at the wooden octopus, "*pulpo!*" she exclaimed.

"Yeah, that's purple," I echoed back to trying to affirm her as she learned her colors.

She pointed again at the purple octopus, but looked directly at me, "No, *puuulpo.*"

I nodded and redirected her, "Yes, sweetie it's a purple octopus."

Her frustration level rising, she screamed, "NOOO, *PULPO!*"

"Okay, *pulpo.*" I conceded.

I did not want to be arguing with my toddler about the pronunciation of the color purple. We finished the game and moved onto another activity.

Later that evening after she was asleep, and the table was cleared off and the dishes done, I leaned over from behind my computer.

"Hey, *mi amor*, how do you say 'octopus' in Spanish?" I could see my husband's eyebrows furrow with confusion, but without missing a beat, he responded, "*Pulpo.*"

She had been right.

My two-year old's Spanish was quickly surpassing mine. I knew it was only the beginning of learning alongside my child in a language and culture that are not my own. Often what still feels foreign to me is completely familiar to her.

My daughter is growing up buying freshly squeezed orange juice in the morning from Doña Marta and listening to the buses beep loudly every time they roar past the plaza. When we leave the gates that guard the front of our house, she greets the horses crossing the road, piled high with the farmer's earnings for the week.

She knows where we stop to buy tortillas and which bakery has the best *pan dulce*. She speaks English at home, Spanish at preschool, and a mix of Spanglish everywhere else. She throws her toilet paper in the trash can, as is necessary here, and corrects me when we're in California, "Mama that doesn't go in there," when I toss it into the toilet. She prefers beans over peanut butter and is often happiest running around the central square in the shadow of a 500-year-old cathedral and a towering volcano. Guatemala is the only home she's ever known. And it's the only place I've been a mother.

I moved to Guatemala as an independent 27-year-old carrying two suitcases and a dream of teaching overseas. I told my parents, "I'm just going for a year." They were supportive, and yet naturally cautious. I had expected to fall in love with the country, but was quite surprised to find myself falling for a man. During rides to work in his truck and conversations curled up on my couch, we shared hopes and ideas for the future as we chatted over a plate of leftovers.

I hummed along to Jack Johnson, and he introduced me to Maná and Jarabe de Palo. We spoke mostly in English, texted in Spanish, and found similarities in the worlds that existed between us. Early on he told me, "I like the way you think." I smiled. There was no kinder compliment in my book. I remember watching him one morning sitting on the stairs playing jacks with the students at the school where I taught, "He's going to be a great dad," I thought, but didn't dare say out loud. That's when I knew I really liked him. We got married a year and half later in Guatemala.

It's now been over six years since I first moved here. My external life has changed greatly. I often cruise around town on my scooter, wait in line at the bank to pay bills and am extra cognizant when I grocery shop, knowing I will have to carry my child and whatever we purchase across the street, because the grocery carts are not allowed to leave the store. The challenge for me has not been adapting to the external differences in this country and culture, but rather acknowledging the deeply woven layers of internal differences.

Becoming a mother outside of the country I grew up in has made me miss things I didn't realize were important to me and forced me to acknowledge expectations I didn't know I had. A mentor once told me, "The distance between expectation and reality is marked by both disappointment, and the potential for growth." I had never considered how disappointment could lead to growth.

I sometimes catch myself scrolling through Instagram, envious of stroller walks on smooth sidewalks and playgrounds with secure railings. There are times I worry my daughter is missing out—on story time at the library and Mommy and Me music class. But when I am honest, maybe I am the one who fears I am missing out—on the ease of friendships with other moms who speak my language and the convenience of having my family close by to help.

Last week my sister FaceTimed us one evening. As the phone rang, my daughter jumped up from the table where she was coloring, "I can push the green button!" Of course she can. She has been staring at the three-inch screen on my phone since before she could talk. Apart from yearly visits, she interacts mostly with my family through technology. A gift of the modern times for sure, but one that always leaves me painfully aware how much it lacks. Little hands and long hugs and the smell of freshly washed baby hair cannot be transmitted, even with the best WiFi signal. My sister, brother, and parents were together celebrating my mom's birthday. They waved into their screen.

My daughter held the phone with two hands, "Hiiiii Nana."

I whisper from behind her, "Tell Nana, Happy birthday!"

The screen goes blank. *Poor connection,* it reads.

"Nana, can't see me," my daughter whines.

I take the phone and try to call back.

I wish that my family could see and be a part of our daily life here. I miss the casualness and comfort of simply being able to swing by for dinner or get together for birthday celebrations. Whenever my daughter is sick or we get stuck without a sitter my first instinct is, "Oh I'll just call my mom." I never realized how much I needed my mom until I became one. We make the most of our visits and fill up those two weeks in California with as much time together as we can, but there is just not enough bandwidth to carry us back and forth through the phone.

The truth is I am choosing to live in Guatemala, a world away from where and how I grew up. Mothering in Guatemala has forced me to reevaluate not just how I parent, but how I live. When I was preparing to go back to work after having my daughter, I stopped by the local *tienda* (store) one morning to grab a few things for the office. With my daughter perched on one hip, I asked the woman behind the counter for paper clips, black pens and some whiteboard markers.

"How many paper clips?" She asked me without looking up from the glass counter that she crouched behind.

"How many?" I repeated the question back in confusion.

She held up a paper clip and once again asked, "*Cuántos?*"

I understood the words, but was baffled by the question. I shrugged, "Just one box," I clarified.

She stared back at me, but didn't say anything as she dumped out an entire box on the glass counter top and began counting each one. It was at that time I learned paper clips are sold by unit, not by box.

I purchased 98 paper clips that day, much to the dismay of the store owner.

I came to realize that not just paper clips, but also Band-Aids, sheets of paper, rolls of toilet paper, pens, and even diapers are each sold one by one. The idea of filling a pantry or valuing the convenience of purchasing in bulk doesn't really exist in small towns, partly due to economic instability and a system that doesn't support the idea of credit card debt. Most Guatemalans only spend what they have and buy what they need.

For most mothers in Guatemala, raising young children is just a part of life; it does not become the focus of your life. The majority of Guatemalans do not have fancy baby carriers or baby swings in their living rooms. Rather they have the wealth of extra arms to hold a fussy newborn and many hands to stir a pot of soup simmering on the stove. Where there is often limited physical resources, human resources are in abundance.

What I have often thought of as guarantees, most Guatemalans view as privileges. Things like clean water, shelter from the rain, a door with a lock, and not having to choose between sending one child to school or buying medicine for another have never been sources of stress in my life and probably won't be for my daughter. However, my own thoughts about mothering are often filtered through these realities.

Anytime my husband's family gathers together for a meal, my father-in-law prays. He always begins by giving thanks for "*otro dia de vida.*" Another day of life. He doesn't give thanks for experiences or things, but rather for life. Because for most Guatemalan families, even life is seen as a gift, not a guarantee.

Cross-cultural motherhood is not seamless, there are loose edges and expectations that sometimes don't seem to fit, especially when you're weaving together multiple languages, cultures, and countries. At best it is a blend of patterns that hopefully begins to form something new and beautiful; at worst it is a confusing mix of unpacking your own definition of what is normal.

My daughter is now three years old and still uses the *cargador* each night. However, that same fabric that at first felt cumbersome and awkward has grown on me over time. Like the *cargador*, I have softened and become more comfortable with life here.

As she lays her head on her pillow, I wrap her up in the comfort of the well-worn pink and purple fabric. I kiss her tan cheeks, "Good night, *Mija.*"

My expectations haven't changed entirely, but they have been stretched and shaped in new ways. On my better days, I trust that something is being woven together. Some part of me and my own cultural expectations and some part of my husband and this country that we call home are forming my daughter's world.

Because the truth is she is growing up different from how either one of us did.

My daughter's life story is being woven together here, between two countries and two cultures.

And mine is, as well.

Michelle Acker Perez is a California girl, who now calls Guatemala home. Her writing has appeared in The Washington Post, Scary Mommy, and Inculture Parent. She works in the non-profit world and writes about life between two cultures at Simply Complicated and documents daily life abroad on Instagram, Facebook, and Twitter.

*Author's note: There is a great risk and deep responsibility when writing about cultures, especially one that's not your own. It's easy to make a sweeping generalization for the sake of brevity. However, I feel it necessary to mention that Guatemala is a very diverse country. Mothers who live near large cities and have access to more resources may not identify with all of the descriptions in this essay. Generalizations, however limiting, are helpful in understanding cultural values attributed to the majority. And that is what I am referring to here, the majority of Guatemalans.

CHAPTER 19

A GIRL AND HER GUARD

Sara Ackerman
Nationality: American
Parented in: Ethiopia

This morning, my four-year-old daughter woke me. "Can you open the door, Mama?" she asked, standing next to my bed and tapping my arm. She was wearing pajama shorts, a superman shirt, and my flip-flops. In her arms, she carried a duck puzzle and a plastic bag of Jenga pieces. I got out of bed, unlocked the front door, and squinted into the sun as she made her way to the gate, my shoes slapping against her feet.

In Ethiopia, children are adored and communal. You can pick up, or kiss, or ruffle the hair of any child in reach, whether you know them or not. You can stroke their cheeks murmuring, "*Yene konjo.*" How beautiful.

If the same child misbehaves any adult is free to intervene. Slapping a random child is not unheard of. In fact, many local schools station a tardiness-slapper-guy at their entrance whose sole employment seems to consist of hitting late children on their way through the gate. *"Ende?"* is a useful phrase to have for those moments when a rowdy child crosses your path. This question sadly lacks an exact English equivalent, but it's convenient to have in your arsenal for any time you want to express disbelief. When you say it to a child, it means roughly, "Are you kidding me? Did you really just do that? Were you raised by wolves?"

When western friends ask about my parenting style, my immediate thought is I have neither the time nor money to possess one. In terms of personality, I'm a mix of aggressive introvert, American anxiety, and Jewish guilt. None of this lends itself to being comfortable sharing my child with strangers. But my daughter, American by passport, Congolese by birth, and Ethiopian at heart is nothing like me. Plus, she's adopted, so I am not exactly in a position to comment on the difficulty of sharing one's children with strangers.

Some people see her smooth brown skin and are sure my daughter is Ethiopian, while others assume at a glance that she is as foreign as I am. Many point to her and ask bluntly. *"Habesha?"* they say, the term Ethiopians use to refer to themselves. I shake my head lightly, but don't reply.

Nonetheless, my daughter has been *konjoed* and kissed more times than either of us can count. In restaurants, people at other tables feed her from their hands if they see our order is slow to come. The woman at the fruit stand down the street gives her a banana or orange most times we stop there, pulling from a pallet box whichever one I didn't buy that day. If my daughter's face is dirty, someone will tell her. If she did the buttons on her shirt crooked that morning, someone is sure to let her know. If her hat flies off when I dash across a busy street clutching her in my arms, a driver will slam on the brakes, stick his hand out the window to stop the traffic in the other lanes, and honk us back into the road to retrieve it.

Bereket, a mentally ill man who paces our neighborhood shrieking at the sky and anyone who passes, approached my daughter one day, his fingers positioned like a gun. "I'll kill you, kill you, kill you," he shouted. When my daughter burst into tears, another man walking our direction knelt down, wiped her face, and demanded she stop crying. He went on to explain in Amharic that there is no sense in crying over something a crazy person said. He said it as if Bereket, with his shrieking and finger gun, was simply a puddle of spilled milk. But it worked. My daughter sniffed and nodded, and we were on our way again.

Part of living in Ethiopia, and not just as a foreigner, is employing domestic workers. Mulugeta is the driver who takes my daughter to and from school while I work. Our nanny, Cathy, a refugee from Eastern Congo, looks after my daughter from the end of her school day until I get home. Expats and Ethiopians alike are often shocked that I don't have an additional person or two to cook and clean. While Ethiopia is not known for crime, a security guard introduced himself to me on my first day in the country. He kissed my hand and handed me a letter written in English by his previous employer. Atnafu, it seemed, came with the house.

Atnafu is small, stooped, and largely deaf. He may be in his fifties, or possibly his eighties. Unable to hear me knock, he has left my daughter and me outside our small house in Addis Ababa in the pouring rain, late at night, and occasionally chased by dogs while I pounded the dead-bolted gate. Whenever he finally hears me, he jogs down the driveway. His limp is audible in his footsteps and threatens to topple him. Step-*step*, step-*step*, step-*step*. I hear his gait faintly at first, and then louder.

"It's okay. Don't run," I yell through the corrugated iron gate, imagining a broken hip or a cracked-open skull. But of course, he doesn't hear me. Sometimes when he opens the gate, he apologizes and bows his head. Other times he squats and makes awkward noises to indicate he was detained in the bathroom. "*Shintebeit*," he shrugs, literally translating to "house of urine."

Atnafu shakes a stick at the snarling, psychotic pack of dogs that roams our street, pulling me inside the gate by my arm with his gnarled, rock-hard hand. "*Cheger yelem*," he says. No problem. It's kind of a *yelem* though. Dogs here can be vicious, not to mention rabid. I shelled out nearly $1,000 so my daughter could be vaccinated against rabies, and having only $1,000 at the time, I decided I would just not get bit. But even with a vaccination, a bite would still mean an emergency trip to the clinic and post-bite shots, possibly out of the country.

Recently, the most viscous dog in our neighborhood was put to sleep. When I came home, Atnafu, having suffered an attack years earlier, couldn't wait to pantomime the news. His Amharic came out in a hyper, breathless string. I could only make out the word for dog, but when Atnafu drew his finger across his throat and then pretended to throw a heavy object over the wall, I got the gist. My daughter, with a fear of dogs and an ear for Amharic, began chanting *Lord of the Flies*-esque, "Atnafu killed the dog. Atnafu killed the dog."

"He did not," I snapped. "A vet did it. And it's sad," though I only half-believed the last part.

To compensate for a general lack of guarding skills, Atnafu washes the car far more than is conscionable in a country that is battling drought. He shifts my hanging laundry on an hourly basis using complicated calculations of sun, clouds, temperature, and time. "It's fine, leave it," I say, and try to pretend he is not holding a handful of my bras.

Faced with hours alone each day, he rips out the lawn to plant vegetables. They never grow beyond thin, yellowing sprouts. He builds a fence for the sickly garden with sticks and bits of garbage he found by sifting through my trash. Every time I see the sad garden with the garbage fence, I suck in my teeth. My daughter scoots around it as she plays, probably only taking note of how the plastic wrappers and bits of foil sparkle in the late afternoon light.

Fencing materials are not all Atnfau finds in the trash. One day I pass by his room and see that it's filled with empty alcohol bottles. They are mine. About three years' worth. Sometimes you can make money from selling the bottles, but these ones are just sitting there and have been for years. In a country where few people drink, I am embarrassed by the sheer amount I have consumed. I start throwing the bottles away furtively at work before realizing it likely runs counter to my efforts not to appear to be an alcoholic.

In addition to having a security guard, our house is surrounded by a high cement wall. The ledge of the wall is embedded with shards of broken glass and topped with looping barbed wire. Two years ago I began leaving our front door open during the day so my daughter, then 18 months old, could freely wobble between the house and the yard. Atnafu was always her first stop. He kicked a soccer ball to her, and she would fall on top of it, laughing hysterically like falling on a soccer ball was the punch line to a good joke. After exhausting themselves, they lay together in sunny patches of grass. If he thought the ground was too cold, he made her sit on a scrap of cardboard he pilfered the day our shipment arrived, a treasure trove of discarded boxes and bubble wrap.

When my daughter couldn't find him outside, she soon took to standing in the doorway of his detached room waiting to be invited in. She sat on his drum, swinging her feet, and staring at him for hours.

"You let her in his *room*?" other expat moms gasp.

"Sure," I say, shrugging. "But anything could happen," they whisper.

Anything *could* happen, and the thing that does happen is my daughter repeats Amharic words after him. The thing that happens is my daughter stares mesmerized at his set of collectible cards featuring, instead of baseball players, Ethiopian Orthodox saints with short afros and enormous eyes. St. Gabriel is the patron saint of our local church. I say our church not because we attend, but because on a regular basis they wake us up with enormously loud liturgical chanting at odd hours of the night.

The worst thing that happens on these visits is that my daughter begins asking for an "angel for my neck. Like Atnafu." After some investigating, I figure out she is talking about the ornately carved wooden cross he wears on a black string. It is tucked against his chest most days, a little knob rising beneath his t-shirt.

"Why not?" she asks when I refuse to buy her one.

"Because we're Jewish. And atheists."

So she asks for a *mefakia* instead, a small piece of wood that is traditionally used in lieu of a toothbrush. "Maybe," I concede.

One weekend morning when my daughter was two years old, I realized in a panic that she was gone. She was neither in the house nor in the yard. After seconds of hysterical searching, I discovered, horrified, that she had learned how to unlatch the gate. I dashed out of the gate and only started breathing again when I found she was 1) there and 2) not run over by a car. After she didn't find Atnafu outside or in his room, my daughter went looking for him in the street outside our house, rightly suspecting he would be perched on his favorite bit of curb.

Now the two of them spend afternoons in the street on a pair of cinderblocks Atnafu recently souped-up into a cardboard armchair with an awning made of Styrofoam takeout boxes. Atnafu let my daughter draw on it with a pen. Together they nailed on a decorative bottle cap. When I ask my daughter what they do together, she shrugs. "Play with keys," she says, or, "I weared his watch."

He continues Amharic lessons, reading to her from a book. He taught her how to find chalky white stones and draw on the driveway with them. He feeds her unidentifiable fruits that fall from a tree so high they seem to drop from the clouds.

They sit with Atnafu's radio between them tuned into Amharic talk radio. Or they listen to Ethiopian pop music on his phone. Sometimes they sing, "Let it Go" from the movie *Frozen*. Neither knows the words. "Weddy go, weddy go," they harmonize. My daughter rests her hand on Atnafu's knee and her cheek against his windbreaker as they sing. She thinks this is beautiful and hilarious, and it is.

When the temperature drops to a certain degree only Atnafu can intuit, he sends my daughter to fetch her jacket. "Jacket," along with "hello," "thank you," and "generator" constitute the entirety of his English vocabulary.

Our maroon gate has become a neighborhood hangout. The driver who works for a Japanese family on the corner, a man who delivers crates of coke in his small red car to the building across the street, and our neighbor's guard, Belay, are regulars. I call them the cinderblock club. A cook from the nearby pizza place parks his prayer mat at our curb at 4:00 p.m. most days and prays.

Sometimes the chanting from the church and the call to prayer from the mosque meet in the air above our home and weave together so we can't tell which is which. These men race my daughter down the street. They play a game she made up in which they all shriek "Go Belay! Go Belay!" and run around in semi-circles. They pull apart woven plastic bags and use the shreds to tie sticks together into toy weapons.

Just as I was getting used to my toddler having street adventures that don't include me, she announced one day when I returned home from work, "Bekele gave me gum." She showed off a small rectangle of Trident in her palm. "Who the heck is Bekele?" I ask. "The man in the peach taxi," she answered as if it was obvious and not at all concerning.

I have yet to meet Bekele, but I know how often he passes our house by the frequency of my daughter's gum chewing. My expat friends are once again aghast. Substitute the Trident for candy and the "peach taxi" for a white van, and we have the cautionary tale we all attended elementary school assemblies about. So they have a point. But a point is all it is. In reality, a man I don't know gives my kid gum that is not poisoned and does not abduct her after. End of non-traumatizing story.

I could stop it if I want. I could lock the gate and hide the key. Forbid my daughter from hanging out in the street with a bunch of men I largely do not know. I can, but I don't. I am not raising my child in the United States, and although she loves Thanksgiving pie and Fourth of July fireworks as much as the next person, she is American by citizenship only.

When I left Congo for a new job, I wanted my daughter, Congolese by birth and heritage, to at least stay on the continent. While there is a danger in viewing Africa as a monolith, and Congo and Ethiopia are vastly different countries, staying in Africa has allowed my daughter not to be the only black child in her preschool class. It has allowed her to be a four-hour plane ride from her birth country, something I plan to take advantage of while we are here. And it has allowed her to grow up in a place where children are the community's to teach, and to love, and to give gum without giving a damn about parental permission.

The men get quiet whenever I open the gate. My daughter drops her chin when I call her inside for dinner, and before we've even made it to the door, she asks when she can go out again. I am not a part of the cinderblock club, and I don't need to be. I don't have to worry constantly what my daughter is doing when I can't see her, and can instead do the dishes, pour a drink, and get another bottle ready for Atnafu's collection.

Atnafu may lock us out sometimes, disconcertingly rifle through our trash, and destroy the lawn with his gardening efforts. He is unlikely to protect us from a physical threat in the off chance one presents itself or even hear it coming. But then I think about my daughter in the cinderblock easy chair, surrounded by gentle souls who zip her jacket all the way to the top, listen to her, race her, and always have a place for her to sit. Atnafu might not be a good guard, but the security he provides is unparalleled.

Sara Ackerman is a writer and a kindergarten teacher. Her writing has appeared in Creative Nonfiction, Brain Child, and River Teeth, The New York Times, and The Washington Post.

CHAPTER 20

THE OTHER SIDE OF ADOPTION

Cecile Dash
Nationality: Dutch
Parented in: The Republic of Congo

Breda, the Netherlands, 1990

I don't think I remember exactly how or when I was told, because I was only seven years old at the time. As a family, we were preparing for the arrival of two newcomers, my new brother and sister from Port-au-Prince, Haiti. This strange lady came to the house to observe us, and my mother told me that this woman would decide if our family was suitable for adoption.

Strange when you think about it—any woman can get pregnant and put a baby into this world, no questions asked—but if you want to adopt, the process is endless. I understand why this is important but at the same time, I feel it is a bit excessive. Especially for my parents, who already had four children, the adoption agency had a hard time under-standing why they wanted more.

I am the eldest, and I already had three sisters, so with our new brother and sister coming there were going to be six of us! My parents got the green light and were stamped "suitable for adoption." Slowly the date approached and then changed again and again. We received their pictures and names, but those changed a few times too. My father had visited the orphanage in Haiti and had made a video while he was there. My sisters and I watched this endlessly as this was all the information we had. My parents found an organization called *Le sourir d'un enfant* (the smile of a child) that was based in Brussels, Belgium and dealt with adoptions through this orphanage. My parents wanted two children and did not specify ages or gender; for all they knew we could end up with two 16-year-old boys. This was not the case, though.

My mother was getting the room ready for my new brother, my room to be exact. My new sister would share a room with my youngest two sisters. So my new brother got my room and my bed, and myself and yet another sister had to share a room. I then had to sort through my toys and make three piles, which I did. My mother then took one pile and put it in a box, telling me that she would send it to the orphanage in Haiti, the middle pile went to my new brother and sister and the last pile I got to keep. I never got to pick out my favorite toys! (At the age of seven, I did not understand what she was doing.) Thankfully, my grandmother understood, and she saved my precious doll from the bag that was going to Haiti and kept her safe for years.

Before the adoption, the same lady came to interview my grandparents and other relatives to get more information about us. My grandparents on my mother's side told the woman that perhaps we should just buy a new car instead of spending so much money on adopting two children. The other grandparents were a little upset about the fact that our family name would now continue in a race of different color. Coming from a colonial Indonesian background, this was hard to accept for my grandfather. As you can imagine, my parents must have been so proud of their parents at this moment.

After a long wait, my parents finally received the date on which my new brother and sister would arrive at Brussels Charleroi Airport. All we knew was that my sister, Isnada, was three years old and had spent most of her life in the orphanage. My brother Joseph was five years old and had been in the orphanage for about a year. Oh, and that they both spoke a different language: Creole, sort of like French, but with a twist. The full explanation of the Creole language is another story, but do look it up, as it is fascinating.

The waiting at the airport seemed to take forever; not sure if I made this up in my mind or if their flight was delayed. We met another Dutch couple at the airport who were waiting for three children from the same orphanage.

Then finally, we saw a woman with lots of children passing through customs, and from what I could see the children looked beautiful. They had dresses on made from lace and were wearing shiny black shoes. I have always wanted a pair of those, but my mother would never allow for me to have such shoes. The boys were wearing dress shirts and pantaloons.

I cannot seem to remember our actual "first" introduction, but I do remember trying to get Isnada, my new sister, to let go of another girl who came off the plane with her. The girls were both screaming as my mom, and the other Dutch lady were trying to take home their new daughters. It was heartbreaking. I also vividly remember the drive home and how my new sister kept throwing up. The smell in the car was unbearable.

The next months were all about us adjusting as a family, and my parents had asked our friends and family to give us the time and space to do so. These months were the hardest as we didn't speak the same language. Isnada and Joseph were both extremely malnourished, and many hospital visits followed. In the end, the entire family went on a diet of mainly soup and white bread so that Joseph and Isnada could slowly adjust and process "regular" food. All other food was hidden in the house, as they would eat themselves to death if they found it.

For the first two weeks, I was persistent to keep my room and my bed and would quietly get out of bed after my parents went to sleep and crawled into my own bed with Joseph. I finally realized they were here to stay and stopped doing this. Joseph would wake up almost every night and scream different things that none of us understood. My father finally figured out he was asking (screaming) for water. Once he realized he could drink the water from the tap, this stopped too.

My mother taught us only to give them things if they repeated the Dutch word for it, and within no time, they could speak Dutch. After six months, my parents finally felt like we had become a family of eight. So to celebrate, we had a dinner with pots and pans on the table, something that we couldn't do in the beginning. My father was dishing out the food and asked us who wanted to go first. My sister Renee replied, "Well, how about you serve the guests first," pointing at Joseph and Isnada. I guess we still needed some more time.

Time does a lot as it has almost erased my memory from those first months; it feels as if they were always with us. I am not sure if my parents asked me to look after all of my siblings, or if being the eldest just made me feel more responsible for them. Today, that weight of responsibility is something that I am proud of and struggle with at the same time. God forbid something happens to any of my sisters or brother, and they fail to inform me about it! I get furious! Why? I don't know really.

We fought each other all the time, and with six children you can actually have different sides/teams. So we were always busy bribing others to be on "our" side. However, when challenged by an outsider, we became one very large and strong team. You did not want to get in a fight with one of my sisters or brother, as you knew the other five would follow.

We were incredibly sensitive to racism, wow! Any comment just hinting at racism, we were on it. Yes, unfortunately, this still happens. One time our family was coming back from a summer vacation and on the way back my parents were trying to find a *Zimmerfrei* (bed-and-breakfast) in Germany for us to spend the night. My father left us in the car and went in asking if they had rooms available. No problem, they had rooms—until they saw us. Now, we were already uber-sensitive toward racism so whether they changed their minds after seeing six children or the mix of races between us we will never know.

A lot has happened over the years, but I found that six children equaled six times the amount of fun but also six times the amount of shit happening. Despite it all, we are a team. A family.

Needless to say, all grandparents came around after Isnada and Joseph arrived and welcomed them into the family with love. I truly believe that the concept of adoption scared them more than anything, as this was new to them.

Pointe Noire, the Republic of Congo, 2014

We are on our way to the ministry to meet the "judge" who will give us the first baby for Mwana Villages. My friend, Cheryl, opened up an orphanage in Pointe Noire, the Republic of Congo in May 2014. I was helping her, and since the orphanage was ready to open, she now needed babies. This is where the judge comes in, she is the one that decides whether you as an organization are suitable enough to take in these orphans.

The judge had already visited the orphanage as part of her inspection and was pleasantly surprised by it. She even asked if her grandson could come here during the week. So all went well with the judge, and now we had to wait. Then the call came, and Cheryl called me, "We can pick up the first baby today; will you come with me?" Yes, of course I will!

This felt so strange and special, I truly felt honored to be a part of this. You go to a ministry knowing that you will leave again with a baby! Not just a baby, but a baby that is (from what we understood) only two days old, was found on the side of the street with the umbilical cord still attached and no information on the family whatsoever. It was hard to wrap my head around this. Cheryl would be responsible for this tiny baby, and I felt proud to be with her that day.

We arrived and went up three flights of stairs and then entered a hallway where we were told to wait. I am not sure what I had expected but certainly not a busy office building where everyone went on about their work, lines in front of every door, and of course no air conditioning. We are here to pick up a baby? Why are we waiting? Surely this is a priority case? No, silly me, it is not!

After waiting for at least an hour, we were asked to step into the judge's office, while another lady left to get the baby. There she was—only a day or two old and so tiny.

She had the most precious eyes, and yes, I was in love! I decided there and then that I would take her home with me. Cheryl and I stood there, crying, and fussing over this beautiful baby girl. Cheryl named her Grace, and when we left, I got to hold her.

One of the helpers of the orphanage was waiting for us downstairs by the car, and while Cheryl was on the phone, I told him I would take Grace home with me. He looked confused, and this could have been due to two reasons: 1) he didn't understand my disjointed French and 2) he thought I was crazy.

He looked over at Cheryl and then back at me. Oh man, if I was going to continue to help Cheryl I had to toughen up, as I couldn't take every baby home with me. But believe me, I so badly wanted to! My daughter was newly potty-trained, and I had so much baby stuff. I could easily do this! Poor Grace, she was so little, and the car seat was so large that it felt wrong putting her in it. We decided to hold her instead.

Over the next few months more and more babies slowly came to the orphanage. Then there was Amandine, this little (almost) two-year-old, who was so sick and so malnourished her hair was falling out. We picked her up from a different orphanage that couldn't handle the cost of her medical care, and so she came to live at Mwana. She was barely alive and slept in my arms the whole ride back. Among some others, Amandine has a very special place in my heart. I watched this child go from almost dying to becoming a fun, cheeky toddler with a very strong will. It was a struggle to get her to eat, and then she started biting her own arm, leaving big marks, from stress. This little girl looked so stressed, even when asleep, in the first few months. She reminded me of my own sister, Isnada. A tough but sweet little girl with an incredible survival instinct. This was the first time I realized I was now on the other side...the side where children get adopted from. After this realization I became quite emotional whenever I visited Mwana Villages.

I have seen children, and babies come and go, and I admire the strength of the mamas working there, as for me it became harder and harder. I formed such strong bonds with some of the children, and after seeing them off, I felt heartbroken. I am not sure why, as they went on to better lives with new families. These experiences made me realize that I could never adopt, though a part of me feels I should, especially being brought up in a family with two adopted children. But if I am being completely honest, I don't think I can.

We bring home one of the orphans once a week for a playdate and swimming lesson, and my children keep asking me, why can't he stay? I can't answer this question, and therefore avoid having to answer it. My children see no problem; they count the beds, are willing to divide their toys, and really know how to sell it.

Adoption can be a beautiful thing, but like everything else, it also has its dark side. I have seen both my brother and sister struggle with different aspects in life. To me, without going into too much detail, it feels that a big part of that struggle is due to the fact they were either abandoned or adopted. I wouldn't want to go through with adoption with the realization that this could also happen to my family.

Now, more than ever I realize how brave my parents were, and I am proud of what they did.

Never in a million years did I think moving to Congo as an expat mom would have such an impact on me. An emotional journey that has shown me "the other side" of adoption! Thank you, Congo!

Cecile Dash is a mom, volunteer, English teacher and yes, another mother blogger who put aside her professional career three years ago when an opportunity presented itself for her family to move to the Republic of Congo. Living the expat life in Central Africa has been both challenging and fun, and Cecile quickly established a new and very different life. She began keeping a journal from the first day, and some of her stories were previously published in the anthology Once Upon An Expat. Cecile continues to share her writing with the world through her blog at www.supermomabroad.com.

CHAPTER 21

BABY POLLUTION JAIL

Cristina Pop
Nationality: Romanian and French
Knocked up in: Austria, France, and China
Birthed in: Austria
Parented in: China

The day we arrived in Beijing with our two-month-old baby, the pollution was thick. I was almost unable to see through the window of our car on the way from the airport. It was my worst fear: being stuck inside our apartment with my baby because of the bad air.

And I was. Five long days. Each morning I woke up, looked outside, and returned straight to bed. The Air Quality Index (AQI) was climbing—250, 300, and then 350. One hundred particle mass at 2.5.

Before I moved to Beijing, I was pollution innocent. I didn't know the meaning of AQI. I didn't know that the microparticles of 2.5 millimeters (the numbers after the particle mass) can stick in our lungs. Into our baby's lungs.

I learned very fast how to evaluate the AQI just by looking out the window of our flat. I knew for sure that if I saw the mountains of the Great Wall, the air quality was under 50. Freedom! I could take my baby out for a walk; the air was clean. If I could see the Ritan Parc (the Park of the Temple of the Sun) in a milky fog, then the AQI was around 150, which for me meant no walk in the park, but possibly a short trip to the shop on the corner. And if I couldn't see the buildings in front of our window then it was bad, really bad: 300 or more.

"What does the app say?" (Yes, we had an app for air pollution.) This was often the first thing I said to my husband, Nicolas, even before saying, "Good morning."

Baby Pollution Jail aka BPJ was how we described it among the mothers in Beijing. On these days, we would wake up, look out the window, and go straight back to bed. What's the point in getting dressed anyway? The air was too polluted to get outside with a baby. Sometimes we took bets before looking at the app, "How much do you think it is today?"

340

340?

Yes, another day inside.

Living in Asia was my dream. For four years Nicolas and I traveled to South Asia, discovering Indonesia, Malaysia, Laos, Thailand, and Singapore. It was our passion in common. One day, when we had just come back from Laos, a trip that we both enjoyed immensely I said, "Why don't we just move somewhere in Asia?"

At that time we had been living in Vienna, Austria for three years, and we were bored. Vienna is the No. 1 city in Mercer's Quality of Living Ranking, and I just couldn't get it. Why? Restaurants close at 10 p.m.; bars close at midnight; and there is nobody on the street on a winter evening at 6 p.m. Coming from hectic and restless Paris, I kept wondering to myself, "*Where are the people?*"

In reality, I was missing my life in Paris, a city with the same number of inhabitants as all of Austria. I lived in Paris for seven years before I met Nicolas. It was a funny story. I was the Romanian woman with dual citizenship (French and Romanian) living in France, and he was the French guy living in Romania. Beautiful mirroring—that's how we met.

After one year of continuing round trips between Paris and Bucharest, we moved together to Vienna. We split the geographical distance—fair enough. Our life in Vienna was peaceful, but we were longing for more adventure and curious about living on a different continent.

So when Nicolas walked in the door from work one evening in January and said the word "China," I immediately said, "Let's go!" In one second I forgot about my two years of struggle to create and run my own company and build a name as a life coach in Vienna. About the nine months of intensive German lessons and our plans to have a baby and live peacefully in a house with garden. Aye!

We had decided to get married in July in Vienna, but since Nicolas' new position was supposed to start the following year, we thought we had one year to prepare for our move to China. But things began to accelerate, and Nicolas was expected to start his contract earlier—in May.

Ten days before our wedding in July, I traveled to Paris to look for a wedding dress. A bit late you may think? Well, we were planning on a small and casual wedding, and one of my friends was a designer, so I knew I would find a beautiful "regular dress" in her workshop (to wear a "regular dress" at my wedding was important for me). And since I had a whole week to spend in Paris, I decided to make an appointment with my gynecologist and have a medical check-up because I didn't trusted my doctor in Vienna at that time. I couldn't believe my ears when she turned on the ultrasound and told me, "This is the heartbeat of your baby."

I had to fight the urge to call Nicolas or send him the picture of the ultrasound and text, "Guess what?" I wanted to tell him in person. As soon as the arrival gates of Schwechat Airport in Vienna opened, I whispered (or maybe shouted?) "I'm pregnant!" I should have known then that a pregnancy announcement made at an airport would lead to a frequent flyer baby. Since that day, we have flown together 54 times: 28 times in utero and 26 times within the first 13 months of her life.

After our wedding, I went to Beijing to see our new home. I was very excited about this new adventure and very curious about China. But I was two months pregnant and constantly felt like I was on a boat in a stormy sea, suffering from constant nausea. The new environment, with strongly fragranced malls and lobbies, exotic smelling fruits (like durians), and pipe-scented streets was exhausting! On top of it all, taking the subway with thousands of people on hot summer days made me feel suddenly claustrophobic.

The day I arrived in Beijing, the air pollution was very high. My app showed an AQI over 300, "hazardous air quality." It was hot and humid. Nicolas had already made an appointment for us to see a gynecologist of an international clinic called International SOS and discuss the birth. I had a wonderful doctor from Venezuela, and she spent around two hours doing a medical check-up, answering all my questions (I had dozens), and trying to reassure me about life in China. In the meantime, I Googled "food scandals in China,"—bad idea!

She didn't really manage to reassure me 100%. Quite the contrary. She mentioned that International SOS does not recommend to their clients to give birth in Mainland China for two reasons: difficulties in having access to blood transfusion in case of an emergency, and the lack of Neonatal Intensive Care Units in international clinics. This meant that in the case of an emergency, a newborn would be transferred to a local hospital, and therefore the mother and the baby would be separated for days or even weeks. I knew from an experience in another Asian country what it is like to be in a hospital where communication in the local language is a real issue. There are moments in life when misunderstandings due to language are cute and funny, and then there are others that can be very scary.

Plus, the idea of natural birth and breastfeeding had already entered my mind, and I knew that I needed to be in an environment and a culture that supported both aspects. Thanks to Google again, I discovered that China had one of the highest rate of C-sections in the world—which was, again, not exactly compatible with my choice of natural birth.

We left her office completely lost: Where do I give birth if not in China? Particularly since we wanted to experience the process of giving birth together, as we would be living in China.

When I came back from my trip to Beijing and entered our flat in Vienna, I went straight to the window, opened it, breathed in the clean air, turned on the tap, and drank a huge glass of spring water (yes, in Vienna, the tap water is spring water). At that moment, I suddenly understood why Vienna is ranked No. 1 in Mercer's Quality of Living Rankings.

It dawned on me that I actually enjoyed living in Vienna (despite the fact that restaurants close at 10 p.m.) and how much I absolutely loved simple things: eating organic, local food, drinking spring water from the tap, swimming in the Danube, and hiking in the Alps within an hour's car ride. I lived my entire childhood in the countryside, surrounded by trees, mountains, and fresh air, and it took me 20 years to realize how important these things were to me. I sat down on the floor surrounded by boxes for the move...and cried...and cried. I saw no escape. We were past the point of no return. The movers were coming in three weeks, our flat in Vienna was terminated, and we had already rented a new one in Beijing. Nicolas had already started his job, my company was almost closed, and we no longer had health insurance in Austria.

For three weeks I kept dreaming and picturing our life as if I could give birth in Austria, have a natural birth like many of my friends in Vienna, and stroll with them in the parks. To complicate things further, my friend introduced me to her midwife, Magalie. As soon as we met, I knew that she would be the perfect midwife to support me through my birth. She was French but working in Vienna for a while, so she knew the system very well and spoke both languages. She understood exactly the kind of birth I wanted, and I felt she would be the perfect birth partner for me, along with my husband.

In Austria, midwives have an extended power, especially compared to France. In many public hospitals, they support women through the whole birthing process without being seconded by an OB/GYN. Nevertheless, in hospitals and clinics, at least one doctor and an anesthesiologist are on duty, just in case a C-section is necessary. Birth is considered to be a normal state, and it's expected to evolve naturally unless something goes wrong, in which case they turn to the latest medical technology to take over. That was exactly my way of approaching birth. Suddenly, I felt at home in that culture, just as we were about to leave.

Once we realized that Austria was the perfect place for this birth, we started having discussions with our health insurance provider. Because birthing in Beijing was not recommended by our medical assistance, our health insurance offered to send me to others cities in Asia considered to be in accordance with what they called "international health care standards." Luckily for me all of the clinics they suggested were much more expensive than a natural birth package in Vienna. So after they weighed the pros and cons, they finally decided to cover the birth costs in Austria. We were over the moon.

At the beginning of December, on a cold winter day, I moved back to Vienna to a small rented apartment. After experiencing 28 flights—many long-distance flights—during my pregnancy, it was time for me to settle down. Nicolas arrived two weeks later, and we spent our winter holidays as usual in the beautiful Alps. After New Year's Eve, I stayed alone in Vienna as Nicolas returned to Beijing for work, but I was busy preparing for my natural birth.

My only concern was the arrival of our baby: Will she wait until Nicolas returns to Vienna? She did. Nicolas arrived on a Friday evening, and the next morning my contractions started. We continued our normal routine as long as possible: We went for long walks, we bought the last things we needed for the baby, and had a delicious Viennese breakfast in one of our favorite restaurants under huge palm trees and sunlight. All this time I was in labor. My wish was to stay as much as possible at home and go to the clinic only for the delivery. When con-tractions started to become close and perfectly timed, I called my midwife, Magalie. She came to our home and we decided together it was time to head to the clinic.

Everything was so peaceful and quiet when we entered the old Viennese-style building at 2 a.m. Almost all of the lights were out in the clinic. It was as if the entire building was sleeping. I heard the sound of our feet pattering on the old wooden floor. Magalie, had arrived just before us, and together with her two colleagues that night, they prepared everything: Perfect temperature in the room, the bathtub with hot water and candles, a small night-light in the delivery room, essential oils. No other woman was giving birth that night, so we had Magalie and two other midwives dedicated to my birth. They played my CD with hypnotherapy music I had been using to prepare myself for the birth over the past six months.

When we arrived at the clinic, I thought that I would give birth very quickly, but it turned out that my baby needed six hours of intensive labor. I was exhausted at the end, but I didn't ask for an epidural. I had a moment of doubt around 4 a.m. because we were heading toward the birth so slowly and my contractions had started 48 hours before. But Nicolas told me, "I think you can do it without." It gave me the strength to continue.

I don't remember much of these last hours; everything was a bit blurred, but I do remember that when the sunbeams entered the room, our daughter came into the world—just like in my dreams. Magalie asked me if I wanted to pull her out. My hands were there to welcome her into the world, and I put her on my chest. I still remember the very first moment when I touched her and pulled her out of my body. Her wet but very hot skin, her little body a bit slippery, her big eyes looking for mine. She stayed with us the whole time, sleeping on our chests. The next day we went back to our rented Viennese apartment.

We moved back to Beijing when our daughter was two months old. I felt so alone, isolated, and lost. The whole city looked haunted on polluted days, like in a bad science fiction movie. I stayed inside endlessly. Sometimes up to 10 days in a row.

That was the general recommendation new expat moms received when arriving in China: During polluted days, you need to stay indoors with all your air purifiers running. How do we define "polluted"? Well, I have found out that this definition was very subjective. Officially the air is considered "good" when the AQI is below 50, but when you live in a city where the average AQI is 150, this seems like a challenging goal.

Some people were very strict and stayed indoors as soon as the air was officially considered unhealthy for sensitive groups of people (like babies), which is anything above 100. Others ventured out even when the AQI was 300 or 400 (considered "hazardous"). I was part of the "strict moms" group, and I didn't want to take any risks for my baby.

But my decision to stay indoors whenever the AQI was above 100 meant I was trapped inside our flat without seeing anybody except for my baby, my husband, and occasionally our building's Chinese cleaning woman who sometimes popped in to take the garbage. Despite only speaking a few words of Chinese, I was looking forward to these rare interactions with someone from the "outside world." She had a warm smile, and I was desperately happy to see her.

The days were long. From our apartment I sometimes couldn't see anything except for the pollution cloud, a thick cloud—sometimes a bit yellow, sometimes gray, sometimes milky.

There is no shortage of things to do with a baby in Beijing and interesting people to meet. I found such a warm and supportive community of mothers in Beijing and many fun activities with babies: gym, yoga, baby massage, playdates, music workshops, and Montessori workshops. But very often I had to cancel the appoint-ments. I would wake up and anxiously, impatiently wait to see if the air would improve. Sometimes there was a pleasant surprise—wind from the mountains might rise and blow the pollution to the sea. However, frequently canceling my meetings due to the poor air quality made a void around me. After a while, many people stopped suggesting we meet up. And my friends, who like me were very cautious about the air quality, were trapped indoor as well. This added frustration to my increasing isolation.

Being stuck inside with a curious baby who loved interacting with people for 10 days in a row was beyond challenging. I rose up against those days. I was angry. I was scared. I was desperate. I wanted to go out. Breathe. Just breathe. I wanted to run on the grass. Touch the trees. Listen to the wind. But around me, the milky air smelled like metal. I felt as if my head was being crushed under a heavy hammer. Migraines. I started to have them all of the time. Sometimes, I had difficulty breathing. The effects of the pollution were manifesting in real ways, and I began to worry. Not only for me but my baby.

I surrendered. The air pollution was stronger than me. I even started to enjoy the quiet days indoors. The strange ambiance where I couldn't distinguish the buildings from the sun and the sky. It was just the two of us—my baby and me. Like being suspended in time and space. It was peaceful inside where it was safe.

On those days, the phone vibrated continuously. All the others moms were on WeChat, a popular texting app in China. People (mostly moms and few dads) chatted frantically, "I'm sorry, I can't make it to the playdate today, we are in BPJ (Baby Pollution Jail) again." "How do you get your bread delivered?" "Which activities do you recommend to keep an 18-month-old interested while indoors?" "He is playing football in the living room—help!" "What is the pollution forecast for tomorrow?"

When I realized that we are talking about air pollution as if it was the weather, I really started to worry. Am I going to get used to thinking this is normal? Am I going to describe these days as "foggy"?

One day someone messaged me about a tool that measures the air quality inside the flat. We bought the laser-powered air quality monitoring tool and placed it our baby's room. My heart sank. It was almost the same level of pollution inside her room as it was outside. I thought we were safe inside; we were not. Now I understood where my migraines came from. I thought that by staying in my pollution jail I was protecting my baby, but I realized that the hundreds of hours spent indoors were useless. I might as well go outside. After all, it was no safer inside as it was outside.

The next day we bought very powerful air purifiers. I researched information on air pollution and related illnesses and symptoms. I learned about asthma and cancer and many other risks. But with the new air purifiers, we managed to keep the air clean inside. I started to smile again, and I felt safe with my little laser machine that showed me the air quality wherever we went.

Then winter came. In China, on the north side of the Yangtze River, the official heating system is turned on on November 15, no matter how cold it is outside. But I noticed that our apartment felt a bit warmer in the morning after some very cold days. The AQI on our little laser machine started to skyrocket. Once again, the air was as bad inside as it was outside despite all of our new air purifiers running on maximum speed. One day I placed our daughter in the smallest room with three big air purifiers inside. It was as loud as a Boeing 777, and the air was still unhealthy. There was no escape anymore. I felt trapped and desperate, but I didn't give up.

I hired a consulting company in air pollution—very popular among expats in Beijing. They came to our apartment, measured the air quality everywhere, and searched for leaks and pollution sources. After a week of measuring and researching, we discovered that the building had an unofficial heating system that ventilated polluted air through leaks in the walls and ceiling into the flats. We spent a fortune and sealed the whole apartment, and purchased hospital-grade professional air purifiers designed for Chinese levels of pollution. Only then did the air start to improve.

Since our building was supposed to have an air-purifying system for the building, I met with the manager to try to understand why it was not working. After several meetings, she admitted that they did have filters in their ventilation system, but that they hadn't been changed for years (aha?) and they didn't intend to change them anytime in the near future. Oh? Well, then.

A reversed climatization system heated our flat. When the official heating system was turned on in the winter, the polluted air from outside was pushed directly through our heating system in the flat—coming through the air vent just above our beds. Pollution during the winter was increased because homes in Beijing were heated with coal. Nicolas and I finally decided to take a radical action.

Our daughter and I left China.

It was not an easy decision. We knew that each move was a significant disruption in our lives and our baby's life. We had already experienced numerous moves and knew the challenges they posed. However, the known (and unknown) challenges of a nomadic life were not greater than risking the health of our baby. My daughter and I lived in France for a month and then we moved to South Korea. Nicolas worked in Beijing and traveled to Seoul every weekend to be with us. Being a single mom in Seoul was another massive challenge in my life, but we were free...to breathe and go outside.

The night we flew over Beijing and left the city forever, the AQI reached 1,000.

Cristina Pop has lived in Romania, France, Austria, China and South Korea and she always has a hard time answering the question "Where are you from?" She is a life coach, and she supports expatriates, expat partners, and their kids through the great adventure of living abroad: finding their identity and what makes them come alive. Her greatest adventures, parenting and nomadic life, brought her to create Mothers Abroad, a blog where she reports from the trenches of motherhood while navigating different cultures and where she invites mothers to share their wisdom and their stories. Cristina is now preparing to move to Germany and start it all over again. You can follow what happens next and connect with her on www.mothers-abroad.com.

CHAPTER 22

THREE COUNTRIES AND SEVEN
APARTMENTS IN TWELVE MONTHS

Sarah Hansen
Nationality: American
Knocked up in: India and Hong Kong
Birthed in: India
Parented in: India, Hong Kong, and Switzerland

Everyone always asks me, "How did a nice girl from Minnesota end up in Beijing?" I tell them, I studied Mandarin in college and when an internship opportunity came up to work in Beijing with a corporate sponsor for the Beijing 2008 Olympics and during the spring and summer of 2007, I jumped on the opportunity. I ended up meeting my husband in Beijing. After moving from Minnesota, where the majority is blued-eyed and of Scandinavian descent, I found a Swede in China. After three years we were more than just friends, and I followed him to India, and that's where we started our family.

Being pregnant in India was blissful in terms of fantastic food to eat, but not in terms of culture shock. Luckily I found a doctor I liked and a prenatal and labor coach who told me to prepare for the birth culture in India and to discuss a birth plan as soon as possible. For example, it is mandatory that women shave their hair down there and take an enema before birthing in a hospital. Episiotomies are routine, and IVs are mandatory. We still do not know all of what was put in the IV.

I remember standing in line at the private hospital for hours for ultrasounds and blood work. I will not go into more details about the health care system in Chennai in 2012 because it still upsets me. At the end of the whole thing, though, our perfect little boy was born, and we forgot anything else. Oh, and my mother was flown out to be there for support—best decision ever, even though she burned most of the food she made for us.

We brought our baby home after one night in the hospital, which we had to fight for since it's the law that women have to stay for four days and this surprised everyone, but when we got home, we could finally relax. He was very alert and an absolute joy. When he was around four months old, we joined a playgroup with other babies, and when a journalist came and observed, she decided to write an article featuring him and how we bonded during play. He started making up a kind of language around this age as well and would "talk" to us. Unfortunately, his language never progressed into real words, and by age two, he still only had about 10 words he used, and he started to become frustrated with the way this limited his interactions and play. He was evaluated by an American speech pathologist in India, and she recommended speech therapy, which he did three to five times per week, and which really did not improve the speaking at all. It did make him happy to have the attention, though, and he learned to control his oral muscles to a better degree.

We were told by everyone who met our son not to worry and that he was obviously only language-confused since he had three languages at home: English, Swedish, and Hindi (we had moved near Mumbai when he was 10 months old). He was very social and happy nonetheless. I became pregnant with our second son on the day of his birthday, which was planned! So, during the next months I found out that the hospital in Pune, India where we lived would not abide or agree to the *International Pregnant Women's Bill of Rights*, so I found a midwife and doctor team recommended through friends, and my best friend was able to get us a discount at a five-star hotel suite to live in for a couple of weeks around my due date.

I ended up having the birth I wanted and was extremely lucky to have had a water birth in a neonatal hospital in Mumbai. My husband's mother came to help and ended up doing all the Christmas baking, since he was born a month before Christmas. Soon after my cousin, who is a chef, came and continued the cooking. It was truly a pampered experience to have gourmet meals prepared and a refrigerator full of food.

Two days after our new baby was born, we found out that we were moving to Switzerland! To say goodbye to India, all of our friends there, and all the moments and highs and lows were a little too much to take in. It took about six months to get all the paperwork and visas in order—including getting a new passport for the baby, with the perfect newborn headshot with both eyes open, both ears showing, on a white backdrop.

Living in India had some perks. Even though we did not have great access to speech therapists and early intervention programs, I did have a housekeeper who came every day to do the dishes and laundry and help me cook. Another woman came to clean every day, and I had a driver and a part-time nanny to help in the afternoons after our little one came home from nursery school. I had full support in every aspect, except for medical professionals.

Our almost three-year-old was not progressing much with speech, and friends, doctors, and professionals all reassured us that he would speak soon. Around the time we moved to the serviced apartments to prepare for the move, his behavior became increasingly difficult and again was explained away by adjusting to being a big brother and the move. By the time we finally arrived in Zurich, I had reached my wit's end. Our pride and joy turned three, and two months later we moved to Switzerland.

The contrasts between Switzerland and India are stark, and his whole world was ripped out from under him, not to mention he was still dealing with the new responsibility of becoming a big brother. He lost his friends, nanny, teachers, and all the people who adored him. Indian culture is so welcoming to children. Almost everywhere we went, he got attention and loving cheek pinches.

The move across the world did not do much for his speech, and often his tantrums lasted hours. Anything could set him off, tidying up toys, transitioning to a new activity, dinnertime, not getting to wear the right shirt, having to walk when he was tired or not interested in moving.

It got to the point where I could only leave the house with him once a day to avoid public meltdowns and tantrums. His concentration was intense, so he did seem to love to play indoors and could play alone for hours. His speech therapists in Zurich were confused. He was obviously not autistic since he made eye contact and was social, but his speech was not classic apraxia. After visiting different speech therapists, private practice and through the government, it became clear that we needed to act fast and start him on a kind of behavior therapy that is used with autistic children to help them learn to speak.

The realization that our little boy could be negatively affected the rest of his life if we didn't get him proper help was the scariest thing we have faced as parents. We have family members who have Autism Spectrum Dis-orders and are nonverbal at eight and 11 years old. We knew this might be a possibility for our son, and we were desperate to find an early intervention program.

After five months and not finding a therapy program in Zurich, Switzerland, or Central Europe with an English applied behavior therapy program, we started to consider that I would take the children to Hong Kong and start an intensive program for him there. Our close friends had helped their child immensely at this center, and it was run and overseen by experts in autism diagnosis and program management. We came to the right place and somehow got into a full-time program without the typical wait time of a few months or more.

On our third day in Hong Kong, we started a 30-hour a week program for him. He was now three and a half years old. In the beginning, he would only make vehicle sounds, *beeb beeb, weeooo weeoo*, etc. He was happy to have people to play with but did not like being told how and when he could play.

He would have tantrums multiple times a day and had to learn words and concepts from scratch. I think the realization that he did not understand language for me was when I observed him in session, and he could not identify the photo of a foot kicking a ball. I had always assumed he knew what we were talking about, but he was very good at following along with the social situation. And when he didn't know what was going on he retreated into playing alone with tantrums. I was so relieved that we had brought him to this center.

On the flip side, I had brought them to Hong Kong without my husband, since he had to stay and work in Switzerland. Thankfully his company was supportive, and during this time he flew to either Shanghai or Mumbai every two weeks and spent two weekends every month in Hong Kong with us. The commute every day was one hour each way, including a 25-minute ferry ride from Discovery Bay to central. In the beginning, the dreaded morning walks to the ferry included me having to drag our three-year-old screaming to the boat from our apartment while pushing a stroller with my almost one-year-old. We lived on a green island where cars were not allowed, only buses and golf carts. While this was a great way to live environmentally, it posed difficulties with two children under four years of age.

The progress with his speech was so fast and intensive that the therapy program became our only life. I started to become impatient. If he could make so much progress, then maybe it could go faster if the therapists did everything perfectly, and I continued the program at home. I had trouble sleeping more than five hours a night, and my nerves were wearing thin.

We also realized that our younger son, who at the time was 11 months old, was at risk for delayed language development as well, based on family history on both of our sides. Younger siblings are more likely to be on the spectrum. He was also not getting enough attention with the focus on his older brother at this time.

We had both the boys' brains scanned to look for abnormalities in the way they perceive stimuli. They both showed abnormalities consistent with high-functioning autism. Despite the scans' results, I still had a lot of questions and did not take this test too seriously.

Our youngest son started his own ABA therapy for six hours a week and immensely enjoyed it. He started talking and communicating on time, and we feel we trained his brain before any pathology showed.

Amazingly, he improved so much after three months that we felt we should continue the program and stay in Hong Kong. He was now talking in three-to-five-word sentences and the tantrums were getting less severe. After another three months, he was speaking in eight to 10-word sentences and rarely having tantrums and able to play with other children appropriately. After six months of the intensive ABA program, we felt it was time to move back to Switzerland and live as a family again. The timing was perfect in a way, since an ABA center in Zurich had just opened and was accredited through the government. We started to go through the formal process of having our older son diagnosed so we could apply for funding for his therapy, which we had spent about $70,000 on already in the past six months.

Through this process we were nervous. Was our little boy autistic? Did it matter? Was a speech disorder the only explanation for all of his complexities with learning the language and communicating with others? Was the problem with transitions and social cues and norms something he would outgrow or a life-long struggle? Getting an autism diagnosis would give us access to around $45,000 in the next two years but also shattered hope that this was just a childhood language disorder.

The whole process in Switzerland has been very thorough and efficient, with hours of observation, testing, interviews, IQ tests, and has now finally ended with an official diagnosis. Our little boy is on the autism spectrum. High-functioning, high-IQ, now verbal. Lots of promise, but still, hearing the words crushed my husband and I. We didn't know who to tell or how to take it.

Autism can now be cared for in many ways, but it is a lifelong struggle to understand social behavior and overcome rigidity in routines. Since our boy is high-functioning, he can blend in quite well with his peers, as long as he doesn't get overwhelmed. Then, an outburst or tantrum can still occur.

At football practice for four- and five-year-olds, he doesn't understand that he needs to go to the back of the line when he finishes kicking the ball. We hadn't taught him the concept yet, and he didn't learn it from being told or observation. He has a conflicting interest in looking at the way the light reflects through the window of the gymnasium, so he just doesn't even hear the words effectively, "Hey! Go to the BACK of the line...no, the BACK of the line." Say it a hundred more times and he won't get it. To him, he is standing at the line, and just behind it. That's what you mean, right? What exactly is the *back* of the line anyway?

At another practice, he saw two little boys having an argumentative play fight, and thought it looked fun to him to run and join the slapping game. He didn't realize they were only slapping hands, and he slapped the boys in the arms. They got mad, and the coach intervened. After the practice, the five-year-old boy asked me why my son was so mean to them. I explained that he is not mean, he just doesn't understand the rules yet.

It's especially tough because these are all new children, new parents; they don't know us, and we are making first impressions. Leaving India was difficult for us all, another country, another opportunity, but for a little boy to be exposed to so much and travel the world, three countries and seven apartments in 12 months has had a great impact on him.

However, he will have plenty of good stories to tell, how he used to come along with his mother to teach at a rural school in India. How he lived in Hong Kong and took a ferry to school every day. How he climbed the Alps in Switzerland and learned to ride a bike on Lake Zurich.

I believe that when he looks back at his childhood, he will say it was a good time.

Sarah Hansen was born in the US, and after studying Mandarin, she moved to Beijing, China to work setting up events for the 2008 Olympics. She eventually worked with Donatella Versace and other celebrities in Beijing. Since then, Sarah has lived in India, Hong Kong, and Switzerland. Along her expat journey, health and wellbeing have become a central focus for Sarah, and in 2014, she earned her Yoga Teaching Certificate in India. During her time in India, she taught yoga to children in the public school system and now supports a school in India to supply fresh drinking water. See her work at www.helayoga.com.

CHAPTER 23

UNEXPECTED ENCOUNTERS OF THE PLAYGROUND KIND

Olga Mecking
Nationality: Polish
Parented in: The Netherlands

As soon as I arrive at the playground, I know that something is wrong. I don't mean wrong in that creepy sort of way, just that things seem slightly off.

I scratch my head and look around. The equipment looks as usual; it seems to be in order. The kids who play at the playground make a pretty normal impression as well. I shrug my shoulders and am ready to let it slip. Maybe, in my sleep-deprived state, my imagination is playing tricks on me. I would not be surprised.

There are three other parents in attendance. As a way of introduction, I look up at one of them and smile. He smiles back. How nice, I think to myself. A father at the playground.

I move on to the next parent. Again, the same protocol: smile. Make your presence known. After all, I am lonely, and we just moved to this neighborhood. Maybe I can make friends? And then maybe my kids would have someone to play with on the days they don't go to daycare? Yes, I could really use that.

The parent in question—another father—looks at me and smiles back, after which he promptly returns to playing with his little Anne-Sophie or whatever her name is.

"This is weird," I am thinking, but am somewhat uplifted. I love this country!

The third parent is also male.

That's when it dawns on me that I am the only mom at the playground surrounded by fathers. I feel both happy and weird.

Happy because I am glad to see involved fathers. The moms must be at work or maybe at home either doing chores or simply doing sweet, sweet nothing. Or maybe they're meeting friends. But who cares, and why does it even matter what the moms are doing? Would I have the same questions if the parents at the playground were moms?

Weird because I am even having these thoughts. Why is that when I see three—I must add, smashing-looking—men chasing their equally cute kids around the playground that I suddenly feel so defensive?

"What are you doing on my turf?" I want to ask them. I shut off these thoughts. I am ashamed of them.

After all, in Poland, my father took me for walks in the park when I was little while my mom was working in the lab, or simply enjoying some time alone. Polish grannies at the park would give him the evil eye and silently judge him a child abuser or worse.

But here, in the Netherlands, I see real equality in action, and it bothers me for some reason that I can't pin it down. My situation is made even more awkward when my baby starts screaming. She's hungry, and I need to nurse her.

I open my shirt just enough to let her drink and pray to whatever powers that be that my wild eldest daughter will behave herself for the 15 minutes it takes me to breastfeed the baby, thus sparing me the embarrassment of having to run around the playground with one boob sticking out of my T-shirt.

Please, please, please, I pray. I really like this playground, but if something awkward happens, I can never come back here again. I am originally from Poland and have ancestors from all over the place, but I must, in reality, be British because I am just as polite as I am socially awkward.

Luckily, my toddler is on the swing, and I relax. The swing is good. She'll stay there for at least two hours. If she had her way, she'd live on a swing, and I'd let her if I could, because peace and quiet are everything to me. At the same time, I begin to feel proud. I can do something these fathers can't! If wasn't such a damn prude, I'd probably stick my boobs out even more, as if to say, *"You think you can do everything, don't you? Well, get over yourselves because you can't do that! You can't birth a baby, and you can't nourish it with your body!"*

The fathers ignore me, my breastfeeding, and my internal statement, of course. They're too busy chasing their kids around the playground.

And now everything becomes clear to me: I know why I was feeling so badly about the whole situation. I am jealous. Jealous as hell.

These dads are out-parenting me. They seem to have everything under control in a way I never seem to master. Their children are not having tantrums, they are behaving themselves and are basically much less work than my rambunctious toddler and the baby, who while of calm disposition is just a few weeks old and, just as infants like her are wont to do, screams a lot.

It probably didn't help that all of the fathers at the playground looked as if they spent more time on their looks in one day than I had done my whole life. While Dutch women are happy to sport jeans and T-shirts at all times (not to mention the ever-present boots), the men go for more courageous choices like red pants and pressed shirts.

Me, on the other hand, I look as if I just had a baby six weeks prior, which I had. I don't even remember what I wore that day, but I'm sure it must have had dried spit-up milk on it somewhere. My hair is probably its usual mess, and the blue bags under my eyes are the only colorful element on my face.

I am usually very low-maintenance when it comes to clothing, but having a baby is not the best thing you can do for your looks, and I look the part. But I wouldn't look as smartly dressed on the best of my days as these men were on that very normal day at the playground.

The fathers seem so confident, so calm and I, on the other hand, am a mess. Having a baby can do that to you, but for me, there was another reason for my lack of confidence in my parenting skills.

Just a few days prior, a woman called the police on me for my toddler's temper tantrum. The experience shook me to the core. Having the police called on you is already terrifying, but if it happens abroad, it is so much worse because you're considered an ambassador for your country and the rules of behavior are much stricter for you. I'm feeling very much under the microscope of Dutch parenting culture and afraid I am not measuring up.

Never again will I be able to go out in public with my children without praying they will behave themselves, or looking around me in search of someone who will judge me instead of helping me out. I will always be afraid of this happening again. Back to the playground, though.

The fathers behave as if they belong here, and they do. It is I who is an intruder—both in their country and on their playground.

Of course, I get over myself quickly. I even manage to make chitchat and say nice things about the kids. I read so many articles how weird and awkward fathers often feel at the playground. These fathers don't consider this weird at all.

Later, I realize that they must be taking what is known as *papadag*, daddy day. The idea is that Dutch fathers have one fixed day a week they can stay at home with their kids. My Dutch mom friends often mention the *papadag*, "My husband is with the kids while I work," or "We're spending this day as a family." Now my husband does the same.

He stays home Wednesdays, which very conveniently is the day the kids have short school days. No longer must I dread trying to figure out what to do with them while also trying to do house chores, cook, and work. Instead, we wait until the kids come back from school and take them for surprise day trips to the various cool places the Netherlands has to offer. Having this break in the middle of the week does wonders for the whole family.
I am grateful to live in a country where men and women are seen as equal.

This is not to say that sexism doesn't exist in the Netherlands. It does, and it happens on a very subtle level. I was talking to a friend who works as a guide in one of the Netherlands' most beautiful cities. She wanted to ask her boss for more responsibilities. The boss, herself female and a mother of two, answered, "Oh well, why would you want that? You're a mother already, maybe you'll have another child?" The next time my friend came back with several practical ideas she came up with and was told, "Oh these are great, I'll think about it. How's your family by the way?"

Women in the Netherlands want to have a good life, which for them means having the time for work, children, and other interests. But it also means that in compliance with the overall "just be normal" mentality, the social expectation for them is to work, but not too much. As a result, both stay-at-home mothers and women who consider their jobs to be their main priority may get scorned.

Not to mention that while the Netherlands is known for its short working hours (the shortest in Europe in fact), it's mostly women who cut back on work hours, especially after having kids.

According to The Economist, "More than half of the Dutch working population works part time, a far greater share than in any other rich-world country." With 75%, women are in the majority when it comes to part-time work, but 26.8% of men work less than 36 hours a week. That is slightly more than one in every four men. Many of these men are fathers, which would explain the high visibility of fathers in the Netherlands, and at the playground. But even in a seemingly gender-equal country like the Netherlands, women are still the primary care providers.

During pregnancy, fathers are very welcome during midwifery appointments and in the delivery room. But while I love the Dutch postpartum experience where a nurse comes over to your house and helps with chores, as well as checks on baby and mom, it simply can't be a coincidence that Dutch fathers only get two days of paternity leave. Two days? Yes, really it really is a joke.

However, despite the ridiculously short paternity leave, Dutch dads are extremely involved, and they are everywhere: shopping at the supermarket, on the streets, or picking up their kids from school or daycare.

That day at the playground, I learned a few important lessons. First of all, I am sadly not as forward-thinking as I thought I was about gender equality in parenting. That was a hard one to swallow, but the first step to solving a problem is actually acknowledging the problem.

Second, I realized that fathers are just as competent caregivers as are mothers—if not more so in many cases. I think I must have always known this but for some reason, I had expected that I would somehow magically become the "traditional mother" when I had kids. I would be their primary caregiver, do everything myself, and of course, enjoy my kids while doing it. My failure to achieve that was epic, and I drove myself ragged. As a result, I felt threatened by the fathers' effortless parenting.

In the end, I felt inspired by these men on the playground and other Dutch dads. Their parenting skills made me realize that I don't have to do it all alone and that I was wrong by assuming that just because I'm a woman I'm better adapted to parenting. The truth was that I was terrible at being a "traditional mother." But I see it as a good thing because it gives my husband a chance at being more hands-on.

As the Dutch show us, where fathers are involved, everyone's happier for it.

Olga Mecking is a Polish woman living in the Netherlands with her German husband and three trilingual children. She is a blogger, writer, and translator. The European Mama is a blog about life abroad, raising children and traveling. She also is a regular contributor to Multicultural Kid Blogs, where she is also a member of the board. Her writings have been published on Scary Mommy, Mamalode, and The Huffington Post.

When not blogging or thinking about blogging, she can be found reading books, drinking tea, or cooking. You can join her on Facebook, Twitter and Pinterest. She is editor of Dutched Up: Rocking the Clogs Expat Style and contributor to Knocked Up Abroad.

CHAPTER 24

THE LIFE OF RILEY (AND HIS SIBLINGS) IN BENIN

Sarah Murdock
Nationality: American
Parented in: Benin, West Africa

My husband, Matt, and I were married in Virginia, US in 1996, and after a few months, he whisked me off to Benin, a small francophone country in West Africa, where he was a missionary. I was not completely unprepared for life in Africa, since I had spent time in Morocco and Kenya as a child, and I had a good foundation in the French language. I think my biggest adjustment was just to being married—I was 31 years old and used to being independent and living in a cosmopolitan city with a busy social life. Moving to the rather isolated town of Tanguieta, in the agrarian northern part of the country, was quite a contrast. I had no friends yet besides Matt, there was nowhere to go for fun, and life slowed down dramatically. The town was mostly made up of mud brick dwellings, an open-air market with scant offerings, a few stores with imported food items, and a well-known hospital. We had our work, and we had each other, and, really, it turned out to be quite satisfying. Nevertheless, we anticipated the day we would welcome another member into our family.

We waited a long time, five years in all. In 2001, I was finally pregnant. A year earlier I had had a big disappointment, something the doctor called an *oeuf clair*, which is translated as a blighted ovum in English. I had to have a dilation and curettage (D&C). This was my first-ever hospital experience since I was born, and it was in a fairly primitive facility (at least by Western standards). I remember lying and being prepped on one of two delivery tables (where six years later I would give birth to my daughter, Bridget, whose story is published in *Knocked Up Abroad*). Nearby on another table, separated from me by a screen, was a woman in labor. I was already going under the anesthesia when I heard her crying out, and finally, *"Alleluia! Gloire à Dieu!"* ("Hallelujah! Glory to God!")—her baby was born. The jubilant doctor, an Italian man, then bounced over to me, pinched my cheek and cheerily said, "Now it's your turn!" right as I faded into unconsciousness.

Regardless, here we were, this time for real. I decided to have the baby in the US because I needed some familiarity, and also so our parents could be with us, particularly my mother, who had cancer. This turned out to be a special blessing, as she was with me when I gave birth to my son, Riley, and then she passed away just four months later.

While waiting for Riley, a friend took me shopping for supplies, and I was completely overwhelmed. Did I really need all this stuff? The subtle hints on the various

packaging made it clear that I would not be a good mother
if I did not purchase each item, but all I could think was,
"The mothers in Benin have none of this, and their babies
are just fine." Actually, they have nothing special at all,
maybe just some talc and perfumed soaps, and a string of
beads to go around the waist (to help measure weight gain).
I agonized over my purchases, tried to be modest, and
probably still overdid it.

The one thing I definitely had way too much of was
clothes. So many people gave us clothes! They were all so
adorable, I was thrilled, but when we returned to Benin
after Riley turned two months old, I realized that in the
sub-Saharan heat, he hardly needed any.

Nor did he need shoes. The first time I put him outside
in the dirt to walk, when he was about a year old, the
Beninese protested, "Oh no! Don't! He must have shoes
on!"

"Why?" I asked, "Your children don't wear shoes."

"Yes, but he's white!"

I resisted their entreaties, and he essentially went
barefoot for nine years, until we left Benin, and never had
any problems. His feet got as tough as a camel's, of which
he was enormously proud.

For lack of any other advice, I subscribed to the baby-
raising school that promotes putting your baby on a
sleeping schedule, in his own room. Both these things were
very upsetting to our Beninese friends, although they
graciously tried not to let on. For one thing, their babies
never sleep alone; they are always with mom and/or
siblings.

Someone once told me a story about an African man
visiting in an American home in the US. At bedtime, the
hosts' child was taken to her room and put into bed. She
got out a few times and was firmly led back in. A little while
later, when the adults were going to bed, the African saw

that the family dog was invited to jump on the parents' bed. This was completely backward to him.

To let Riley cry himself to sleep was incredibly agitating to our night guardian, who could hear him. Beninese babies sleep whenever they want, wherever they happen to be, for as long as they want. There is no schedule at all, and they never cry going to sleep, because they just fall asleep when they are tired. In fact, until a child is about two years old, they are always pacified when they cry, with the breast usually, or with food, with cuddling, or simply by giving them what they want. So whenever I refused Riley anything, with the result that he cried, I was looked at askance and with slightly veiled disapproval. After a child turns two, though, he is on his own. He can cry till the cows come home, and no one pays any attention. I am not sure why this is so.

Little Beninese boys often rule the roost. They are allowed to be rude to their mothers, and often defy them. Couple this with the early practice of giving in to them when they cry and the results can be quite comic. One day Mariam, our house help, came to me asking for some advice on how to wean her son, who was probably around three at the time. When she had gone home the previous day she was greeted by him pulling out a stool for her, pointing at it and ordering her, "Sit down—I want to eat!"

I found out that there were some taboos and myths that kept mothers from solely breastfeeding their babies. For a number of reasons, they usually supplemented their babies' diet with a watered-down corn porridge, or plain water, which was often contaminated. Consequently, even week-old infants got sick with diarrhea. They sometimes got pneumonia from an especially horrifying feeding habit of plugging the child's nose and forcing porridge down the throat. I had been asked to write a booklet for publication in a local language on the importance of breastfeeding alone for the first year of life, per World Health Organization standards, so I was researching these practices along with the help of a Beninese midwife. The booklet was published shortly after Riley's birth. The timing was fortuitous, particularly because he was a very chubby baby: a stellar example. Neighbors asked Mariam what I fed him, and it was fabulous advertising to say only breast milk.

During my first pregnancy, I was trying hard to do everything by the book. I made great efforts to maintain a proper diet, and protein was the hardest element to get. Meat was just so unpredictably available, and we tried not to eat too much because it was so expensive by local standards. I ate peanut butter and sardines (not together!), and—to my father's horror—the leaves of the Moringa tree. This tree, which is starting to become better known in the US, was one we had been promoting as a superbly nutritious and healing plant. It contains copious amounts of vitamins, minerals, and amino acids and is highly recommended for pregnant and nursing mothers, but my father just could not get past the idea that his poor daughter was forced to resort to eating leaves. I eventually fed the leaf powder to Riley when he began on solids, stirring it into his porridge made of locally available grains, and into his scrambled eggs, which turned them green. Too bad we didn't have some ham to go with them! For a while, he didn't realize eggs were actually yellow.

Even after Riley was born, I continued to try to follow what the books told me to do. There are no well-child visits to the pediatrician where we lived, but I did take Riley to a friend at a maternal health office to get him weighed on a top-loading scale once a month, ostensibly to reassure myself that he was gaining weight properly. Since he was so chubby, I think it was more just to congratulate myself when I found he was off the charts. Later I did the same with the other two, and they got weighed at the local clinic in a sling that hung from a spring scale, not unlike ones you might see in the produce section of some grocery stores.

As a new mother, I was overly zealous with trying to protect Riley's health when he was a baby. I suppose in the back of my mind I felt I had something to prove to all of our family and friends in the US by having healthy children since many of them believed we were crazy to have children in "dangerous" Africa. Since he was my first, he got an enormous amount of attention from all the people we knew and got passed around quite a lot. Whenever I got him back, I tried to apply hand sanitizer surreptitiously. I watched him like a hawk to keep him from putting things in his mouth. What with all the domestic livestock wandering around, the lack of toilets, the habit of spitting…the dirt was just filthy.

When Duncan came along, I was pleasantly surprised to find that he had no desire to explore with his mouth, so I never had to worry about him. By the time Bridget arrived, I was just not so worried about it, and wouldn't you know it, she turned out to be the worst one for putting objects in her mouth. I would catch her sucking on mango seeds we had thrown out to our animals, or eating fruit she found on the ground. Is it a coincidence that she is the only one of the three who has never had any intestinal issues at all?

I decided to get their vaccinations in the US, since the schedules were different, and I didn't want any confusion. This was a little hard on the children, who always had oodles of shots to catch up on when we came to the US every two years. We were required to get yellow fever shots, however, and we did comply with the UN nurses who came door to door with polio drops since there were still cases popping up in the region. Bridget, the only one to be born in Tanguieta, also got a shot the day after she was born, on her left forearm, which left a scar like the old small pox vaccines—a permanent souvenir of Benin.

Riley was quite stubborn when it came to potty-training. He was completely not interested. We used cloth diapers because 1) disposables were not readily available and were expensive, and 2) there was no good way to dispose of them. There was no garbage service. Instead, we had a trash pit that we regularly burned, and diapers do not burn! Washing the cloth diapers, boiling them, and ironing them was a major chore that I wanted to eliminate. The diapers were washed twice a week and hung out to dry on our clothesline. During the rainy season, anytime I heard even the faintest rumbling of thunder or saw rain clouds coming, I prepared myself to dash outside and madly rip them all off the line before they got soaked. We had to string them all around the living room like so many small curtains so they could continue drying, and avoid getting mildewed.

Duncan arrived when Riley was two and nowhere near being potty-trained. I am sure Mariam thought he was a delinquent in this area. I did not want a repeat if I could help it, so when Duncan was about six months old, I asked her how she potty-trained her children (all the Beninese kids were "potty-trained" very early). She told me that when her children became mobile, she bought a little plastic potty and the minute she noticed anything about to happen, she would put them on it.

So, once Duncan began crawling at eight months, I decided to do the same. By the end of the very first day, he learned he was supposed to produce something when he sat on that potty. It was amazing! When he was a year old, he was nearly fully trained—about the same time as Riley. Competition helped! It also helped that the warm climate meant the children could remain scantily clad if necessary and that our cement floors were easy to clean up!

When my children were young, I didn't take them grocery shopping very often, mostly because it was so much easier to navigate the market without them, and also because they just preferred to stay home. If Matt was home, I usually left them behind. Otherwise, they had to accompany me. We lived just a mile or so from the center of town, down a wide, shady avenue. I sometimes walked, or went on my bike, either by choice or necessity when the car wouldn't work. If I had to take the boys on my bike, I got rather unwieldy. I had two seats on the bike, one attached to the crossbar, and one over the back tire. I also had a basket on the front. By the time my shopping was done, in addition to the boys, I usually had a full basket, a full backpack, and bags hanging off of the handlebars. It's a miracle I never fell over.

Another reason the boys did not like to go into town was that whenever I took them, they were stared at quite a bit. At the time, there were two other white families with children in town, but white children were still relatively rare. Most people were merely friendly in their curiosity, others got slightly aggressive in their well-intended, but unwanted, attention.

Sometimes women tried to pry a child out of my arms so they could hold him. When he inevitably cried in protest, she would say, "See, he doesn't like black people," to which I would reply, "No, he just isn't comfortable with strangers." Which was true. By far, the most common skin color my children saw was dark, and they hardly even noticed.

My children also did not appreciate the local manner of joking by saying, "Give me your child," "Let's trade babies," or, "Your son can marry my daughter." I tried to explain to the boys, when they were old enough to understand, that it was just a joke, and the best thing to do was just go along with it, we'd all get a laugh and then go our own ways, but they couldn't seem to manage it.

Once in a while, the attention from other children got to be quite upsetting, especially if we were in a stationary car and the windows were completely covered with faces looking in. Even now, almost five years after repatriating to the US, my children are averse to any activities which involve them being watched.

Observing them become aware of language was quite interesting. Riley was a precocious talker, while Duncan was very quiet (and thus earned the nickname *Le Sage* [the Wise One]). Frequently, Riley mixed English and French when talking to the Beninese, substituting for words he didn't know in French. I was fascinated to see his grasp of how verbs worked when one day he saw a hug beetle dead in the dirt. As he squatted next to it, he observed, "*Le bug est deadé*" ("the bug is dead")—"bug" in English (with a French pronunciation), and an English verb with a French past tense verb ending!

When the children were two, five, and seven, we moved from town to a 100-acre farm about five miles away. It was near a tiny village, but for all intents and purposes quite isolated. This was an ideal place, in some ways, for the kids to have a simple country life. Their entertainment involved whacking termite mounds, splashing in the reservoir in water the color of chocolate milk, making palaces for bugs (oh, the plethora of colorful bugs!), playing in the rain and mud, making wigwams with tree branches, and playing ball or tag with the other kids who lived on the farm.

We were often brought little animals, often orphaned by hunters, or just found in a nest. In this way, we adopted ducklings, baby birds, rabbits, hedgehogs, duikers (miniature deer), and kittens. We were offered baby monkeys as well, but having had some negative experiences with them before the children arrived, we always declined those. The kids helped their dad plant a cornfield by hand, babysat a baboon, rode our old horse when they could catch her, tried their hand at milking bony cows, fed pigs and chickens, and also read a lot and played Legos. Thankfully, none of them ever got bitten by a snake or stung by a scorpion as they ran all over the farm with bare feet.

As I already mentioned, there were very few places to go for fun in town. We went for walks, bike rides, picnics, sometimes to a nearby waterfall. For a while, there was a little library, but of course, all the books were in French. Trips to the big cities were always a treat. Usually, these trips happened only once a year for official reasons—to obtain our residence visas or to pick up visitors at the airport. On these occasions, we got to spoil the kids a bit at restaurants, and we went to the beach or swimming pools.

One huge treat was being able to use air conditioning in the guest houses. At home, we only had fans, and never were able to escape the heat fully during the worst time of year, when temperatures could reach 120°F (almost 49°C) during the day and stay at 90°F (32°C) inside at night. Swimming was an activity that we usually only indulged in once a month during the hottest season, when we went to the nearest town on a bank run. We did have two different inflatable kiddie pools at home that we used a little, but it was a guilty pleasure. The hottest time of year was, of course, the time when local water sources dried up, and because we had our own well, we often had requests for water from people in our neighborhood and others who walked several miles to our place. We gave out a lot, but did turn some people away, and having a pool full of water for kids to play in at the same time made for conflicting emotions.

The Beninese don't celebrate birthdays, but we had parties for our kids. Riley's first birthday consisted of 20 or so teenagers who were living on our compound at the time. After that, they got more kid-friendly. At first, they usually consisted of Belgian, Italian and Beninese children. Once the Europeans left, we continued with the Beninese boys. We never expected them to bring anything since they knew nothing of birthday parties, and my boys usually ended up giving toys away.

With only biannual trips to the US, and shipping being prohibitively expensive, birthday and Christmas presents were a challenge. A few relatives managed to send boxes once in a while, but they were never expected. And there was nothing much available locally. So Matt and I would have to buy two years' worth of gifts before we left the US, usually in one last-minute trip to Target or Toys "R" Us, and just try to guess what they would like down the road.

The holidays were generally very simple affairs, and I felt happy that our kids seemed so unspoiled. Our first year after moving to the US, though, I think we tried to compensate for those "deficient" years by organizing big birthday parties and overdoing the Christmas presents a bit. They were ridiculously happy over their birthday cakes which for once were more than just a plain rectangle with candles.

Raising children in rural Africa was an incredible experience. No, we didn't have playgrounds, or libraries, or museums, or places of entertainment, much of which we appreciate now, and they didn't have any friends that spoke English or liked to play the same way they did. But they grew to be each other's best friends, learned how to entertain themselves with very simple resources, grew some impressive imaginations, learned how to communicate in another language (or without words), and became super travelers. I wouldn't have had it any other way.

Sarah Murdock was glad to escape from eight years of working in Washington, District Columbia to life in rural Africa as a newlywed, where she lived as a missionary for 15 years. She feels at home just about anywhere, having also grown up overseas, and dislikes being asked, "So, where are you from?" Sarah hopes to travel more with her family in the future, but for now she is happily settled in Wyoming, with her husband and three children, enjoying the wild outdoors, seizing opportunities to pretend to be a cowgirl, and seeing moose from her bedroom window. She is a contributing author to Knocked Up Abroad.

CHAPTER 25

PARENTING IN THE LAND OF THE NOT-SO-POLITICALLY CORRECT

Mihal Greener
Nationality: Australian
Parented in: The Netherlands

My first we're-not-in-Kansas-anymore moment came a few months after arriving in the Netherlands on Christmas Day 2008. Surprisingly enough, the shock didn't come from the brutal European winter or attempts to eat raw herring, head first. The biggest moment of culture shock came from the seemingly innocuous task of finding a school for my eldest daughter.

I had assumed that the biggest challenge I had to negotiate in this process was deciding between an international school and a local Dutch school. It turned out that I was facing a much bigger obstacle. In the Netherlands children usually start school on their fourth birthday, slotting into an established class. It turned out that with a three-year-old I had missed the optimal time to put her on a school waiting list by roughly three years, three years and nine months in some cases. Desperate for help I called up the *gemeente* (the local council), after hearing about a school that specialized in helping children from other countries learn Dutch so that they can later integrate into a Dutch school. I chatted briefly with the gentleman, explaining our circumstances and telling him about the school I was looking at. In his dry, direct and very Dutch manner, he told me, "You don't want to send your daughter to that school. It's a black school."

It turns out that black schools are a thing in the Netherlands, at least unofficially. I told Dutch acquaintances this story, and they didn't flinch. Schools with high populations of immigrant children are referred to as black schools, and they're usually not very good. The council official wasn't just making the big assumption that I was white, he was basing his response on the fact that I wasn't a migrant from Turkey or Morocco and therefore would not be wanting to send my child to a school designed to integrate an immigrant underclass, not educated expats.

I was taken aback by what I took as a cavalier racism, bandied about as casually as if he was telling me not to try the Gouda cheese. But, truth be told, I also appreciated his directness. He was right; I wouldn't have wanted to send my daughter to that school, and his forthright response saved me a trip out there to find this out myself.

It turns out that political correctness is not a thing in the Netherlands. The Dutch approach is to be direct, blunt, and say it how it is.

Over the next seven years, I was often reminded of the double-edged sword that is Dutch directness. The Dutch don't tie themselves up in knots making sure that their opinions are couched in politically correct language or acceptably neutral. At times it's a slap in the face, at other moments, it's blissfully refreshing. Imagine all the time that can be saved by saying it how it is, no malice intended, just the unfiltered truth, *naturlijk* (of course).

By the time my daughter's fourth birthday arrived, I was relieved to have found her a place at a local Dutch Montessori school. My daughter was the only non-native Dutch speaker in the class. Her teacher was up for the challenge of getting her up to speed; although she clearly expressed her disappointment with how little Dutch I had managed to learn so far. It is genuinely difficult for multilingual Dutch people, whose English is nearly world-perfect, to appreciate that some of us find picking up a second language an exhausting, unpronounceable struggle.

The Dutch kids at my daughter's school were some of the happiest and most assured kids I've ever met. Most of the sea of blond-haired and blue-eyed kids in the classroom carried themselves with a remarkable self-confidence, even at the age of five or six. My guess is that a lot of it comes from the home and the emphasis Dutch families place on time spent together as a family. The Dutch are known to work reasonable hours, with most women working part-time (by choice), and a *papadag* (an unpaid daddy day) legally available for dads who want to work four days a week in order to spend a day with their children.

Dutch kids are also listened to—there's none of this "kids must be seen but not heard" business going on. Dutch children are raised in an environment where it's common for everyone to be home for a family dinner at 6 p.m., and, as they sit around their plates of *rookworst* and *stamppot* (smoked sausage and potato mash), children will have a voice, and their opinions will be listened to. There is respect, love, and a healthy dose of self-worth that's firmly instilled. But there's no mollycoddling approach of the you-are-a-special-and-unique-snowflake variety.

My education continued alongside my daughter's, and I soon realized that Dutch directness also extends into the school system. At parent-teacher interviews the greatest praise ever lauded on my children from various teachers was that they are doing *fijne* (fine). I would ask about their reading or math, transparently seeking out praise for my kids in areas where they seemed to be doing well, only to be met with a "*fijne,*" or "There is no problem." If there's nothing wrong with their progress, then they are doing fine—delivered with what I interpreted as a subtext of "don't be a needy English person who needs to be told how precious their prodigy is."

The Dutch national ethos of "just act normal, that's crazy enough" (*doe maar gewoon, dan doe je al gek genoeg*) is alive and kicking at Dutch schools. Back home the kids' report cards spanned the range of satisfactory to very good and excellent; in our Dutch school it starts at below average and the best you can hope for is a solid good.

Once you adapt to the idea that the greatest compliment you, or your child, will receive is that something is *fijne* or good, it is oddly liberating. The pressure to stand out, to feel a sense of accomplishment is lifted when all the praise and value on offer can be grouped together in a broad *fijne*. Being exceptional doesn't make you better than anyone else in the Lowlands. If you're sticking to the "just be normal" anthem, preferably donning the national uniform of jeans and boots and helping yourself to only one cookie with your coffee, then everybody's happy.

The upside of the bullshit-free Dutch approach is that if someone says something nice, you know that they mean it. There's no agenda that has to be deciphered. If you're fortunate enough to get a compliment, accept it on face value and relish the moment. It may be a while before it happens again. Living in the land of the not so politically correct means not being cushioned from confronting language and questionable attitudes toward race. But it also means reducing the propensity for misunderstanding, leaving you actually able to address the issues at hand. I may have been uncomfortable hearing a school be labeled as a black school, but it means open conversations can be had about the integration of immigrants into Dutch society and the challenges it poses, rather than hiding behind language that obfuscates the real issues causing tension. After a few rounds of parent-teacher interviews and report cards, my expectations were re-shaped, and I was able to feel satisfied with a good or a fine, rather than temper my pride with an analysis of the shades of the A-minus to A-plus continuum.

When I picked up my daughter from a playdate from a school friend's house and asked how it was, the parent would actually let me know if she had been difficult or grumpy—matter-of-factly, no implied judgment, just that they fought over the Lego for a bit, but then it settled down. In the end, this directness is most of the time just designed to help. I also realized that if I didn't really want to know, I didn't have to ask.

The Dutch directness is part of a bigger attitude that looks to cut down anyone who seems too full of themselves, and no one is above it. This "be normal" attitude is a great equalizer, removing the value placed on status or achievement. In the Dutch worldview, the office cleaner should be treated with the same respect as the CEO. Many people argue that this approach puts the reigns on success and achievement and if your child is a prodigy the shackles of conformity may be oppressive. My suspicion is that this is a big part of why Dutch kids have been found by UNICEF to be the happiest in the world. When your value is not tied up with your school results or status in society, it's pretty hard not to be happy with what you have.

One afternoon my daughter and I took advantage of the June sunshine to visit Amsterdam for an afternoon of museums and shopping. We stopped at a sunny café along a canal to recharge on some famous Dutch *appeltaart* (apple pie). As we ordered at the counter we saw photos of President Clinton on the wall and a framed letter of thanks from his office. My daughter excitedly asked the waitress if we were eating in the same café as a former US president. "Yes," she replied, "although it nearly didn't work out."

The story, as she told us, was that Clinton's people had called the café and said that the president was in town and would like to come in for some apple pie. They asked that the café be closed down so that the secret service could come in and make sure it was safe before he arrived and ate. The owner responded in the way of a true Dutchman, encapsulating the lack of hierarchy in Dutch society. "That won't be possible," he said. "Our regulars would be very upset if we closed down. But the president is welcome to come with everyone else."

As the photos captured, Clinton came in, enjoyed his pie, and was apparently able to sit and enjoy the cozy atmosphere of the small café for a couple of hours, virtually undisturbed. Who, after all, was going to make a fuss over a man who was no better than any of us just by virtue of his job? For all the parenting lessons I could share with my daughter, this story struck a chord with her. She was as valuable a customer as a US president. This attitude, I suspect, may be go a big way to explain the seemingly innate confidence so many Dutch children appear to possess in spades.

It turned out that we had made the right decision to make the most of the good weather. The brief summer was only a sun kissed memory as autumn bought with it sharp winds and heavy grey skies. This time we were ready for it, armed with layers of wool beneath our waterproof jackets and pants, to not only keep warm but also stay dry on our bikes. To my great pride, and everyone else's amusement, in my mid-thirties I had finally learned to ride a bike. When out at night I'd fly along on my second-hand gazelle, enjoying the freedom and fresh air racing through my helmet-free hair. During the day I would cart my daughters around in my *bakfiets*, the three-wheeled box bike that could easily fit a combination of children, shopping bags, scooters, and room for our newest daughter who would be joining us the following spring.

Despite the weather, everyone's sprits in our household were high. October had closed with Halloween celebrations and was followed shortly after by Sint Maarten. From my perspective they were much the same, both an opportunity for neighborhood kids to amass an impressive collection of sweets. Sint Maarten is, however, a much quainter celebration. Children parade door-to-door, holding colorful paper lanterns lit up with a small electric light, while singing traditional Dutch songs for candy instead of challenging parents to a trick or treat. After the lanterns had been packed up and the candy demolished there was only one word on the mind of every child in Holland, whether Dutch or expat: Sinterklaas.

Sinterklaas is the highlight of the Dutch year, far surpassing Christmas celebrations. As an old white man with a beard delivering gifts, Sinterklaas is clearly a distant relation of Santa Claus, yet there are no reindeers or elves in sight. Sinterklaas travels on a white horse called Amerigo, and carries a golden staff. He is religion-free, at least in practice, despite the big cross adorning his pointed red hat, meaning all children could join in and celebrate his arrival—a nice change for this time of year. Every year Sinterklaas arrives in the Netherlands by steamboat from Spain in mid-November and stays until the big celebration of gift-giving held on December 5. My daughters quickly realized the opportunity that three weeks of gifts provided. At night they would fill their shoes with carrots for Amerigo and drawings for Sinterklaas, and leave them by the fireplace. In the morning they would rush downstairs to see what candy or small toys Sinterklaas and his helpers had left for them in their shoes.

For a small minority in the Netherlands, however, Sinterklaas is one of the most awkward and offensive celebrations of the year. Despite being a virtual three-week version of Christmas, there is one element of the ritual that is just too non–politically correct for many expats and for a small part of Dutch society: Sinterklaas has helpers, but they're not elves. They are called Zwarte Pieten—literally "Black Petes." Yep, white Santa has black helpers.

These helpers who visit schools and are readily spotted all over town and decorating shop windows aren't actually black. Together with their bright shirts and knickerbockers they don black face paint, big gold hoop earrings, bright red lips, and top off the ensemble with a black Afro wig.

The Dutch, being the Dutch, don't see why their Zwarte Pieten are the focus of any controversy. As the Dutch Prime Minister explained it, "Black Pete is black and I cannot change that." On one version of the story the Petes are black because they are Moors, North African Arabs brought on a ship from Spain by Sinterklaas (I'm not sure how this version makes it any better). Another explanation readily offered is that their faces are black from soot, from climbing down all the chimneys delivering presents. One year our local council, in an attempt to dull the opposition to Zwarte Piet, suggested that the Petes actually come into school with black soot on their face rather than actual black face paint. The school duly passed this message on to the parents. We turned up to the school celebrations where not only were lots of blonde children walking around with painted black faces, but so were the Zwarte Pieten.

Most of the Dutch people I spoke with don't know what all the fuss is about. The Dutch directness is intertwined with their lack of political correctness. They take issues on face value and don't understand the controversy when people read into situations things that they don't see are there. Especially when these people are immigrants or expats. During Sinterklaas our 16-year-old neighbor Molly came over to babysit and shared the children's excitement as they put out their shoes and earnestly sung songs welcoming Sinterklaas up into the fireplace. Once the kids were asleep we spoke about another council decision years earlier to address the controversy by introducing multi-colored rainbow Petes instead of black Petes, which was naturally dismissed by the Dutch as illogical, politically correct posturing. Molly didn't understand the sensitivity over Zwarte Pie*t*. "Sinterklaas is okay," she readily offered, "but Zwarte Pieten are the highlight of the celebrations. They are the ones that are fun and cheeky, handing out gifts and causing chaos. They aren't second-class slaves; they are the best bit."

When Sinterklaas arrives in The Hague every year, huge crowds gather at the harbor to see his steamboat arrive. Sinterklaas then rides Amerigo through the neighborhoods and down to the city center. The Zwarte Pieten run through the streets, full of energy and antics, throwing *pepernoten* (spiced cookies) into the crowds of children, most of which are dressed up in a full Pete costume or at least Pete's jaunty beret with a feather sticking out. On our first parade I pushed to the front of the crowd to take a photo of Sinterklaas and the kindly old man looked down, made eye contact with me and…winked. I wasn't sure what to make of this dirty old man version of Santa. The only part of the celebrations that I found even more difficult to process were the handful of black children I saw in the crowd, who were also wearing black face paint with their Zwarte Piet outfits.

Over the next six years, Sinterklaas remained the highlight of the year for my children and helped ease the lethargy that began to kick in as we settled down for a long winter. Each year they would dress us up Pete but, against their vocal objections, they were never allowed to paint their face black.

The Dutch are famous for their tolerance and directness, but as I gradually realized over our time there, it is skewed toward a particular perspective. The Netherlands was the first country to introduce gay marriage, they have open prostitution in the red light district, voluntary euthanasia is legal, and you can buy joints at the local coffee shop. But if you rock the boat and put your rubbish bin out before the designated time, expect to be slapped with a hefty fine.

A big part of Dutch permissiveness is that they like having things out in the open where you can see them and then regulate them. No game playing, no couching things in acceptable language and definitely no political correctness.

As an adult, the Dutch attitude was often refreshing, sometimes challenging and always something I had to adjust to. For children, this is their default setting. Being direct and telling the truth with no harm intended is how children naturally communicate before we introduce them to white lies and good manners. Letting go of this makes it easier for everyone, child and adult alike, leaving time for the more important things like riding your bike down to the local shops and filling yourself with *friet* (fries) slathered in mayonnaise. No wonder Dutch children are so happy.

Mihal Greener is a freelance writer, now back living in Melbourne, Australia after seven years and one pregnancy in the Netherlands. She's missing the cycling, cheese, flowers and the price of wine, but happy to be back enjoying Melbourne's cafes. Mihal apologizes to all the Dutch people she offended over the years proclaiming Melbourne's coffee to be far superior. But she was right. Mihal writes at www.mihalgreener.com.

ACKNOWLEDGEMENTS

A huge thank you to the contributors and all 277 of our Kickstarter backers who believed in these stories and helped us bring them to life. It is because of the names below that this book exists, and I am extremely grateful.

When I published *Knocked Up Abroad,* I had to convince parents, some of whom had never written a personal essay before, that sharing their pregnancy, birth, or parenting story abroad would connect with readers around the world. Personally, I loved reading the inherent drama that accompanies every birth story. The cultural complexities layered on top was like eating a cupcake with thick frosting. I couldn't get enough. I guessed that others would also enjoy these stories. I wasn't wrong.

Knocked Up Abroad Again came together a bit like my second pregnancy—knowing what happened before only partially prepared me for what was to come. What I love most about collaborative projects is the network of women I get to meet. For once, I felt not so alone as this book came together. We were all along for the ride.

The success of the crowdfunding campaign resulted in positive social proof that I'm not the only person out there who loves reading about other people's lives—the stranger and more foreign, the better. Right? Readers demanded this book into existence.

Special thanks to my husband, Jonathan, and my family for all of their support as I continue to take on more and more ridiculous challenges. I send all of you virtual hugs every day.

Do you want to continue the
Knocked Up Abroad journey?

Read the first book in the *Knocked Up Abroad* series, *Knocked Up Abroad: Stories of pregnancy, birth, and raising a family in a foreign country* and please leave a review. You can also visit the contributors' websites and blogs located in the bios at the end of each chapter. They'd love to hear what you thought of their chapter.

You can read more stories about pregnancy, birth, and parenting abroad in numerous ways:

WEBSITE:
https://knockedupabroad.com

FACEBOOK:
http://www.facebook.com/knockedupabroadbook

INSTAGRAM:
http://www.instagram.com/knockdupabroad

The best way to help is to leave a review on Amazon and Goodreads and let other readers know what you thought about the book.

Made in United States
North Haven, CT
26 April 2024

51770951R10189